Council for Standards in Human Service Education (CSHSE) Standards Covered in This Text

The Council for Standards in Human Service Education (CSHSE) developed 10 national standards that guide human service departments and help students understand the knowledge, values, and skills as developing human service practitioners. These guidelines reflect the interdisciplinary nature of human services.

STANDARD	CHAPTER
Professional History	
Understanding and Mastery...	
Historical roots of human services	1, 2
Creation of human services profession	1, 2
Historical and current legislation affecting services delivery	
How public and private attitudes influence legislation and the interpretation of policies related to human services	1, 2, 3
Differences between systems of governance and economics	1, 2, 3
Exposure to a spectrum of political ideologies	1–8
Skills to analyze and interpret historical data application in advocacy and social changes	1, 2, 4–8
Human Systems	
Understanding and Mastery...	
Theories of human development	1, 2, 3
How small groups are utilized, theories of group dynamics, and group facilitation skills	2
Changing family structures and roles	4-8
Organizational structures of communities	
An understanding of capacities, limitations, and resiliency of human systems	1–8
Emphasis on context and the role of diversity in determining and meeting human needs	1–8
Processes to effect social change through advocacy (e.g., community development, community and grassroots organizing, local and global activism)	1–8
Processes to analyze, interpret, and effect policies and laws at local, state, and national levels	1, 2, 3
Human Services Delivery Systems	
Understanding and Mastery...	
Range and characteristics of human services delivery systems and organizations	4–8
Range of populations served and needs addressed by human services	4–8
Major models used to conceptualize and integrate prevention, maintenance, intervention, rehabilitation, and healthy functioning	1–3
Economic and social class systems including systemic causes of poverty	1, 2, 4–8
Political and ideological aspects of human services	1–8
International and global influences on services delivery	1–8
Skills to effect and influence social policy	1, 3–8

Adapted from the October 2010 Revised CSHSE National Standards

Council for Standards in Human Service Education (CSHSE) Standards Covered in This Text

STANDARD	CHAPTER
Information Management	
Understanding and Mastery...	
Obtain information through interviewing, active listening, consultation with others, library or other research, and the observation of clients and systems	
Recording, organizing, and assessing the relevance, adequacy, accuracy, and validity of information provided by others	
Compiling, synthesizing, and categorizing information	1–8
Disseminating routine and critical information to clients, colleagues or other members of the related services system that is provided in written or oral form and in a timely manner	
Maintaining client confidentiality and appropriate use of client data	3
Using technology for word processing, sending email, and locating and evaluating information	2
Performing elementary community-needs assessment	3
Conducting basic program evaluation	
Utilizing research findings and other information for community education and public relations and using technology to create and manage spreadsheets and databases	
Planning & Evaluating	
Understanding and Mastery...	
Analysis and assessment of the needs of clients or client groups	2
Skills to develop goals, and design and implement a plan of action	2
Skills to evaluate the outcomes of the plan and the impact on the client or client group	2
Program design, implementation, and evaluation	2
Interventions & Direct Services	
Understanding and Mastery...	
Theory and knowledge bases of prevention, intervention, and maintenance strategies to achieve maximum autonomy and functioning	1–8
Skills to facilitate appropriate direct services and interventions related to specific client or client group goals	3–8
Knowledge and skill development in: case management, intake interviewing, individual counseling, group facilitation and counseling, location and use of appropriate resources and referrals, use of consultation	3
Interpersonal Communication	
Understanding and Mastery...	
Clarifying expectations	
Dealing effectively with conflict	
Establishing rapport with clients	
Developing and sustaining behaviors that are congruent with the values and ethics of the profession	

Council for Standards in Human Service Education (CSHSE) Standards Covered in This Text

STANDARD	CHAPTER
Administration	
Understanding and Mastery...	
Managing organizations through leadership and strategic planning	3
Supervision and human resource management	
Planning and evaluating programs, services, and operational functions	
Developing budgets and monitoring expenditures	
Grant and contract negotiation	
Legal/regulatory issues and risk management	
Managing professional development of staff	
Recruiting and managing volunteers	
Constituency building and other advocacy techniques such as lobbying, grassroots movements, and community development and organizing	1, 3
Client-Related Values & Attitudes	
Understanding and Mastery...	
The least intrusive intervention in the least restrictive environment	
Client self-determination	1, 2, 3
Confidentiality of information	
The worth and uniqueness of individuals including: ethnicity, culture, gender, sexual orientation, and other expressions of diversity	1–8
Belief that individuals, services systems, and society change	1–8
Interdisciplinary team approaches to problem solving	
Appropriate professional boundaries	
Integration of the ethical standards outlined by the National Organization for Human Services and Council for Standards in Human Service Education	3
Self-Development	
Understanding and Mastery...	
Conscious use of self	3
Clarification of personal and professional values	3
Awareness of diversity	1–8
Strategies for self-care	
Reflection on professional self (e.g., journaling, development of a portfolio, project demonstrating competency)	3

Designed to help students advance their knowledge, values, and skills, the Standards for Excellence Series assists students in associating the Council for Standards in Human Services Education (CSHSE) National Standards to all levels of human services practice.

FEATURES INCLUDE

- **Standards for Excellence grid**—highlighting chapters where various standards are addressed.
- **Standards for Excellence critical thinking questions**—challenges students to think critically about the standards in relation to chapter content.
- **Multimedia links**—correlates content to multimedia assets throughout the text, including video, additional readings, and more.
- **Self-study quizzes**—found throughout the text, self-study quizzes test student knowledge and comprehension of key chapter topics.
- **Chapter review**—links to a scenario-based chapter review, including short-answer discussion questions.

Advocacy for Social Justice

A Global Perspective

Michelle E. Martin
DePaul University

Boston Columbus Indianapolis New York San Francisco Upper Saddle River
Amsterdam Cape Town Dubai London Madrid Milan Munich Paris Montréal Toronto
Delhi Mexico City São Paulo Sydney Hong Kong Seoul Singapore Taipei Tokyo

Editor in Chief: Ashley Dodge
Editorial Assistant: Amandria Guadalupe
Managing Editor: Denise Forlow
Program Manager: Carly Czech
Project Manager: Erin Donahue, PreMediaGlobal
Executive Marketing Manager: Kelly May
Marketing Coordinator: Jessica Warren
Procurement Manager: Mary Fisher
Procurement Specialist: Eileen Collaro
Art Director: Jayne Conte

Cover Designer: Karen Noferi
Interior Designer: Joyce Weston Design
Cover Art: Shutterstock/alexcoolok
Digital Media Director: Brian Hyland
Digital Media Project Manager: Tina Gagliostro
Full-Service Project Management: Sudip Sinha/PreMediaGlobal
Composition: PreMediaGlobal
Printer/Binder: RRD/STP Crawfordsville
Cover Printer: RRD/STP Crawfordsville

Credits and acknowledgments borrowed from other sources and reproduced, with permission, in this textbook appear on appropriate page within text.

Many of the designations by manufacturers and seller to distinguish their products are claimed as trademarks. Where those designations appear in this book, and the publisher was aware of a trademark claim, the designations have been printed in initial caps or all caps.

Library of Congress Cataloging-in-Publication Data
Martin, Michelle E.
    Advocacy for social justice : a global perspective/Michelle E. Martin, Dominican University.—
        pages   cm
    Includes bibliographical references and index.
    ISBN-13: 978-0-205-08739-6
    ISBN-10: 0-205-08739-6
  1. Social justice.   2. Social advocacy.   3. Public welfare.   4. Social service.   I. Title.
    HM671.M37 2013
    303.3'72—dc23

                                                                          2013035637

3   18

ISBN-10: 0-205-08739-6
ISBN-13: 978-0-205-08739-6

Contents

· ·

6. Advocacy for Children   106

7. Advocacy for Lesbian, Gay, Bisexual, and Transgender Populations   135

8. Advocacy for Refugees and Migrants 154

Preface

Ten years ago I had an unjust experience with a societal system that left me feeling powerless and victimized. One day, when I was bending the ear of a very good friend for about the 50th time, lamenting my encounter with social injustice, my dear friend, who just so happens to be an African-American woman, responded to my outrage with patience and wisdom saying, "The difference between you and me is that you expect justice, whereas I do not." She then went on to describe the hard lessons she learned throughout her life, many learned collectively through her parents and grandparents—"my people do not expect justice, but when we experience it, we're grateful."

Her words stopped me cold and led me on a journey of deep reflection and contemplation—what would it be like to be born with the "wrong" color skin, in the "wrong" country, as the "wrong" gender, in the "wrong" caste, with "wrong" sexual attractions, in the "wrong" religion, and on the "wrong" side of the border. What would it be like to possess traits or be born into conditions that I had no control over? During my entire childhood, I was told that I could be anything I wanted to be, as long as I worked hard enough. I heard that so many times growing up (as did my friends) that by the time I was 10, I was certain I could be the president of the United States, or a president in a board room, if I just worked hard enough. And while I was born female, I was also born white, in an upper-middle-class family, in an upper-middle-class community, so my belief wasn't completely unrealistic.

Although I was well aware of social injustice from my long career as a social worker doing poverty work, it wasn't until I visited India that I finally "got it." No one tells the children from the "untouchable" caste that they can be the prime minister of India one day, or president of a company, if they just worked hard enough. No one tells them that, because it isn't true. For most of these kids, it doesn't matter how "hard they work"—they will never have the luxury of dreaming. And as difficult as this reality may be for those of us who grew up in the United States, the truth is that the majority of people in the world live with the dim reality that they have few choices in life, except acceptance.

But why write this book? Why not just leave it at a personal journal? After 25 years in the human services and social work field, I have become increasingly aware of the need for clear guidance in how to advocate for those who need it, because they have no voice. We are in the era of globalization. The world is shrinking, but it's also becoming more violent. Armed civil conflict is prevalent throughout the Global South causing millions into forced displacement, some as long as three decades or more, languishing in tented camps. Children are being conscripted into war in alarming numbers, some as young as five. I read recently that there are more slaves now than at any other time in history—through a billion-dollar moneymaking scheme called human trafficking. Transnational corporations are now more wealthy and powerful than some sovereign nations, some of which are linked to sweatshops that work young girls to death, so that Westerners can buy jeans for $25.

When I became interested in advocacy, particularly the area of global advocacy, I became quickly frustrated because I could not find many books on the subject. So, after considerable soul searching and some talks with my editor, I decided that this was a book that needed to be written—a book that would answer the questions—what is advocacy for social justice? Who in our world needs advocacy the most and why? And how can advocates help? It is my hope that I have honored not only my personal passion for this subject but also all the people in the world who do not have the luxury of expecting to be treated justly. So while I am writing this book for you, the student, and future advocate, I am also writing this book for them, the survivors of social injustice, and I hope I have made them proud.

Learning Outcomes

Students will be able to achieve a variety of learning outcomes by using this book and its resources, including:

- **Critical Thinking Skills**—students can develop their critical thinking skills by reviewing the standards boxes (indicated by the Standards band) throughout the chapters.
- **Oral Communication Skills**—students can develop their oral communication skills by engaging with others in and out of class to discuss their comprehension of the chapter based on the chapter's learning objectives.
- **Assessment and Writing Skills**—students can develop their assessment and writing skills in preparation for future certification exams by completing topic-based and chapter review assessments for each chapter.
- **CSHSE National Standards**—students can develop their understanding and mastery of CSHSE's national standards by discussing the standards box critical thinking questions.

Acknowledgments

I would like to thank many people who made the writing of this book possible and who helped me along the way. I would like to thank my friends and colleagues Leticia Villarreal Sosa and Kathy Clyburn for their sharp minds, their compassionate hearts, their loyalty, and their honesty in giving me valuable feedback. I would also like to thank students in my global advocacy class, Ali Moore, Maxine Davis, and Francis Arthur, who asked all the right questions and challenged me to think more deeply. I would like to thank my friend Mark Burge for reviewing my LGBT chapter. I would also like to thank my colleagues at Pearson, my editors Carly Czech and Ashley Dodge for their patience and support. I would like to thank my friends and family for their support and patience. And finally, I would like to thank my son, Xander, who is now 18 and has learned to see the world through a different lens because of all of our world travels, and my surrogate children, Sharon Rurangirwa, Elodie Shami, and Annabella Uwineza, who taught me that love does not depend on shared blood ties or culture.

CHAPTER 1

An Introduction to Advocacy for Social Justice

Local and Global Implications

ADVOCACY

alejandro dans neergaard/Shutterstock

Kendall has an associate's degree in human services and provides case management and generalist counseling services at the local Veteran's Administration (VA) office in the Dallas area. Recognizing the need for increased services for vets returning from Iraq and Afghanistan, Kendall has decided to attend a convention and rally sponsored by *The Circle of Friends for American Veterans*. The convention will address a national veterans' platform to raise awareness and advocate for veteran's issues. The goal of the convention organizers is to push veterans' issues to the top of the national agenda. In preparation for the convention Kendall engaged her colleagues and friends in supporting this cause by sending them an email asking them to attend the convention with her. In support of her advocacy efforts she prepared a fact sheet detailing relevant issues and goals of the convention, which included increased funding and legislative action on various important issues. Of those who could not attend the convention, Kendall asked for a donation and asked them to sign a petition asking federal legislators to support a Veteran's Bill of Rights, which advocates increasing veterans' medical care reimbursement rates, counseling for posttraumatic stress disorder (PTSD) for returning vets, and making veterans' issues a top federal priority.

Caleb has worked in the human services field for years—first as a counselor at a community mental health clinic, and then as a victim advocate in domestic violence court. Caleb is currently on the faculty in a social work program in the Chicago area. While in his Ph.D. program Caleb met another student who was equally passionate about advocating for victims of domestic violence. Caleb and his fellow student collaborated, engaged community partners, and founded the Center for Domestic Peace, an organization committed to working with communities to raise awareness about domestic abuse and challenge attitudes and social norms that enable family violence. Caleb recently ran a marathon in Chicago as a fund-raiser for the organization. Prior to running, he raised donations by gaining sponsors willing to donate a certain amount of money per mile. Caleb used email and social networking sites, such as Facebook and Twitter, to recruit sponsors and increase awareness of both the Center for Domestic Peace and its anti-violence message.

Leticia is a licensed psychologist and works at Heartland Alliance, an organization that advocates for human rights and the needs of oppressed, poor, and displaced populations on a local and global level. Leticia works with victims of trauma, particularly refugees and political asylees who have experienced government-sanctioned torture. Leticia travels internationally, training mental health workers in post-conflict regions to work with survivors of trauma. Leticia recently organized a community coalition of human services professionals, including counselors, social workers, grassroots organizers, psychologists, university professors, and attorneys all committed to ending government-sanctioned torture. The coalition is advocating for the passage of legislation that would criminalize torture inflicted by a government official (acts currently not considered a crime in many nation-states). Leticia and her coalition partners plan to advocate for the passage of anti-torture legislation on a state level initially, but will then push for national legislation, and then ultimately advocate on an international level. Leticia's activities range from conducting research, developing fact sheets, and contacting state legislators in the hope of finding possible sponsors. The coalition is currently meeting once a month to contribute perspectives, opinions, and ideas. Once their action plan is developed they will move forward with their advocacy efforts.

Karen is a Child Protection Advisor for the United Nations Children's Fund (UNICEF), an organization charged with the responsibility of protecting the rights of children globally. Karen is currently assigned to the Tashkent office, Uzbekistan, located in Eastern Europe, a member of the former USSR. Guided by the UN Convention on the Rights of the Child, Karen is responsible for providing program guidance and support on issues related to child protection in humanitarian emergencies. She will be in Uzbekistan, a country in post-conflict, for approximately three years, and will then be reassigned to another country experiencing a humanitarian crisis, such as armed conflict or a natural disaster.

What Is Advocacy for Social Justice?

What do these fictionalized case studies have in common? They all feature human services professionals working on micro, mezzo, and macro levels, engaging in advocacy work with the goal of achieving social justice on behalf of their clients, in regard to a particular issue, or on behalf of an entire population experiencing a crisis. Whenever I teach a course on advocacy one or more students ask the same question: "What exactly is advocacy?" The answer is not an easy one because the activities associated with advocacy work are very broad and can (and often do) include a variety of activities. I answer my students' question by starting with the basics. What is advocacy? Advocacy in general typically involves acting or arguing in support of something in order to influence outcomes. So in a sense, one might say that virtually all people advocate for something consistently throughout their lives. When people engage in job interviews, they are advocating for the employer to hire them. When teens beg their parents to let them stay out past curfew, they are advocating for their parents to change their minds. When leaders of a corporation lobby for some policy change, such as increased corporate tax breaks, they are advocating for a change in government legislation.

This book is not concerned with the everyday types of advocacy that we all engage in as we attempt to get our needs met, or get our way in some respect. Rather, in this book I will be exploring ways in which human services professionals advocate for causes that are believed to increase the quality of life for people who are vulnerable, displaced, marginalized, oppressed, or in some way suffering and in need of a voice. In other words, I will be exploring ways in which human services professionals advocate for social justice.

Advocacy for social justice is a concept that has been defined in many different ways. Loewen and Pollard (2010) define social justice movements as "striving for dignity." Other authors have described advocacy for social justice as being grounded in values of fair treatment, equality, social inclusion, and human rights (Longmore, 2003; Miller, 2001). Advocacy for social justice on behalf of oppressed populations then is concerned with power relationships, equal participation in society among all members, personal rights inherent in being human (i.e., human rights), and a just and decent society.

Perhaps one of the most comprehensive descriptions of advocacy for social justice is the one put forth by David Cohen and colleagues, a longtime social advocate. Cohen, de la Vega, and Watson (2001) define *advocacy* as a process where advocates work to change outcomes. They do this through organized efforts, such as lobbying for change in public policy and legislation as well as increased funding for causes in order to effect change within a variety of social institutions. Advocates are particularly concerned with social problems that may be submerged, ignored, or dismissed within society. Cohen et al. note how advocates start with reality ("what is"), and then advocate for change based upon "what should be" if the world were a just and decent place for all people. They cite the importance of using a human rights framework with the ultimate goal of giving a voice to the voiceless, and improving the lives of all people within society.

This definition provides a very descriptive and thorough picture of the all-encompassing nature of advocacy for social justice. What Cohen and colleagues are essentially saying is that advocates begin with a vision of what a just society *should* look like. The underlying foundation for this *just society* is the belief that equality is a right of all people and is not something that must be earned—certain rights are inalienable by the mere fact that someone is human. This ideal of course does not represent reality, as virtually all societies involve some level of inequity. Unfortunately, it seems that human nature is such that the more powerful members in any given society tend to marginalize the more vulnerable members. There is great variation though in levels of societal oppression, with those societies possessing more developed social structures generally experiencing fewer injustices . But ideally, all societies should seek to have injustices identified and strategies developed to make the "playing field" more level. The goal of these advocacy efforts is to directly improve the lives of the displaced, marginalized, and oppressed populations. Thus, the advocate for social justice establishes a standard of social equity within a just society (the ideal), identifies ways in which

Human Systems

Understanding and Mastery: Processes to effect social change through advocacy (e.g., community development, community and grassroots organizing, local and global activism)

Critical Thinking Question: Advocacy for social justice has been defined in a variety of ways. Per Cohen's definition, in what manner is the change process dependent upon one's envisioning of society?

the society fails to meet that standard (the problem), and then sets about to effect change in an organized manner (the solution).

The terms *advocacy* and *activism* are often used interchangeably, both within the advocacy world, as well as in this book. While these terms are overlapping concepts, there are some distinctions. For the most part advocates represent groups and advocate on their behalf (Masner, 2008; Tusinski, 2007). Activism on the other hand involves direct action, such as participating in a demonstration, protest action, or boycotts (Zeitz, 2008). While much of this book focuses on advocacy as a whole, when intervention strategies involve direct action, then the reader can assume that activism is likely involved.

> Assess your comprehension of **The Definition of Advocacy for Social Justice** by taking this quiz.

A Human Rights Framework: Inalienable Rights for All Human Beings

Before human services professionals can effectively advocate for social justice, they must first become aware of what a just society looks like. What is an ideal society? As Cohen et al. (2001) point out, social justice advocacy is based upon a human rights framework. Thus, at the root of any discussion of human rights violations is the assumption that all human beings have inalienable rights simply because they are human. Yet, history is replete with examples of egregious human rights violations, often waged in the belief that such concepts are justified on some level. Slavery, a caste system that deems one group of people more worthy than another, a patriarchal system that subjugates females within society, the genocide or "ethnic cleansing" of a particular cultural group, the sale and exploitation of women and children are all examples of the gross mistreatment of individuals, often because there is some perceived defining characteristic about these individuals that makes them different from those of another group. Such differences are often used to justify their mistreatment, where members of a more powerful group place themselves above the members of a more vulnerable group. Members of a just society recognize that no one group should have oppressive power over another, and that all human beings have basic rights that must be protected. Since some groups of individuals are more vulnerable than others, social justice advocates take responsibility for being the voice of the voiceless.

Kheng Guan Toh/Shutterstock

Human rights are typically organized into three basic categories—personal rights, political rights, and social and economic rights. *Personal rights* include the right to the "integrity of the body and security of the person" (Steen, 2006, p. 101). Violations against the person may include torture, arbitrary detention, and extrajudicial killings (Steen, 2006). *Political rights* include the right to vote, protest, and express one's opinions freely (Donnelly, 1984). Violations of one's political rights may include oppressing political space and denying individuals the right of responsible free speech and the expressing of dissenting political opinions. *Social and economic rights* include the right to community resources necessary to achieve one's full potential, such as access to education, health care, and employment (Donnelly, 1984). Examples of violations of social and economic rights include not allowing girls to attend school, or excluding ethnic minorities from the labor market, thus barring them from achieving basic sustenance.

The Roots of Social Justice Advocacy: Early Advocates and the Development of a Human Rights Framework

It's difficult to identify the genesis of social justice advocacy movements. Certainly, social movements have likely been around since humankind first realized what personal gains could come from exploiting others. Throughout history social movements have occurred, leading to everything from the overthrowing of governments to the initiation of wars. For the purposes of this book, the roots of advocacy for social justice will be explored within the context of the human services profession—an interdisciplinary profession evolving from an organized effort to effect change in society by addressing both human and social problems, by helping "people meet their basic physical and emotional needs that for whatever reason cannot be met without outside assistance" (Martin, 2013, p. 4).

Several key activists rose to prominence during a social reform movement, a type of collective action where ordinary people participate in organized efforts to effect social change (Tilly, 2009), and some engaged in activism independently in response to a personal call to action. It would be impossible to include an exhaustive list of social justice advocates in this brief historical review, but the work of a few key advocates who emerged in the midst of significant historical trends, or in response to key societal events, will help to provide some historical context in our exploration of how social justice advocacy has evolved throughout history. Also, understanding the historical context of social justice advocacy, including the social, political, and economic conditions and ideologies that have influenced social reformers throughout history, is vital to gaining a true appreciation of the multifaceted nature of social justice advocacy and social justice movements.

Jane Addams and the Settlement House Movement

Jane Addams (1860–1935) is probably one of the most well-known advocates of social justice (at least in human services circles) and is often considered the "mother" of sociology, social work, and human services disciplines. Addams was responsible for beginning the U.S. settlement house movement in the late 1800s—a project based upon a European model of caring for poor immigrants. Addams' advocacy efforts were widespread and varied, but focused primarily on poverty alleviation and social inequity (Lundblad, 1995).

Addams was born in Cedarville, Illinois, to upper-class parents who valued gender equity, higher education, and philanthropy. It was Addams' father who inspired in her a love of social action and advocacy. After her father's death, Addams became quite passionate about the plight of immigrants in the United States, but due to her poor health and the societal limitations placed on women during this era, she did not believe that she had a role in social advocacy.

During the late 1800s through the early 1900s, the United States experienced a large wave of immigration, with approximately 23 million people emigrating from Europe. Many of these immigrants were from non-English-speaking countries and were unable to obtain skilled work; they were thus forced to work in factories in unsafe and quite harsh conditions. Many were also forced to live in deplorable conditions, in tenements where several families shared small rundown rooms. For example, in the early 1900s in New York's Lower East Side, there were approximately 330,000 inhabitants per square mile (Trattner, 1998). Employment abuses, such as unsafe working conditions, extremely low wages, and child labor, were rampant with no labor laws to protect the vulnerable.

Addams was aware of these conditions and responded in a variety of ways. She founded the Hull House of Chicago with Ellen Gates Star, which served as the first settlement house in the United States. The Hull House served as a social hub and residential home to hundreds of poor immigrants who were victims of industrialization and the booming population in Chicago (Knight, 2010). Addams also engaged in advocacy on a variety of levels, focusing primarily on targeting the underlying causes of poverty such as unfair labor practices, the exploitation of non-English-speaking immigrants, and the absence of social programs or laws sufficient to protect the vulnerable.

Addams' advocacy went far beyond local efforts, as she advocated on a state, national, and international level for personal, social and cultural, political, and civil rights of women, children, immigrants, and African Americans. She was a strong advocate of the women's suffrage movement, advocating for women's rights in general and specifically for the woman's right to vote. She served as the president of the Women's International League for Peace and Freedom and as an officer in the National American Woman's Suffrage Association. She attended international conferences, where she spoke on human rights issues across a broad range of political and civil rights issues. She was an antiwar activist cofounding the Women's Peace Party and the Civil Liberties Bureau (which was renamed the Civil Liberties Union). She consistently advocated for approaches to international conflict resolution that involved "courageous advocacy" rather than violence or complete passivity. She also advocated for workers' rights and the eradication of sweatshops through several women's trade unions that operated out of the Hull House (Steen, 2006). Addams collaborated with other social justice advocates in her advocacy efforts. For instance, she worked with Ida B. Wells on issues related to racism and racial oppression.

Professional History

Understanding and Mastery: Historical roots of human services

Critical Thinking Question: Jane Addams was one of the first social justice advocates to recognize social causes of personal struggles. What were some of the social conditions that motivated Addams to action?

Ida B. Wells and the Anti-Lynching Movement

Ida B. Wells (1862–1931) was an African-American woman and nineteenth-century social advocate who was also influential in the field of social justice advocacy. In fact, Wells' campaign against racial oppression and inequity laid the foundation for the civil rights movement of the 1960s. Wells was approximately the same age as Addams, and ultimately coordinated efforts with her, but their lives could not have been more different.

Wells was born to parents who were slaves in rural Mississippi in 1862, and although her parents were ultimately freed, Wells' life was never free from the crushing effects of severe racial prejudice and discrimination. Wells was orphaned at the age of 16, and went on to raise her five younger siblings. This experience not only forced Wells to grow up quickly but also seemed to serve as a springboard for her subsequent fierce advocacy against racial injustice. Early in her advocacy career, Wells was the owner of a black newspaper (the only one of its kind) called *Free Speech*, where she consistently wrote about matters of racial oppression and inequity, including the vast amount of socially sanctioned crimes committed against blacks (Hamington, 2005).

The indiscriminate lynching of black men was prevalent in the South during Wells' lifetime, and was an issue that Wells became quite passionate about. Black men were commonly perceived as a threat on many levels, and there was virtually no protection of their personal, political, or social rights. The black man's reputation of an angry rapist was endemic in white society, and many speeches were given and articles written by white community members (including clergy) about this "growing problem." Davidson (2008) references an article published in a mainstream newspaper in the South, the *Commercial*, entitled "More Rapes More Lynchings," which cites the black man's penchant for raping white women. The article cites how Negros were losing their sense of "awe" of the white race; thus they no longer had any restraint in their behavior; thus they acted in ways that were consistent with their "nature" and their "bestial" desires. The constant characterization of black men as having an aggressive and insatiable sex drive, with their alleged inability to control their sexual desires (particularly in relation to white women), was linked to increased freedoms they had gained during the Civil War, which served as justification for what became an all-out slaughter of African-American men generally. These negative stereotypes continue to permeate contemporary society, and often contribute to challenges many black men face throughout the United States, even today.

Wells wrote extensively on the subject of the "myth of the angry black man," and the myth that all black men raped white women (Hamington, 2005). She challenged the growing sentiment in white communities that black men, as a race, were growing more aggressive and "lustful," leading to increases in the rape of white women. These accusations were often used as a justification for lynching black men throughout the South. Ironically, it appears as though another reason why white men were

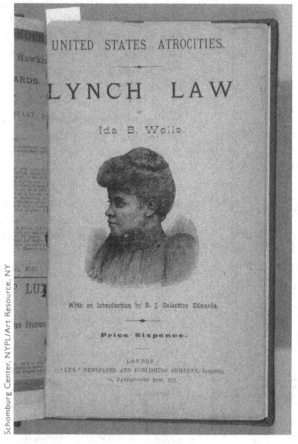

Schomburg Center, NYPL/Art Resource, NY

increasingly leveling these accusations against black men in part due to an increase in biracial relationships (Hamington, 2005). Wells' advocacy was not received well in her community, and the response to her articles was swift and harsh. A group of white men, enraged that a black woman challenged the status quo in this way, surrounded her newspaper building shortly after a particularly powerful story was published. Their intention was to lynch Wells herself, but when they could not find her they burned down her business instead, effectively stopping her career as a journalist and newspaper owner (Davidson, 2008).

Despite the fact that this act of aggression appeared to successfully halt Wells' journalism advocacy, what this act of revenge really did was to motivate Wells even further. After the burning of her newspaper business, Wells left the South and moved to Chicago, where she continued to wage a fierce anti-lynching campaign, writing books and articles on the subject, and challenging societally entrenched notions that all black men were dangerous (Hamington, 2005). Wells and Addams worked together in their advocacy efforts, coordinating their fight for civil rights on a variety of fronts. For instance, Wells and Addams ran the Chicago Association for the Advancement of Colored People, and worked collectively on a variety of projects, including fighting against racial segregation in schools.

An evaluation of the advocacy efforts of Addams and Wells reveals why categorizing advocacy efforts can be so challenging. Rarely do advocates act on behalf of a single issue, or engage in only one type of advocacy, on only one level. Rather, advocates such as Addams and Wells are involved in advocating for multiple social justice issues related to personal rights, political and civil rights, social and cultural rights, and economic (labor) rights. Addams and Wells engaged in micro-level work by working directly with vulnerable and impoverished populations (immigrants, African Americans, and those jailed for civil and political issues). They engaged in macro-level work through her engagement in community development projects, such as her work at the Hull House; her extensive writing of articles, position papers, and books; attending protests; forming advocacy organizations; and attending and speaking at local, national, and international meetings and conferences.

Assess your comprehension of The Roots of Social Justice Advocacy by taking this quiz.

Advocacy for Social Justice: Using a Human Rights Framework

The belief that all human beings have basic rights to just treatment within society, and the belief that these rights have been horribly violated in the past, ultimately led to the United Nations (UN) General Assembly drafting the *Universal Declarations of Human Rights* (UDHR) on December 10, 1948, which was passed a few years after the Second World War. Once the declaration was written the General Assembly disseminated it to all member countries, asking them to publicize the text throughout their country. In essence, the UN General Assembly was engaging in the type of advocacy Cohen et al. (2001) refer to in their definition of social justice advocacy—recognizing "what is," envisioning "what should be," and engaging in an organized effort to create awareness, with the goal of effecting change on a variety of levels (UN General Assembly, 1948).

corgarashu/Shutterstock

The preamble of the UDHR establishes an underlying assumption in the inherent dignity and inalienable rights of all human beings. The preamble also establishes the justification of its development based upon the existence of egregious human rights violations being committed against some human beings. And finally, it indicates the solution, asserting that the highest aspiration of common people is to be free to say what they want and believe what they want without fear. The declaration's universal nature is made clear in the statement that the various human rights listed in the treaty are to be treated as a standard for all peoples in every society, throughout the world (UN General Assembly, 1948).

The UDHR consists of 30 articles, each setting forth a particular human right. Article 1 establishes the inalienable nature of human rights afforded to all human beings simply because they are human. Article 2 establishes its universal nature, citing that all people without regard to race, color, gender, language, religion, political beliefs, nationality, property ownership, or state of birth are entitled to the rights and freedoms set forth in the declaration. The remaining articles outline specific human rights, and their parameters. For instance, Article 4 states that no one can be held either as a slave, or in servitude. Article 5 states that no one should be tortured, or subjected to cruel or unusual punishment. Article 15 grants the right to a nationality, Article 16 grants the right to marry by choice, Article 19 grants the right to freedom of opinion and expression, and Article 23 grants everyone the right to work.

The UDHR is a part of a larger bill, which also includes the *International Covenant on Economic, Social and Cultural Rights* and the *International Covenant on Civil and Political Rights*, both of which were adopted by the General Assembly in 1966. The UDHR and its two covenants constitute what is called the *International Bill of Human Rights*. This bill is the core covenant in a number of human rights treaties, called treaty bodies, each making a statement of "what should be" in regard to a particular type of human right or human rights violation (an example would be the *UN Convention on the Rights of the Child*).

Taken as a whole then, in response to a recognized history of egregious human rights violations (culminating in the Holocaust), the international community established a comprehensive list of basic and inherent rights for all humans that if respected would lead to a just and decent society. Falk (2009) points out though that the declaration did not address the issue of self-determination "so as not to challenge, even obliquely, the legitimacy of colonial rule" (p. 3). Thus, the declaration was never meant to be implemented on a compulsory basis with enforcement strategies, but was designed as an expression of future goals, with voluntary implementation.

Nonetheless, the UDHR provides a basis upon which human services professionals throughout history have built a legacy of advocacy, fighting for the rights and protection of the economically, politically, and socially vulnerable, including women; children; lesbian, gay, bisexual, and transgendered (LGBT) populations; ethnic and/or cultural groups; and refugees, stateless individuals, and migrants. The UDHR and the subsequently drafted set of treaty bodies also provide an effective framework for advocacy in general, establishing a *what-should-be* standard for which human services professionals and other advocates can aim, as they work diligently to change outcomes, thus improving the lives of those for whom they advocate.

Human Services Delivery Systems

Understanding and Mastery: International and global influences on service delivery

Critical Thinking Question: The UDHR provides a sound basis for ensuring that all human beings everywhere are treated with the dignity and equity they deserve, simply for being human. Is this a realistic goal, and if so, how can human services professionals use the UDHR to advocate for their clients?

The Downside of the Human Rights Movement

Using a human rights framework requires that we spend some time exploring the current state of the human rights movement. In addition to exploring the underlying assumptions upon which the movement is based, it is also important to examine the deficits, particularly with regard to contemporary human rights models that are based upon Western values. With the dramatic increase in armed civil conflict worldwide, particularly in the Global South, there is considerable concern about human rights violations, particularly of marginalized and vulnerable groups. Thus, the human rights movement has grown considerably alongside the increase in global conflict, in an attempt to address these concerns. The Internet, particularly social media, has made human rights advocacy an activity available to all who are concerned about human rights and has increased the reach and access for professional and grassroots volunteers. But with this increased activity comes increased power, and the potential to cause more harm than good, if a human rights worker, or an organization, is not cautious. For instance, within the context of conflict in the Global South, particularly sub-Saharan Africa, political exiles who resettle in the West often engage effectively with Western human rights advocates, joining forces to fight for human rights around the globe. Unfortunately, there is a significant risk of Western human rights activists being exploited and manipulated by some within politically active diaspora populations, particularly when the origin of the conflict and the cause for which they are fighting have their roots in ethnonationalism or fundamentalist religious movements (Collier, 2000; Collier & Hoeffler, 2002, 2004; Lyons, 2004).

Steven Kinzer refers to the issue of Western human rights workers being manipulated in his 2010 article entitled "End Human Rights Imperialism Now," where he argues that the human rights movement has lost its way, and is at risk of becoming a new form of imperialism, pushing its own agenda without always understanding broader historical and socio-political issues. Kinzer (2010), a former *New York Times* correspondent, who is now on the faculty of the Department of International Relations at Boston University, claims that many within the modern-day human rights movement have veered off from the movement's original mission, and "bathed in the light of self-admiration and cultural superiority," (para. 9), too often make decisions about the nature of human rights violations outside of vitally important cultural contexts. Describing how this attitude can lead to manipulation by rebel groups and their supporters, as well as an increase in conflict and human rights violations, Kinzer states:

> By their well-intentioned activism, they have given murderous rebel militias—not only in Darfur but around the world—the idea that even if they have no hope of military victory, they can mobilize useful idiots around the world to take up their cause, and thereby win in the court of public opinion what they cannot win on the battlefield. The best way to do this is to provoke massacres by the other side, which Darfur rebels have done quite successfully and remorselessly. This mobilizes well-meaning American celebrities and the human rights groups behind them. It also prolongs war and makes human rights groups accomplices to great crimes. (Kinzer, 2010, para. 10)

Another consideration when adopting a human rights framework is whether the current human rights model of "blame and shame" is appropriate for the human services discipline. The human services field is based upon a theoretical foundation that (1) respects a client's right to self-determination (and *client* can refer to an individual, or an entire community), (2) evaluates a client/client system within socio-political and historical context to ensure cultural competence, and (3) promotes home-grown solutions based upon the belief that clients are experts on their own lives and futures (Martin, 2013). Not only is there no room for blaming and shaming in the human services discipline, but using public humiliation as an intervention tool is contradictory to everything the human service field stands for. Thus, the question social justice advocates must ask is whether within a human services context a human rights model can be adapted in such a way that it does not incorporate blame and shame tactics. This is an issue that will be explored throughout this book, as the reader is encouraged to challenge the status quo and engage in advocacy for social justice in a way that reflects the human service values of self-determination, cultural competence, and bottom-up approaches that rely primarily upon "home-grown solutions." This is the only way that advocates can be sure to avoid Kinzer's description of human rights imperialism.

Human Services Delivery Systems

Understanding and Mastery: Political and ideological aspects of human service

Critical Thinking Question: Social justice advocates must balance their ideals of a just society with the need to become sufficiently competent on the contextual details of the issues being focused on. What are some ways social justice advocates can avoid engaging in "human rights imperialism" described by Kinzer?

Certainly, not all human rights organization engage in such polarizing tactics. In fact, there are hundreds, if not thousands, of human rights advocates, that do excellent work, engage professionally, without increasing conflict. Some of these advocates work with organizations are featured in this book, and they exemplify all of the good things about the human rights movement.

Assess your comprehension of <u>Using a Human Rights Framework</u> by taking this quiz.

Concluding Thoughts on Advocacy for Social Justice

The first section of this book will provide an overview of the field of advocacy within a human rights framework. Chapter 2 explores foundational issues that influence how at-risk populations are formed and are viewed, including an exploration of poverty and the attitudes of the poor, the long-lasting effects of colonization, the impact of globalization, as well as current social trends that have had a devastating effect on vulnerable populations, such as neoliberalism and the dismantling of the state. Chapter 3 explores ways in which advocacy practice occurs as well as some of the tools that advocates use to effect change within society. In Part II of this book advocacy practice is explored within the context of human rights violations against particular vulnerable populations, including women and girls (Chapters 4 and 5), children (Chapter 6), LGBT populations (Chapter 7), and refugees and migrants (Chapter 8). The epilogue explores the future of advocacy in light of continued globalization and recent global trends, such as an aging population, and the continued growth of technology and its influence on all of the advocacy fields.

My hope is that after reading this book those entering into the field of human services will have not only a greater understanding of advocacy practice for social justice on a macro level but will also have a greater passion for effecting change—on both small and grand scales, whether in their own neighborhoods, or in the far reaches of Asia, Africa, or Latin America. Passion is at the root of true advocacy, and with passion comes frustration, for all advocates can tell you that passion must fester and grow for some time before it finds its ultimate home—likely working within one of the areas that will be explored in the forthcoming chapters.

Assess your analysis and evaluation of this chapter's content by completing the **Chapter Review**.

CHAPTER 2

Contemporary Issues Affecting Social Justice

Poverty, Globalization, and Neocolonialism

mypokcik/Shutterstock

Dominator culture has tried to keep us all afraid, to make us choose safety instead of risk, sameness instead of diversity. Moving through that fear, finding out what connects us, reveling in our differences; this is the process that brings us closer, that gives us a world of shared values, of meaningful community.

—bell hooks

The area of advocacy is influenced and affected by several underlying issues and phenomena that are important to explore to gain a fuller picture of why advocacy is needed, how it is accomplished, and what challenges advocates for social justice face. These contemporary issues often frame the pursuit of justice by highlighting who it is that needs advocacy and why, as well as targeting particular themes and issues within society that create conditions that increase the risk of injustice for particular groups within a given society.

Before exploring some of the conditions that contribute to various types of injustices in the world, you might be wondering what makes an individual or a group in society more at risk of injustice in the first place. Why is it that some people seem to have the ability to "rise above" challenges in life and others do not? We all love stories about people who "pick themselves up by their bootstraps" and conquer adversity (a constant theme in North American films), but how do we feel about those within any society who seem to be in constant need of assistance? Are they just weaker than others? And if so, why? This line of questioning is very important because it leads us to explore why some groups of individuals within a society have more power than others, and conversely why some groups are more vulnerable than other groups, and finally why these vulnerable groups warrant special attention and advocacy.

Vulnerable Populations: Who Needs Advocacy and Why?

Vulnerable populations generally refer to those populations that are vulnerable to oppression, discrimination, injustice, and exploitation, "due to lifestyle, lack of political power, lack of financial resources, and lack of societal advocacy and support" (Martin, 2013, p. 317). Vulnerable populations often share unique characteristics not shared by others within the mainstream population (Brownridge, 2009), and it is this uniqueness that can often increase their risk of oppression, discrimination, injustice, and exploitation. Vulnerable populations are thus *at greater risk* of experiencing a variety of social problems compared to other populations within the majority and/or mainstream of society.

Vulnerable populations can vary from era to era, depending on how their uniqueness is perceived by the majority population, but currently groups that are at risk of injustice of some type include:

- Ethnic minorities
- Immigrants (particularly those who do not speak English)
- Indigenous people
- Older adults
- Women
- Children in foster care
- Prisoners
- The economically disadvantaged
- The homeless
- Single parents
- Lesbians, gays, bisexual, and transgendered individuals (LGBT)
- Members of a religious minority
- The physically and intellectually challenged (adapted from Martin, 2013, p. 317)

In addition to these groups Martin (2013) points out that

… in many regions of the world certain groups of individuals are selected and oppressed due to their ethnic background, religious heritage, and caste (their level of status within society, which in many regions of the world is a level one is born into), and although these individuals may not be in the minority as far as numbers, they typically have little to no political power and are subject to mistreatment and exploitation. (p. 318)

Poor widows in India from lower castes are very vulnerable due to a lack of government protection and social stigma.

Xander Martin

Vulnerability increases with what is called *intersectionality*—where an individual possesses more than one social and cultural characteristic of vulnerability, leading to incrementally increased risk of disadvantage. The concept of intersectionality was originally applied to race and gender but is now applied to a variety of additional marginalizing categories, such as level of disability, sexuality, socioeconomic status, social class, immigration status, nationality, and family status (Knudsen, 2005; Meyer, 2002; Samuels, 2008). An example of intersectionality of vulnerability is an African-American lesbian older adult who is economically disadvantaged, physically disabled, and struggling with homelessness. This profile reveals a woman who experiences multiple forms of vulnerability to injustice on a variety of levels, likely warranting various types of advocacy.

Social forces can combine as well, increasing the risk of discrimination, prejudice, oppression, and injustice. For instance, social conditions such as white privilege (advantage experienced by Caucasians to varying degrees), nativism (a bias against foreign-born residents or those who are perceived threats to a country's nationalism), xenophobia (an irrational fear of immigrants and foreigners), and other forms of prejudice often combine to increase a group's vulnerability to oppression, marginalization, and exploitation. Within the human services field, there is a recognition that vulnerable populations often need advocacy because many of the challenges that lay before them are created within society through government policies and legislation, institutionalized racism based on historic disenfranchisement, and stereotyped attitudes that create an uneven playing field, where some groups enjoy greater access to benefits (often referred to as "privilege"), whereas other groups are systematically overtly and covertly excluded from such societal benefits. The ways in which vulnerable characteristics and social forces interact are complex and will be explored in greater depth within subsequent chapters on particular types of oppression, marginalization, and human rights violations, but for the remainder of this chapter, I will be exploring what are often considered contemporary issues and phenomena that are often underlying various forms of human rights violations and conditions in need of advocacy.

One important point that is important to make before embarking on this journey relates to terminology. There are many terms used to distinguish between countries that are considered "developed," such as the United States, and those that are considered "developing," such as some countries in Africa. Terms are important in that they denote regional power differentials. Some literature uses the terms *Western* and *non-Western* to reflect cultural variations; another way of referring to this power differential is using the terms "Global North" and "Global South" which are more descriptively accurate, or "developed" or "developing," and "least developed" countries, which references a country's level of economic development. While these terms which reference are used somewhat interchangeably throughout this book, for the purposes of clarity, when I use the term *Western*, the *Global North*, or *developed*, I am referring primarily to Organisation for Economic Co-operation and Development [OECD] countries—countries considered as having advanced or emerging economies (see *http://www.oecd.org/about/membersandpartners/*).

> ### Client-Related Values and Attitudes
>
> *Understanding and Mastery: The worth and uniqueness of individuals, including ethnicity, culture, gender, sexual orientation, and other expressions of diversity*
>
> **Critical Thinking Question:** When evaluating the range of ways a social problem, such as poverty, impacts the population, it is important to consider the issue of intersectionality. How might characteristics such as gender, age, and race intersect to increase someone's risk of chronic poverty?

Assess your comprehension of Vulnerable Populations: Who Needs Advocacy and Why? by taking this quiz.

The Face and Nature of Poverty

A common theme underlying virtually all types of disadvantage is poverty because of its reciprocal relationship with oppression and justice, meaning poverty leads to and results from various types of oppression and injustice. The process of accurately framing the poverty condition is a challenging one due to its complex nature. Lister (2004) notes that there is no universally applied concept of poverty and describes how perceptions of poverty (and its causes) are often framed ideologically and politically, which then often dictates policy with regard to the societal distribution of goods and resources. Thus, arriving at a universally agreed-upon definition of poverty and method of measuring poverty is challenging, at least in part due to ways in which certain definitions can relate to a "call of action" on a political level. Any definition of poverty must effectively capture the full manifestation and effect of poverty, as well as accurately reflect the reciprocal relationship between the poverty condition and other related forms of disadvantage.

Traditionally poverty has been defined (and then measured) in either absolute or relative terms. Absolute poverty uses a poverty threshold (or reasonable standard of living) where individuals who fall below the established minimum standard of living threshold are considered to be living in poverty (Gordon, 2006; Townsend, 1979). The World Bank's definition of extreme poverty as living on less than $1 per day is example of poverty being defined in absolute terms (Ravallion, 1998). Poverty in developing countries is often reflected in absolute terms, primarily because poverty in many regions of the world, such as Africa, is extreme. These more narrow and concrete definitions of poverty use income and resources as tools with which to define and describe poverty (Lister, 2004). The absolute threshold does not vary from country to country and does not take cultural variations, or cross-comparative living standards into consideration (Lister, 2004; Simler & Arndt, 2006). While defining poverty in absolute terms may be convenient in the sense that it allows for easy intercountry comparisons, this convenience can also be its downfall, as such comparisons are rather arbitrary in nature since the poverty threshold is static, while the actual level of income required to live "adequately" differs widely from country to country, and even community to community can range significantly (Marx & van den Bosch, 2007; Townsend, 1979).

Another way of defining poverty is in relative terms, where the poverty threshold is set relative to the standard of living within a particular community (Simler & Arndt, 2006). Relative measures of poverty recognize that economic disadvantage is best evaluated within the context of regional standards of living (Callan & Nolan, 1991). An advantage of considering poverty in relative terms is that inequality and the level of relative deprivation can be more easily explored that more accurately reflects the complicated nature of poverty (Alcock, 2006; Lister, 2004). Additionally relative poverty measures poverty levels within social context thus the complexity of financial markets, varying lifestyles and incomes, and the fluid nature of social mobility (the ability of someone to move up the "income ladder") are recognized. Most European countries use relative poverty measures where poverty is measured based on economic distance from the median income level.

Despite all of the advantages of using a relative measure of poverty, the United States uses an absolute poverty measure based on what many economists believe is the outdated indicator of using the cost of food (a measure that assumes that the average family spends one-third of its income on food), which does not take into consideration regional differences or other costs of living indicators (which may fluctuate depending on the state of the

Cartoonresource/Shutterstock

"ACTUALLY, CARRUTHERS, IF YOU TAKE THE WORLD AVERAGE INCOME, YOU'RE GROSSLY OVERPAID."

economy), such as housing costs, transportation, and utilities (Lister, 2004). Both types of measures are faulted to a certain extent, with critics of relative measures of poverty arguing that while poverty is relative, it also has an "absolute core" that cannot be expressed in relative terms. Also, critics note how it's possible for some countries to have no relative poverty, but still have significant income inequality (the distance from the "haves" and "have nots"); thus relative poverty indicators can be misleading because they do not always measure actual economic disadvantage (Marx & van den Bosch, 2007). Scholars also criticize absolute measures of poverty, which are seen as too narrow, with somewhat arbitrarily set thresholds that do not take social context and social obligation into consideration, thus limiting the actual definition of poverty by omitting several forms of disadvantage (Townsend, 1979).

Poverty is almost always considered along with the concept of social exclusion, a form of deprivation that involves the marginalization and consequent exclusion of vulnerable groups from various domains within society, such as employment, education, and housing (Lessof & Jowell, 2000; Lee & Murie, 1999). Townsend (1979) characterizes poverty in relative terms, as the primary cause of social exclusion where those in society who are suffering from poverty have such limited resources that they are excluded from mainstream activities customary in one's society, such as having the resources to afford the typical diet, and the resources to maintain typical living conditions with customary amenities. If this is the case, then it makes sense that social programs should be developed to help lift people out of poverty by increasing access to education, employment, and social activities that will reduce their marginalization (thus increasing their income). Consider the woman who is born into poverty thus cannot afford to attend college, which limits employment opportunities. A social program that provides financial benefits used for attending school would theoretically enable her to gain the skills necessary to enter the job market.

Yet, there is another theory that holds that the opposite is true—that social exclusion causes poverty. Thus the woman is poor not because she has been excluded from the labor force, but because her refusal to work is what has made her poor. If this theory is true, then social programs that provide benefits without the mandate of working will theoretically fail. What underlies each perspective are assumptions about those suffering from poverty, and what has made them poor—are they generally good or bad? Are they worthy or unworthy? Are they victims of harsh social conditions or of their own poor choices? Do they want to work, or are they inherently lazy? The answers to these questions will determine the most effective course of action among policy makers, and then often, carves out the work of advocates who challenge these underlying assumptions, particularly when they are based on negative stereotypes and based on incorrect information.

Human Services Delivery Systems

Understanding and Mastery: Economic and social class systems including systemic causes of poverty

Critical Thinking Question: Why is it important to consider elements of social exclusion when defining poverty and evaluating its impact?

Attitudes toward the Poor: Worthy or Unworthy?

Poverty is very complex and is intertwined with many other issues. Unpacking these interconnected dynamics can help identify what groups are more vulnerable to poverty, the types of social exclusion that will lead to the most profound forms of poverty, and what the long-term consequences of social exclusion are. For instance, gaining a greater understanding of how years of excluding African-Americans from the labor market, educational institutions, and the housing market may yield valuable information on the nature of social problems currently being experienced by African-Americans, such as the high unemployment rates among African-American males, or the overrepresentation of African-Americans in the U.S. penal system (Feagin, 2004).

A common argument against advocacy efforts on behalf of the economically disadvantaged is based on the belief that disadvantage is no longer an issue in contemporary society, thus poverty and its related problems are self-made. The belief that the playing field in society is level infers that everyone has an equal chance at opportunity and prosperity. If this assumption is accurate, then it can be argued that misfortune in life is more often the fault of the person (versus society); thus the solution must be a personal one, and not the responsibility of society. This perspective is probably one of the most significant challenges advocates face when attempting to advocate for social justice in regard to poverty-related causes. Such arguments are often relied on in political debates where the merits of self-sufficiency and hard work are passionately argued, and social programs are cited as the actual *cause* of hardship, not the solution. Urgent calls for the end of social programs that enable those within society to remain dependent on "big government" are often the hallmark of conservative political discourse, which again is based on the presumption that every person within society has equal access to the benefits and privileges that societal membership entails. Often such arguments incite an "us versus them" mentality where one segment of the population is pitted against another, and matters of equity are inverted—where the majority population is made to believe that other (often less fortunate and less regarded) groups within society are gaining unfair advantage and obtaining resources unfairly. We have seen such arguments in a variety of arenas, most notably in the areas of public assistance programs and immigration.

Although there has been some shifting in how the poor and vulnerable in society are perceived, two major studies in the 1980s and 1990s illustrated growing negative perceptions of those struggling with poverty, particularly those seeking government assistance. In these studies, those surveyed stated that they supported the general idea of helping the poor, but most were critical of government welfare programs, and welfare recipients in general. In fact, one study found that three-quarters of those surveyed believed that most welfare recipients were dishonest and collected more benefits than they deserved (Feagin, 1975; Kluegal, 1987).

Politicians and others in power have been scapegoating the poor and disadvantaged for years for political advantage. Unfortunately the intersectionality in this regard is often race and gender, with African-American women being the target of much of the public rage over what was perceived as welfare abuse. Ronald Reagan capitalized on this negative sentiment toward the poor during the 1976 presidential campaign when he based his platform in large part on welfare reform ("Welfare Queen," 1976). In several of Reagan's speeches, he cited the story of the woman from the South Side of Chicago who was finally arrested after committing egregious welfare fraud:

> She has eighty names, thirty addresses, twelve Social Security cards and is collecting veteran's benefits on four non-existing deceased husbands. And she is collecting Social Security on her cards. She's got Medicaid, getting food stamps, and she is collecting welfare under each of her names. (Zucchino, 1999, p. 65)

Regan went on to claim that she defrauded the government of about $150,000 per year, while not working. While Reagan never mentioned the woman's race, the context of the story as well as the reference to the South Side of Chicago (a primarily black community) made it clear that he was referring to an African-American woman on welfare—thus matching the common stereotype of welfare users (and abuser) (Krugman, 2007). This story is presumed to have been based on an African-American woman in Chicago named Linda Taylor, who used two aliases and cheated the government out of $8,000 (not $150,000, and no veteran's benefits). Also, she did not get away with anything, as she was caught, charged with welfare fraud and perjury, and sentenced (Gustafson, 2009). Despite the lack of factual information in Regan's assertions, the enduring myth of the *welfare queen* was born.

Journalist David Zucchino attempted to debunk the myth of the welfare queen in his exposé on the reality of being a mother on welfare, but stated in his book *The Myth of the*

Rob Crandall/SCPhotos/Alamy

African American women who struggle with poverty are often stigmatized due to negative stereotypes based on false political rhetoric

Welfare Queen that the image of the African-American woman who drove a Cadillac while collecting welfare illegally from numerous false identities was so imbedded in American culture that it was impossible to debunk the myth, even though the facts do not back up the myth (Zucchino, 1999). Krugman (2007) also cites how politicians have used the myth of the welfare queen to reduce sympathy for the poor and gain public support for welfare cuts ever since, arguing that while covert, such images clearly play on negative racial stereotypes. They also play on the common belief in the United States that those who receive welfare benefits are poor due to immoral behavior and a lack of motivation to work.

Take, for instance, the common arguments for welfare reform (policies that reduce and restrict social welfare programs and services) that have often been predicated on the beliefs that (1) hardship is often the result of laziness; (2) providing assistance will increase laziness (and thus dependence), hence increasing hardship, not decreasing it; and (3) those in need often receive services at the expense of the working population. A 1995 article in *Time* magazine entitled "100 Days of Attitude" captured this "us vs. them" dynamic fostered in the debate on welfare reform in the mid-1990s. In his article, Stacks (1995) states that

> … the country is up in arms over welfare, convinced that while the middle class is struggling, the poor are getting something for nothing. The debate in the House on welfare was symptomatic of that anger. Representative John Mica of Florida's Seventh District compared welfare recipients to alligators and cautioned that "unnatural feeding and artificial care increases dependency." His fellow Republican, Representative Barbara Cubin of Wyoming, decided that the better analogy was to caged wolves: "When you take away their freedom and their dignity, they can't provide for themselves." (p. 3)

Professional History

Understanding and Mastery: How public and private attitudes influence legislation and the interpretation of policies related to human services

Critical Thinking Question: In what ways have historic and contemporary attitudes toward the poor and poverty influenced social welfare policy and provision?

Such perspectives negate the complexity of economic disadvantage often experienced by vulnerable populations, and categorize the poor as a homogenous group that is in some significant way different with regard to character than mainstream working society.

How the poor are perceived in Western societies has everything to do with how they are treated. Since vulnerable populations are often excluded from the labor market and other benefits enjoyed by more privileged members of society, they often experience far greater levels of poverty, which in turn increases their vulnerability, making them targets for human rights violations. In the next section, I explore some political and ideological trends that have significantly influenced how the vulnerable and disadvantaged populations are viewed and treated.

Assess your comprehension of the <u>Face and Nature of Poverty</u> by taking this quiz.

Social and Political Movements Affecting Economically Disadvantaged Populations

Throughout history there have been numerous waves of ideological trends and political movements that have affected the disadvantaged within society. For example, some ideological trends have reflected compassion toward the plight of the poor, while some have been grounded in a more punitive approach citing the moral failure of the poor (Betten, 1973). Such attitudes have been instrumental in influencing how the poor and disadvantaged populations have been viewed and treated, both by politicians supporting social welfare legislation, as well as attitudes held by the general population.

It is incumbent upon human services professionals working with economically disadvantaged populations to become aware of both the historical and contemporary ideological influences of social welfare policy in the United States, as well as the assumptions about poverty and the poor that often underlie social policies, programs, and practices. It is only through greater awareness that those in the human services fields can proactively advocate for social justice and avoid internalizing the ideological biases of the mainstream population and particular political movements.

Social Darwinism and the Survival of the Fittest

Social Darwinism is a philosophy that has influenced how mainstream population has viewed the poor for more than a century, and although the term *social Darwinism* is not as frequently utilized, the power of this theory remains strong, even in contemporary society. Social Darwinism is a theory was a theory developed in the mid-nineteenth century and involves the application of Charles Darwin's theory of natural selection to the social world. Darwin theorized that the process of natural selection ensured that only the fittest members of a species would survive, thus guaranteeing the successful survival of the group (Darwin, 1859/2009). The application of the "survival of the fittest" philosophy to the human social world significantly influenced how poverty and the disadvantaged were perceived and treated within the U.S. social welfare system, and to an extent, Europe as well.

One of the most influential social Darwinists was Herbert Spencer, an English philosopher who applied the concepts of natural selection to the social world prior to Darwin's development of his theory. In fact, it was Spencer who coined the phrase *survival of the fittest* in reference to the theory that human competitiveness for limited resources was a prerequisite for the survival of the "fittest" members of society. Spencer opposed all forms of government intervention on behalf of the poor and disadvantaged based on his belief that such interventions would interfere with the "natural order" of things, thus threatening the survival of society (Hofstadter, 1992). Spencer's theory embraced the concept of social superiority, which justified the existing power structures in society, by citing not only personal responsibility for poverty but biological superiority as well.

Although many people within society may not recognize the term *social Darwinism*, many social scientists believe that this philosophy has greatly influenced how the poor are viewed, and significantly contributed to the belief that helping the poor will only further lead to their dependence and ultimate demise (Martin, 2011). Seeing the poor and disadvantaged as weak and condemned, and not worthy of saving has influenced perceptions of poverty alleviation significantly, something that will be explored in more depth in subsequent chapters in more depth.

The Christian Right's Influence on Poverty Perceptions and Poverty Programs

It seems as though both the Republican Party and a conservative faction of the Protestant Christian faith community may have been influenced by social Darwinism, as well as other religious philosophies that play into social structures of power and hierarchy, without recognizing historical oppression and social exclusion.

A new rather powerful voice within the Republican Party includes what is often called the *Christian Right*—a group of individuals, often fundamentalist Christians, who espouse "conservative family values," juxtaposed to emerging contemporary values embraced by other groups within society (e.g., LGBT populations and other progressive-leaning populations). Conservative Christian organizations, such as the Christian Coalition, the Eagle Forum, and Focus on the Family, have wielded considerable influence within the Republican Party beginning in the 1980s, becoming a core of the party in the 1990s (Green, Rozell, & Wilcox, 2005; Guth & Green, 1986; Knuckey, 2005). These groups were instrumental in the call for welfare reform by voicing concern about the moral decline of society. While many associated with these groups professed to be protecting traditional family values, some believe that their battle cries were in reality a response to growing multiculturalism and growing advocacy movements on behalf of alternative lifestyles (Reese, 2006; Uluorta, 2008). In fact, an examination of many of the claims among many on the Christian Right resonate with nativism, xenophobia, extremist nationalism, and a form of protectionism that often represents the values of the majority population while framing behaviors that often result from oppression and lack of resources as immoral (Uluorta, 2008). Many within the Christian Right professed ardent support for welfare reform measures in the mid-1990s because of the focus on behavioral reform, including the promotion of marriage and sexual abstinence (Reese, 2006).

Complaints of big government, and a nationalist platform that values self-sufficiency, rugged individualism and traditional moral standards (a luxury that often the vulnerable and marginalized cannot afford) underlie the recent trend in privatizing social welfare benefits, a political philosophy referred to as *Neoliberalism*. Neoliberalism is based on the belief that big government is inherently wasteful, inefficient, and enabling, and that poverty is better addressed within the private domain. In general, the argument for the privatization of public services posits that the free market will make it possible for the private sector to provide welfare and public services more efficiently and at a lower cost than the public sector, thus providing a greater benefit to society (Gollust & Jacobson, 2006; Hacker, 2002; Sclar, 2000).

The application of market theory to welfare provision, while growing in popularity, is highly criticized by social justice advocates who challenge whether this capitalist approach can be a solution for all problems in society. In fact, research shows that when social welfare services are privatized, public service ethos suffers, and the most vulnerable members of society are often excluded from receiving services because providing them with human services is often not very profitable (Hacker, 2002; Nelson, 1992; Pack, 1989; Schlesinger, Dorwat, & Pulice, 1986; Shonick & Roemer, 1982; Van Slyke, 2003).

The Tea Party: A New Populist Movement with Old Ideas

The *Tea Party* movement (named in symbolic allegiance to the Boston Tea Party—a protest in 1773 of American colonists objecting to excessive taxation on tea) is a relatively new grassroots conservative political movement that came onto the political scene in about 2009. Although the Tea Party has no agreed-upon political platform, and no designated leaders, they appear to be gaining increasing political clout and membership, with a recent poll indicating that close to 20% of the U.S. voting population identify themselves as Tea Party supporters (*New York Times*/CBS News, 2010).

According to many social advocates, Tea Party members are waging an all-out war against disadvantaged populations, including the poor, single mothers, ethnic minorities, and immigrants. The movement began with a few sporadic protests organized around similar themes, including advocating for smaller government, reduced government spending, and lower taxes. But as the movement has grown, other very conservative (and many believe divisive) political goals have emerged as well that appear to extend beyond economic issues. For instance, the majority of Tea Party backers support immigration reform and stricter border enforcement, and are against environmental protection laws and expanded political powers of the LGBT population (Barretto & Parker, 2010).

A Bloomberg poll conducted in 2010 found that self-described members of the Tea Party movement were far "more likely than other voters to be white, married, 55 and older, and call themselves born-again Christians" (Bloomberg National Poll, 2010, para 10). The poll also found that the majority of Tea Party supporters surveyed consider themselves Republican, and were mid-

dle to upper-middle class with regard to income and education levels. Interestingly, while the majority of Tea Party members supported spending cuts in social programs, including repealing the Affordable Care Act (aka "Obamacare"), the majority were against allowing Bush's tax breaks for higher-income Americans to expire.

Another poll conducted in 2010 by the *Washington Post* found similar results but revealed quite troubling racial perspectives among many Tea Party activists. For instance, when asked whether African-Americans had received less then they deserved in the last few years, 78% of self-described Tea Party members surveyed stated that they disagreed. Similarly, 74% agreed with the statement that while equal opportunity programs for ethnic minorities were important for their success, it was not really the government's responsibility to guarantee equal rights for minorities, and 46% agreed with the statement that "if blacks would only try harder they'd be just as successful as whites." Only 18% believed that gays and lesbians should have the right to marry, and 52% believed they had too much political power. Finally, the poll found that 73% of Tea Party respondents expressed disapproval of President Obama's plan to engage Muslim countries, and 63% disagreed with the statement "We should not single out Muslims or Middle Easterners for airport security stops."

Another poll conducted by the *New York Times* in 2010 found that the majority of Tea Party supporters believe that their views are representative of the majority of Americans (they are not), and over 30% still question whether President Obama was born in the United States. A 2010 analysis of the Tea Party movement conducted by the Institute of Research and Education on Human Rights found that a significant aspect of this movement is based on resentment toward the poor, with over 75% of Tea Party members disclosing that they believe that federal safety nets actually encourage people to remain poor (Burghart & Zeskind, 2010). In fact, Burghart and Zeskind found in their statistical analysis that Tea Party members are majority members of U.S. society who are "angry middle-class white people" who believe that their country has been taken away from them by others in the country who are not "real Americans" (p. 8). In general, Burghart and Zeskind's analysis of the Tea Party movement on a local and national level found strong indications that bigotry and nativism are driving forces in the movement.

Although the Tea Party movement was initially perceived as a fringe segment of the Republican Party, it appears to be growing in size and power. While it is too early to tell whether this movement has true staying power or is merely a reaction to the late-2000 financial crisis and the election of the first African-American president, the results of these opinion polls suggest that supporters of the Tea Party movement embrace values that are antithetical to the values held by most human services professionals, and certainly by those engaging in advocacy for social justice. Further, analyses of this conservative movement also suggests that it is strongly contributing to the "us versus them" politics espoused by social Darwinists and others who negate structural causes of disadvantage.

Assess your comprehension of <u>Social and Political Movements affecting Economically Disadvantaged Populations</u> by taking this quiz.

Global Poverty in Developing Nations

Up to this point, poverty has been explored primarily within the context of a developed or Western countries, also referred to as the *West*, or the *Global North*, but much advocacy for social justice occurs on a global level, thus exploring the nature of poverty in the context of developing countries will provide necessary context for better understanding many of the human rights violations occurring in the world today. Most of the injustices that will be explored in subsequent chapters have extreme poverty as a common thread that is woven through each condition. Many human rights violations are the direct result of contemporary civil wars that create conditions leading to extreme vulnerability. For instance, civil conflict in many regions in Africa and Asia have resulted in mass murders and forced migration that have left children orphaned and vulnerable to everything from sex trafficking, bonded labor, and conscription into armed services (Roby & Shaw, 2006). It is poverty that compels young women and children to work in sweatshop conditions; poverty entices desperate families to cross international borders with the hope of finding a better life in another country, only to be subjected to economic and personal exploitation.

Whenever I teach a global social policy class, invariably there is at least one student who will ask me why Americans should care about what is happening in Africa, particularly when we have so many problems here at home. This is a loaded question of course because it is based on several presumptions—most of which are false. First, the student is operating off the assumption that what happens in Africa stays in Africa. In the last chapter, we explored the effects of globalization, thus it should be clear at this point that events occurring even in the far reaches of the world have global ramifications. Yet the student is also assuming the United States has not engaged in any policies that have contributed to global poverty and other social conditions in developing nations, and may even be under the common impression that the United States loans money to developing nations solely for humanitarian reasons. In this section, we explore each of these assumptions as I attempt to answer the question: *Why should we care?* Exploring such issues as colonialism and postcolonialism and how these practices of exploitation have led to mass conflict and extreme poverty in many parts of the world.

A History of Colonialism

Colonialism is another issue that remains relevant in advocacy for social justice due to its long-lasting consequences. Colonialism is a form of domination popular in the fifteenth to twentieth centuries, involving the practice of one territory claiming control over another, often-distant territory, for the purposes of expansion, exploitation, and profit (Horvath, 1972). The term *colonialism* is often used interchangeably with the term *imperialism,* but there are important differences. Horvath (1972) notes that a territory was considered *colonized* when individuals from the colonizing territory migrated to the new territory and settle there, thus colonizing the "new" land. A territory is considered to have been *imperialized* when there was domination of a territory, but little to no settling by outsiders. Despite this difference, most scholars agree that the practice of colonization and imperialism had similarly devastating effects on developing countries as well as the original people who lived in them. In fact, many of the social, psychological, and physical problems, such as high rates of poverty, substance abuse and child welfare issues, currently experienced by the Native American population in the United States can be traced to the physical and cultural genocide of these indigenous populations during the long process of colonization and domination.

Several scholars agree that many of the problems currently being experienced in many African countries, such as abject poverty, recurrent civil conflict (often resulting in mass forced migration), and continued interstate territorial disputes, as well as vast human rights violations, are the direct or indirect result of years of colonial invasion, exploitation, and rule (Afisi, 2009; Reno, 2011; Yoon, 2009). In fact, in the past two decades, there have been between 16 and 33 armed intra- and interstate conflicts in developing countries, predominantly in Africa (SIPRI, 1993, 2008), and many scholars theorize that such conflicts are a direct result of colonialism.

The colonization of Africa was swift and dramatic. Various European countries colonized the majority of the African continent during what is often called the *Scramble for Africa,* between the latter part of the 1800s and early 1900s, during the Industrial Revolution. There were many motivations for invading Africa, including the valuable resources found in many African regions, ranging from minerals to people, but one primary reason for colonizing Africa was to manage the exports of commodities (Blanton, Mason, & Athow, 2001). Many regions in Africa were invaded or annexed during this time period, and competition was so fierce that there was some fear that a consequence of this rush for territory (and commodities) in Africa might result in war between European countries.

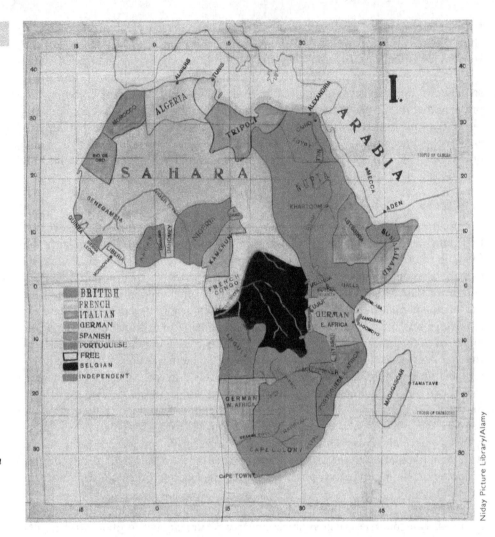

Partitioning of Africa by European Colonizers 1885-1914 (often called the "Scramble for Africa")

The Berlin Conference of 1884 was one attempt to manage the colonization of Africa by regulating its colonization by European powers. Several rules and acts were passed during the Belgium conferences of 1884 and 1885 that stipulated how territories were to be obtained and attempted to address multiple claims that could potentially result in conflict between European countries. Various disputes were resolved at the conference, thus avoiding violent clashes between the colonizing European countries (which could disrupt trade exports), but the conference also had the effect of speeding up colonization (Uzoigwe, 1985). Some examples are Germany's colonization of German East Africa, which included what is now called Rwanda, Burundi, and Tanzania, in 1880; Belgium's subsequent colonizing of Rwanda and a part of the Congo River Basin; the British authority colonizing Northern Rhodesia (now called Zambia), Kenya, and Southern Nigeria; and France colonizing Niger and Côte d'Ivoire (Yoon, 2009). Subsequent treaties resulted in even more colonization and land partitioning, referred to as the delimitation (or establishment) of boundaries.

Colonialism gradually decreased after the Second World War and an era of decolonization began where many African countries were slowly granted independence, managed for the most part by a United Nations mandate. On December 14, 1960, the *Declaration on the Granting of Independence to Colonial Countries and Peoples* was passed, stating that

> The subjection of peoples to alien subjugation, domination and exploitation constitutes a denial of fundamental human rights, is contrary to the United Nations Charter, and is an impediment to the promotion of world peace and cooperation, and that steps should be taken to transfer, unconditionally, all powers to the Trust and Non-Self-Governing Territories so that they might enjoy complete freedom and independence. (UN General Assembly, 1997, para 2)

The goal of the UN mandate was that all colonized territories would be self-ruled as soon as feasibly possible. Two years later, the UN General Assembly established the *Special Committee on Decolonization* to monitor compliance, but despite UN involvement and commitment, the transition toward self-rule was anything but smooth. Territorial boundaries in Africa were for the most part nonexistent prior to colonialism, and colonizers created arbitrary borders (sometimes in straight lines) without much thought to natural geographic boundaries or ethnic communities, thus colonial boundaries often separated ethnic clans that had lived in community for centuries. During the decolonization process, several countries claimed historic lands to regain cultural and territorial cohesion, and many of these claims resulted in territorial and ethnic conflict (Blanton et al., 2001; Yoon, 2009). In addition, research indicates that the ways in which colonial powers ruled, including the structures for managing ethnic clans, have significantly influenced conflict during independence, including exacerbating ethnic polarization (Blanton et al., 2001). Understanding the nature and effects of colonialism on developing countries is important because what occurs in these regions now not only directly affects people all over the world but is a direct consequence of Western countries' earlier exploitation of their lands.

Neocolonialism: A New Form of Colonialism through Economic Policies

A significant amount of advocacy work also centers on human rights issues in countries in postcolonial/postconflict regions. In fact, several advocates believe that many developing countries (particularly those with resources, such as minerals) are still being exploited by Western powers, through what is called *neocolonialism*—a set of policies that have a similar effect as colonialism by controlling developing countries governance through global debt, lending, and UN governance mandates (Cohen, de la Vega, & Watson, 2001), made easier through globalization.

While the United Nations no longer permits overt colonization of countries as was permitted in the past, powerful countries can gain control over a developing country's political structure and resources through investment and lending. For instance, some of the lending practices of global lending organizations managed primarily by Western countries, such as the World Bank, the World Trade Organization, and the International Monetary Fund, are cited by social justice advocates as continuing the legacy of earlier colonial practices by imposing Western values on developing nations with vastly different cultures (Polack, 2004). Virtually all global lending is now facilitated by these world lending institutions, which institute Structural Adjustment Programs (SAPs) (now referred to as Poverty Reduction Strategy Papers) as a financial management tool, with the goal of increasing effective fiscal management and reducing mismanagement, particularly in fledgling democracies. SAPs often favor labor market reforms involving privatization and other neoliberal economic policies that critics claim severely affect education, health care and social welfare programs, thus harming the most vulnerable members of society (Cohen et al., 2001; SAPRIN, 2002). SAPs (or PRSPs as they are now called) are often cited by social justice advocates as representing a form of neocolonialism, alleging that international aid and development programs are being used as a way of controlling developing countries economies, and at times as a way of exploiting resources (Cohen et al., 2001; Polack, 2004).

Such programs have been highly criticized by analysts and foreign governments, particularly those in developing and Muslim countries who have become suspicious of attempts to Westernize their countries through linking eligibility criteria and funding goals for international aid and development programs to Western values (Roy, 2008). Citing Olivier Roy's writings on the democratization of recipient countries, DeCroider cites how donor country development policies are very Western in nature, in particular, reflecting the value of democracy prevalent in the United States. Roy points out how U.S. policies of democratization in international aid and development programs are anchored by neoliberal policies that reflect a general suspicion of indigenous governments, particularly those that are based on values of collectivism. Roy sums up the Western philosophy of governance as a democracy that is based on individualism within a market economy, where common collectivist practices of nepotism, tribalism, and ethnic networks are seen as negative forces, and where religion is seen as an "expression of personal faith and not in allegiance to a community" (p. 33). This doctrine has placed civil society outside of the domain of the state, and into the realm of the individual, which is completely contrary to collectivist cultures commonly practiced in most developing countries.

Such conflicts in cultural values might explain some of the anger directed at Western countries and the international aid organizations funded by them. To those skeptics who claim that if a developing country does not agree with the assistance policies they should simply not borrow money or accept assistance from donor countries or organizations, the issue is not as clear-cut as such an argument may imply. There is mounting evidence that suggests that it is the neoliberal policies in many circumstances that contribute to some developing countries' continued economic vulnerability (Polack, 2004). This issue is discussed in greater detail in the next section, particularly the section focusing on global debt.

Globalization: A Shrinking World

Neocolonialism has been made possible through a phenomenon called globalization, another phenomenon that has significantly affected disadvantaged populations, as well as the field of advocacy. Globalization involves the process of "standardizing social institutions, economic policies and markets, and governments and governmental policies; homogenizing people and their cultures; and substituting uniformity for diversity in policies and practices" (Briar-Lawson, Lawson, Hennon, & Jones, 2006,

p. 296). Generally, globalization refers to the "shrinking" of the world in the political, geographical, cultural, and technological realms. Communication has never been faster. In the past, communicating with someone in another part of the world might take weeks. Now, with email, social media, newsgroups, blogs and cell phones, information and news can get from one part of the world to another almost instantaneously.

Globalization has had a significant impact in virtually every area of our lives—everything from the "deterritorialization" of war (where wars are no longer fought within borders but extend beyond borders, such as through Internet propaganda), to the interdependence of the world's various economic systems. When the United States experienced a financial crisis in the late-2000s, the reverberations were felt worldwide due to the global investment market. Cultures are rarely isolated any longer, and Western music and fashion frequently influences teens in some of the most remote parts of the world. So what is the effect of globalization on the human services fields? The effect is dramatic!

Twenty years ago, when I was an undergraduate I took a class on "Third World Countries." The course focused on Africa, particularly South Africa, which at the time was still practicing apartheid. As a class assignment, we were required to locate information about human rights violations occurring in the country related to the apartheid movement. I spent weeks tracking down newspaper articles from a variety of news sources and other reports from human rights organizations such as Amnesty International. What I had to go through to obtain this information would likely shock current undergraduate students. I had to send written requests to news agencies abroad and to the human rights organizations working in South Africa, via the U.S. Postal Service with a check enclosed to pay for the reprinting and mailing of the requested information. The entire process took weeks and was quite cumbersome. Today, all students (or any interested parties) need to do is go to their laptop, open a browser, connect to the Internet, and "Google" their search terms, and instantly they will likely find over a million hits of websites containing information relevant to their interest.

The ability to disseminate information so quickly and broadly means that advocates in one country can quickly learn what is going on in another country and can almost immediately share this information with others. Additionally, the skills and knowledge of advocates working in Western countries can be transferred to advocates in developing countries, and news of what is happening on the ground can be disseminated almost immediately. A great example of this is the 2009 civilian uprising in Iran in response to the contested presidential election. Once the uprising began, the Iranian government barred all press from entering the country, yet participants were tweeting, blogging, and filming the scenes using their cell phones, and immediately sending their reports to major news agencies, such as CNN, which aired them for the world to see. No sooner did the Iranian government shut down social media sites, hackers within Iran opened up new channels of electronic communication to the West (Schonfeld, 2009). The practice of lay journalism using social media has become so prevalent that CNN has given it the name *iReporting*—defined as a form of public journalism where people from around the world can submit videos of breaking news as they witness it unfolding (Scheim, 2011).

Assess your comprehension of Globalization: A Shrinking World by taking this quiz.

iReporting during Iran's 2009 post-election violence

Cyberactivism: Using the Internet for Advocacy Purposes

The Internet has completely changed the way advocacy is accomplished. It has enabled social justice advocacy to grow in size far faster than in previous generations. And often these movements have no identifiable leader, thus rather than the traditional top-down advocacy movements of the past, the Internet has enabled formerly disconnected groups from all over the world to connect and coordinate through online social networks. In the past, a demonstration had to be organized over several months by a few key organizers who mailed paper flyers and made telephone calls. Yet now the Internet permits information about protests and other forms of activism to be disseminated instantly, and broadly, by a number of people, allowing news of an event to go "viral" through various types of social media, such as e-mail, text, Twitter, listservs and Facebook. The capacity of the Internet to facilitate mass mobilization allows organizers and participants the potential to reach thousands of people in a matter of minutes, something not possible in the pre-Internet era.

The term *cyberactivism* is often used to describe the use of the Internet as a tool in advocacy (Morris & Langman, 2005). In Carty and Onyett's 2006 analysis of the role of cyberactivism in peace and social justice movements, they explore the many ways in which the Internet affects the existing processes involved in traditional forms of social justice advocacy and activism. Rheingold (2002) refers to this type of Internet-driven mass mobilization of people who are most often virtual strangers, but work in concert with one another via the Internet as "smart mobs," which he describes as being the wave of the future in social advocacy movements. In describing how the Internet has and will continue to change the way protest movements are facilitated, Rheingold describes how the mobile devices of today are actually microcomputers that allow people to coordinate their actions with others around the world, wielding social power that enables people to engage in ways that were never before possible.

Another strategy often used by activists using the Internet is *swarming*. Carty and Onyett (2006) describe *swarming* as various social networking groups engaging in different forms of activism, such as protest demonstrations, seemingly spontaneously while they are actually organized through the Internet. It is the very fact that swarming by smart mobs does not require central leadership that makes it so effective, and so difficult for political elites to manage, since it is "multi-headed [thus] impossible to decapitate" (Carty & Onyett, 2006, p. 242). As an example of the power of smart mobs Rheingold cites how President Joseph Estrada of the Philippines was ousted from power in response to mass demonstrations organized through text messages.

Another way that the Internet can assist in advocacy efforts is by shrinking the distance between observer and victim, a challenge that activists have faced for years. This distance typically allows the general public to remain emotionally aloof in situations in need of advocacy. By closing the gap between "us vs. them" solidarity is enhanced "through a shared sense of morality and consciousness of human rights," and as a consequence, average citizens will be much more likely to get involved (Carty & Onyette, 2006, p. 242). This is easily accomplished in an online social networking environment where photo streams, videos, and personal testimonies bring the laptops of everyday uninvolved citizens.

A good example of how the Internet has been used to engage everyday citizens, by increasing the ability for mass mobilization and appealing to constituents by closing the gap between us and them, is *MoveOn.org*, a public policy advocacy organization, founded in the United States in 1998. This virtual grassroots advocacy organization boasts over 7 million online members and consists of a Political Action Committee (PAC) and a civic action website. *MoveOn.org* organizers engage in online activities, such as the facilitation of online petitions where they have collected millions of digital signatures of average citizens not typically involved with activism. One way that *MoveOn.Org* organizers mobilize activists is by sending e-mails and texts to members encouraging them to call and fax their congressional representatives in support or against various causes. For instance, in opposition to the impending U.S. invasion of Iraq, *MoveOn.org* engaged in a virtual civil disobedience campaign resulting in U.S. congressional offices receiving hundreds of thousands of telephone calls and faxes with the simple message "DON'T ATTACK IRAQ!" that not only sent a clear message of dissent among a very large constituency but also illustrated the sheer power of the Internet since this action resulted in Senate office fax machines and telephone lines being clogged for hours (Carty & Oynett, 2006).

The effects of globalization of communication technologies are not always positive though. For instance, criminal activities have become far more easily coordinated. While law enforcement and social justice advocates can now more easily than ever discover and report virtual networks of human sex trafficking, the traffickers can use this same technology to coordinate the sale and transfer of women and children into the sex trade (Kunze, 2010). For example, Craigslist, an online community-moderated forum where people can place free classified ads, quickly became the largest source for pimping

Information Management

Understanding and Mastery: Using technology for word processing, sending email, and locating and evaluating information

Critical Thinking Question: The globalization of communication technologies has significantly changed the way that human service professionals engage in advocacy practice. What are some positive and negative ways that technology has impacted the field of advocacy?

and prostitution. According to Cook County, Illinois sheriff Thomas Dart, vulnerable children and women, including those trafficked from other countries were routinely pimped on craigslist (Kunze, 2010). (*Note:* in 2010 Craigslist removed all erotic adult ads from both its domestic and international sites under mounting pressure from law enforcement and advocacy groups.)

The Internet has also made it possible for rebel groups, terrorists, and other criminal organizations to engage in conflict, often referred to as virtual war (Østergaard-Nielsen, 2006), mobilizing funds and disseminating propaganda on a scale not previously possible. Other negative forms of cyberactivism can include civil disobedience via the Internet, such as disrupting Internet traffic or hacking websites (cyber-disruptions). In its extreme form, cyberactivism can include cyberterrorism, such as the purposeful spread of computer viruses. As the world becomes increasingly dependent on the Internet for global functioning (economic markets, the health sector, defense, transportation, etc.), cyberterrorism has the potential to exact profoundly catastrophic consequences. Despite the potential negative uses of the Internet, overall, technology has served the advocacy world quite well, and in the right hands, can dramatically increase the potential for success in many worthy advocacy campaigns by providing some balance of power within society.

Concluding Thoughts on Contemporary Issues Affecting Social Justice

Assess your analysis and evaluation of this chapter's content by completing the Chapter Review.

Many areas within advocacy practice are affected by broad social phenomenon, such as poverty, neocolonialism, globalization, and technology. Each of these underlying issues will be examined in more detail within the context of the specific human rights issues explored within each of the following chapters. By examining the interplay between these various contemporary issues insights can be gained into ways in which trends within contemporary society affect its most vulnerable members.

CHAPTER 3

Human Services Advocacy Interventions

. . . .

Generalist Practice on a Macro Level

epa european pressphoto agency
b.v./Alamy

Advocacy skills are sometimes called *generalist skills* because they can be applied broadly to a variety of situations and contexts. Thus rather than having a few concentrated skills (such as therapeutic skills), the skills used in advocacy work are broad and varied. *Generalist practice* and *generalist skills* are terms often used in reference to working with individuals, but they are also applied to macro work, particularly since the ultimate goal of generalist practice in the human services fields is to improve the well-being of individuals and populations, with the goal of addressing social justice by working within various systems (Schatz, Jenkins, & Sheafor, 1990).

Generalist practice in macro advocacy work involves working within a variety of systems, such as the political, educational, economic, and legal realms, with the goal of effecting change in one or more of these systems. Advocacy work is accomplished by interacting with the various systems that people operate within, addressing issues of social justice, and ensuring that these systems (such as the economic or political systems) are humanized in the sense that respect for *all* human beings is not lost in the process of achieving other goals (such as earning a profit, or being "fiscally conservative").

Generalist skills are broad and varied because the change being affected is broad and varied. Consider the task of advocating for mentally ill homeless youth. Advocates would need counseling and case management skills but would also need skills that would enable them to be able to understand and engage in various economic and legal systems, including lobbying for mental health programs, housing, and educational initiatives on various political levels. Additionally they would need writing skills, (enabling them to write in various formats for a variety of audiences), researching skills, (enabling them to interpret statistical and demographic reports, and challenging them when necessary), interviewing skills (enabling them to interview talk to individuals from diverse backgrounds), facilitation skills, (enabling them to facilitate meetings, committees, and coalitions), and negotiation skills (enabling them to engage in conflict resolution among rivaling factions, and maintain coalitions despite differing goals). In fact, one might say that the social justice advocate is a "jack of all trades" who to be effective, must be able to master generalist skills that can be applied across a variety of settings, with a variety of people, dealing with a variety of issues.

Skills development and utilization is best accomplished when based on theoretical foundation, where theory informs practice. Theories are frameworks that help us to understand and even predict why things happen. For instance, if advocates have a better understanding of how change occurs, then they can utilize skills in a way that works with natural change evolution, such as addressing barriers to change by focusing on common ways change is resisted, or understanding change cycles and implementing interventions strategies during periods when change is most likely to occur. Theories that help us understand power, gender, and society, can increase our understanding of why injustice occurs and how those who benefit from power structures within society justify its use, including what purpose it serves (e.g., who are the winners and losers). When we operate within theoretical frameworks or are at least aware of the theoretical framework others operate from (whether they acknowledge these frameworks or not), we can be better prepared to challenge the status quo. For instance, understanding the nature of power, and how it is used within the theoretical framework of patriarchy, will help those advocating for gender equity to understand vastly different perspectives and lifestyles as they relate to gendered issues, and then challenge those that are contrary to egalitarian values. In this next section, some relevant theories are explored that will later be used to develop a framework for understanding social issues and how to best apply the skills necessary for effecting authentic change.

Mobilizing for Change: Using Social Systems Theory to Better Understand Social Structures

There are three primary sets of theories that will assist in better understanding the nature of advocacy for social justice and the process of social change. The first set of theories relates to how to envision society by using systems theory. General systems theory is a paradigm that conceptualizes the organization and ordering of various elements in the world (originally just the physical realm) as organized units with similar characteristics. For instance, general systems theory assumes that there is an intelligent ordering of everything in the world, and that all systems are open, thus in some manner, they interact with other systems forming reciprocal or interdependent relationships, which then leads to a continual evolution of the broader systems (Bertalanffy, 1968).

Think of a mobile that hangs over a crib. Each dangling object is independent to a certain extent, but each is also connected to all of the other objects in some way, thus when the baby reaches up and bats at one part, all parts are affected in some way.

Systems theory is of course more complex than that, but imagining the independent yet collective behavior of an infant's mobile helps to understand the basic premise of this theory. Now imagine ocean life from a systems perspective. The marine biologist would categorize various types of animal life into broad categories and then subcategories, and then organize underwater plant-life, crustaceans, and coral reefs into various categories as well, and then they would study how each of these *systems* interacted with and is dependent on the others. Thus general systems theory involves a way of thinking about the world from an organizational perspective. It assumes that the world is structured into a particular order, and understanding the nature of this organizational structures helps to manage and make predictions about the functions of various systems and sub-systems, and what can be expected from them. In other words, systems theory better helps us understand our world, and predict the behavior of those living within it.

Systems theory can be applied to the social life as well, with the various elements of a society being perceived and evaluated from a social systems perspective. Thus a society's various systems, such as its economic and political systems, educational systems, religious systems, family structures, and cultural systems (i.e., cultural norms and traditions) would all be considered social systems that interacted with and depended on each other in some way. Let's consider family from a system's perspective. A family is a network of individuals with relative levels of independence who are all affected by each other in some respect. If a husband loses his job, then the entire family is affected in some manner. When the eldest son, who babysat for the youngest while mom was at work, leaves for college, all are affected. The family is also a part of broader social networks that may include social supports such as an extended family, friends, a neighborhood, the school system, a church community, the labor force. When an event or change occurs anywhere within the immediate or broader systems, a ripple effect will run through the entire system having some type of effect.

Ecological systems theory, developed by Urie Bronfenbrenner, has been used in the human services fields to better understand individuals and their interactions with their environment. In his theory, Bronfenbrenner categorized an individual's environment into a series of expanding spheres, all with varying levels of influence on the individual. The microsystem includes the more intimate world of the individual and his or her family; the mesosystem (or mezzosystem) includes one's neighborhood and school; the exosystem includes more distant influences such as mass media, the health-care system, state government; and the macrosystem would include the broader culture at large, including the political system of one's country. Figure 3.1 illustrates these systems and describes the nature of interaction between the individual and the various entities within his or her spheres of influence. The primary premise of Bronfenbrenner's theory is that individuals can best be understood when seen in the context of their relationship with the various systems operating within their lives.

How does using systems theory help us in exploring the functions and process of advocacy? It is the systems within a given society that are used as the vehicles of social injustice, as well as for counteracting social injustice. Understanding the nature of systemic racism, for instance, is dependent on understanding how social systems operate. How is racism integrated into the criminal justice system? How is racism reinforced within the educational system? How is power used and misused within these systems? And how does change occur within various systems? Discovering the answers to these questions will help advocates know how to work within various social systems to affect social change.

FIGURE 3.1
Brofenbrenner's
Ecological Systems
Theory

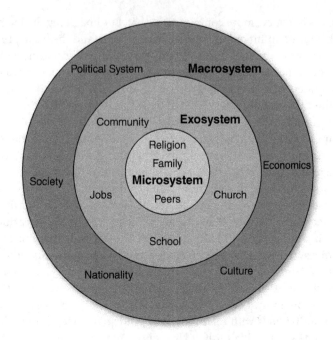

Social systems theory informs us that all social systems have a particular structure in that they (1) have boundaries, (2) have subsystems, (3) interact with other social systems, (4) are porous in the sense that they have input and output that then leads to the development of an interdependent relationship with other social systems (Dale & Smith, 2013). In other words, each social system influences the other, thus when change is instituted within one system, it will have a ripple effect creating change (sometimes wanted and sometimes unwanted) in other related systems.

Human Systems

Understanding and Mastery: An understanding of capacities, limitations, and resiliency of human systems

Critical Thinking Question: How does applying social systems theory to human social functioning assist social justice advocates better understanding the change process?

Systems theory also informs us that social systems have particular functions, meaning that each social system (such as a community's educational or political system) has functions that must be performed for the system to remain viable. Further, it is the performance of the various functions that serves to maintain order within a given society (Dale & Smith, 2013). For instance, if an educational system does not effectively educate the community's children (or certain children within the community), then it cannot remain viable, and from an advocate's perspective, social injustice will undoubtedly occur.

Consider the case of the U.S. school system failing to meet the educational needs of ethnic minorities living in the inner cities. Dr. Jonothan Kozol is an educational advocate who has been fighting for racial equality in the U.S. school system for decades. Kozol considers the deplorable conditions in many inner-city schools as a form of apartheid—where the white children are educated together and enjoy well-funded educations with experienced teachers, and the ethnic minority children who are educated in inner-city schools are forced to endure poorly funded schools, shoddy school buildings, and inexperienced or inept teachers. Kozol argues that many ethnic minority children in such schools are essentially cut off from mainstream society (Kozol, 2012). Kozol's description of the inner-city school system is an example of a system that is no longer viable; thus it is negatively affecting several other systems, including the family systems of those children who are victims of the inept and non-functioning school system, and perhaps even the criminal justice system if students drop out of school and follow the path into the juvenile justice system.

Understanding social systems theory and its relevance to advocacy within the human services context helps us better understand the various systems in society that affect the well-being of people by either empowering or oppressing them. Dale and Smith (2013) cite nine assumptions about the world and social order inherent within the field of social work (which is easily applicable to all of the human services). The following five of these assumptions are most applicable to social systems theory:

1. **There is an underlying general order in the world**—this means that there is even order in chaos.
2. **Social ordering is a constant and dynamic process**—in other words, no system is static—they are always changing and in flux. Finding the entry point that will result in the most significant change can then assist the advocate in creating enduring social change.
3. **All forms of social organization display self-maintaining and development**—characteristics meaning that systems are adaptable in order to ensure their continued existence and evolution.
4. **All forms of social organization can be characterized and studied as social systems**—this means that any social organization that is operating within a given society is subject to specifications outlined in systems theory, regardless of the uniqueness of the particular social organization. For instance, according to Dale and Smith, a family structure, a cultural group, a social welfare system, a criminal justice system, and a political system can all be effectively evaluated through a social systems lens, because they all have "behavioral" characteristics in common.
5. **The social relationship is the fundamental unit of all social systems**—this means that among all characteristics of social systems (educating children, establishing rules and order, providing a safety net), it is the relationships between people that serve as the most basic component of social systems.

Social systems theory can assist us in predicting not only how various systems within a society are interconnected but also helps us be better prepared to create changes within one system when we understand how interconnected systems influence one another. Social systems theory also gives advocates hope for the future since general systems theory would predict, for instance, that even the most closed system, such as a harsh and autocratic dictatorship, can be influenced by making changes in other systems, which will then eventually lead to changes within all other systems.

Assess your comprehension of Using Social Systems to Better Understand Social Structures by taking this quiz.

Theories That Explain Power and Abuse of Power

Advocates for social justice must also be familiar with theories of power, so that they can better understand the range of power dynamics within society. In particular, under what conditions power is most often exploited at the expense of others, and since few individuals or groups readily surrender power once they obtain it, it is important for social justice advocates working in the human services to learn what steps must be taken to confront power sources, and what remedies are effective for mediating power dynamics.

So what is power? Who has it? How is it used? How is it misused? And in particular, how is power wielded within societal systems, such as economic and political systems? Prior to being able to answer these questions, it will be helpful to more fully explore the actual nature of power and power dynamics within society. Power is a complex concept and can be defined in different ways, depending on the context. For instance, a car must have gas in its tank to have the power to run, just as humans must eat to have the power necessary to walk. Yet the type of power we are referring to in discussions of advocacy and social justice refers to power within social structures and systems, where an individual or group has power (legitimate or otherwise) and then uses force to exploit another individual or group, for some type of personal gain. Thus the discussion in this section centers on power within the context of social relationships in a societal structure, so that we can better understand how advocacy can address what appears to be the unfortunate correlation between privilege and exploitation.

Dobratz, Waldner, and Buzzell (2012) cite three different types of power that exist within society: (1) coercive and dominant power, (2) authority and legitimate power, and (3) privileged and interdependent power. In the field of advocacy, we are particularly interested in how dominant power is exploited by privileged groups, which results in certain groups being marginalized, scapegoated, and exploited for the benefit of the more powerful groups. Societal power has been defined in many ways, but one rather straightforward definition frames power as the capacity of individuals, groups, or structures to achieve an agenda through "force, influence, or authority" (Dobratz et al., 2012, p. 3). According to this definition, power can exist individually as well as collectively.

Racism as Abuse of Power

Racism is an example of the abuse of power because it involves the irrational perception that members of certain racial or ethnic groups possess unique negative traits that render them inferior. Racial prejudice refers to the negative attitudes held by individuals, and discrimination refers to the harmful and destructive behavior exacted toward racial groups perceived inferior (Allport, 1954), manifesting in everything from violence to "name-calling, vandalizing, threatening, firing, or refusing to have contact with individuals who are different" (Levin & Nolan, 2011, p. 2). In other words, racial prejudice involves feelings and attitudes, and discrimination consists of behaviors and actions.

Although race is a socially constructed concept, people of various races, primarily racial or ethnic minorities have experienced racial discrimination around the globe for centuries, with their perceived inferiority being used as a justification for harsh and destructive treatment and social exclusion on various levels. For instance, race is often used as a marginalizing factor in determining where someone can live and work, and what freedoms they can enjoy in society. Racial discrimination can be either overt or covert, and is often institutionalized within various social structures such as within the criminal justice system, or the educational system, as noted by Kozol's reference to educational disparities in inner-city schools. In discussing how racially prejudiced attitudes of those in power often evolve into institutionalized policies and practice, Levin and Nolan (2011) state:

> In the atmosphere of an executive boardroom, a real-estate agency, or a university admissions office, verbal bigotry may be just what it takes to stifle the ambitions of individuals who seek jobs, homes, or a place in the classroom. The individual hatred of powerful decision-makers can easily be transformed into company policy. (p. 100)

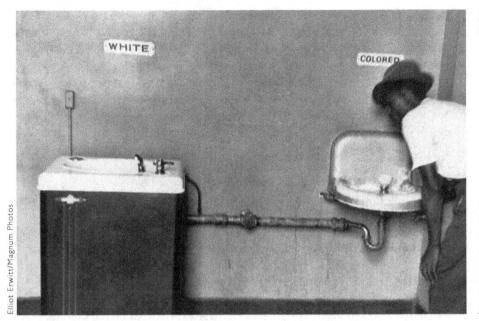

Elliot Erwitt/Magnum Photos

Reserving the best resources for Caucasians, and forcing African-Americans to utilize secondary and lessor resources is an example of white privilege.

Racism exists in society through the abuse of all three types of power referenced by Dorbratz, Waldner, and Buzzell (coercive and dominant power, authority and legitimate power, and privileged and interdependent power), but almost always involves the third type—privileged power. For example, *white privilege* is a social phenomenon where Caucasian members of society enjoy a distinct advantage over members of other ethnic groups. White privilege is defined as "unearned advantages of being White in a racially stratified society" (Pinterits, Poteat, & Spanierman, 2009, p. 417) and an expression of institutionalized power. White privilege is something that most Caucasians do not acknowledge leading many of those who benefit from this advantage to take personal credit for whatever they gain through white privilege, crediting those benefits as being earned (Neville, Worthington, & Spanierman, 2001).

Unfortunately, in addition to taking personal credit for advantages gained through white privilege, many Caucasians also attribute struggles experienced by members of non-Caucasian groups to personal moral failings, such as a poor work ethic, rather than acknowledging the role white privilege plays in establishing social inequality within various societal structures, such as the labor force. In reality, it has typically been white men who has benefited most from the best that life has to offer—gaining access into the best educational systems (or being the only ones to obtain an education at all), the best jobs, and living in the best neighborhoods. Even if white privilege were to end, the cumulative benefit of years of advantage would continue well into the future, just as the negative consequences of years of social exclusion will continue to negatively affect diverse groups who have not benefited from white privilege.

Zetzer (2005) also refers to *racist double binds* as a manifestation of racial prejudice and discrimination. A racist double bind occurs when a person with more power and privilege (i.e., the Caucasian from the majority population) gives someone from an ethnic minority group (with less power) mixed

Human Systems

Understanding and Mastery: The worth and uniqueness of individuals including: ethnicity, culture, gender, sexual orientation, and other expressions of diversity

Critical Thinking Question: Theories about power can assist social justice advocates to better understand why inequity occurs within society. In what ways is racism a form of abuse of power?

and/or contradictory messages, which leaves the latter with no good choices. Zetzer describes how the powerful person will often play the victim if confronted with the racist double bind, accusing the less powerful person of being too sensitive, argumentative, and even hostile. History is replete with examples of racist double binds, where members of disadvantaged and less powerful groups attempted to advocate for themselves in response to no-win situations only to be accused of being uncooperative, oppositional, or hostile. For example, consider the scenario where African Americans are socially excluded from the labor market for generations, and then told, "If you really wanted to get ahead you would get a better job."

Political Power

Political power is another type of power that often exists within political structures of society. There are several theories that focus on political power—what it is, and how it works within society. Pluralist theories of political power assume that power is not concentrated but lay in power centers throughout society, in government certainly, but also with special interest groups, coalitions, unions, even radicals (Miller, 1970). But critics of this theory argue that pluralist theories cannot be applied broadly since pluralism can only exist in democracies that allow people to associate for political purposes, such as the United States (Marger, 1987). Pluralist theories are based on the premise that all individuals have access to groups that can wield political power within society, which for some marginalized groups is simply not the case (Skocpol & Fiorina 1999).

An earlier theory of political power is *conflict class theory*, developed by Karl Marx (1962/1996), a famous political sociologist and economist. Marx framed power in society in terms of competition between social classes, where power held by higher social classes leads to social inequities. This theory becomes less relevant though when a society becomes increasingly diverse, with less of a categorical class structure (Dorbratz et al., 2012). Also Marx's theory does not account for noneconomic such as marginalization based upon gender and race. Yet conflict class theories have led to other theories that are relevant to many of today's societies, such as feminist and race theories of power structures.

The *elitist theory* argues that power lay in the hands of the *social elite* of society (often called the *ruling class*), typically those people who possess certain qualities that are highly regarded within society. Max Weber, the famous political sociologist wrote at length about bureaucracies within society, and what he termed the *managerial elite*, which ruled lower-level workers. Marx also addressed the political elitism in capitalistic society in his conflict class theory, where he described how the "exploited worker" was treated as nothing more than a commodity serving the "bourgeoisie" (Weber's term for capitalist elites).

Elitist theorists, such as Weber, traditionally perceived power as being in the hands of the only one segment of society (the social elites), yet contemporary applications of elitist theory conceptualize networked concentrations of power held by various factions within society. Examples of networked concentrations of power include the "corporate elite," members of the upper socioeconomic strata, and special interest groups. Individuals within these power networks have access to power that the average individual does not have. An example of this would be members of upper management in transnational corporations who have the financial resources and connections to lobby Congress for favored policy and legislation. It is for this reason that Higley and Burton (2006) argue that even in democracies, power lies not with the broader populace but with a handful of individuals who form elitist groups, where with their financial and social status, they garner broad societal support for political action that serve primarily their own elitist interests. An example of this process may be reflected in the current debate on health-care reform where lobbyists representing special interest groups, such as the health insurance industry, and drug companies paid millions of dollars to lobby legislators in opposition of health-care reform, as well as waging a multimillion dollar media blitz to influence public opinion (see CNN's "Health Care Reform Efforts Prompt Lobbying Bonanza" at http://political-ticker.blogs.cnn.com as an example).

Social justice advocates understand that they are rarely in a position where they hold dominant positions in power relationships within society. They also understand that virtually all advocacy issues are a result of unequal power dynamics (Cohen, de la Vega, & Watson, 2001). Yet history is full with examples of the powerless overcoming the powerful. Jane Addams and her fight for immigrants in Chicago in the early 1900s, Nelson Mandela and his fight against apartheid in South Africa in the 1950s and 1960s, and Cesar Chavez and his fight for undocumented farm workers in California in the 1970s and 1980s are all examples of advocates who were not members of the power elite, yet affected enduring social change by using strategies that successfully challenged political power structures within society.

Assess your comprehension of <u>Theories that Explain Power and Abuse of Power</u> by taking this quiz.

Theories That Explain How Change Occurs in Society

For social justice to be achieved, change must occur: a change in attitude, a change in how people perceive a problem (even whether they perceive something as a problem at all), a change in how governments perceive various groups of people, a change in how problems are solved, and a change in how those experiencing social problems are advocated for, even a change the organizations that exist to advocate for those in society affected by social problems. Change theory helps the advocate better understand how change occurs and how it impacts those involved by the change.

Historian Thomas Kuhn (1962/1996) refers to the change process as a *paradigm shift*. Although Kuhn applied the concept of paradigm shifts to the hard sciences, his theory can be applied to the field of advocacy as well. For instance, Advocacy for paradigm shifts can bring about new perspectives, increased awareness, and a new way of thinking that is shared among community members. Change occurs in cycles, and understanding the nature of change cycles will assist the social justice advocate in knowing when to be patient and when to strike. Cohen et al. (2001) reference the following three cycles of change relevant to advocacy:

1. Problem-solving cycle
2. Issue life cycle
3. Organizational life cycle

Problem-solving cycles involve the stages people go through when they attempt to solve a problem. The first stage involves the initial recognition that a problem exists. During this first stage, the advocate experiencing the problem *makes the decision that change must occur*. During the second stage of the cycle, the person *considers alternate solutions and then selects one solution* based on a particular rationale, and in the final stage of the change cycle, *the solution is executed and change occurs*.

Change in an Advocacy Campaign

Another application of change theory relates to how a social justice issue that is being advocated for changes, progressing through a number of stages, from its initial discovery to resolution (assuming that the advocacy efforts are successful). Cohen (2001). use a lifespan development model to describe these progressive stages. When a new social justice issue is first identified, such as advocating for safer schools, or addressing the problem of domestic violence within a particular population, it is in the *birth stage*. During the *childhood stage*, the advocacy issue is nurtured by gaining increasing support and gaining momentum through the development of new ideas and strategies. During an issue's *adolescence*, the momentum is gained and supporters within power positions in society are added to the advocacy campaign. During *adulthood*, the issue reaches maturity with the identification of sustainable solutions, or if solutions cannot be identified, the advocacy campaign is abandoned. During the *renewal* stage, solutions are evaluated for continued need and any necessary change. Cohen et al. point out how different skills and actions are warranted during each stage, from knowing how to initially define an issue during the *birth stage*, to building alliances within the community, working with the media, and analyzing alternate policy approaches during the *childhood stage*, and then managing resources to ensure that a cause has sufficient support, during the *adulthood stage*.

Recognizing that social problems are solved in stages, and that advocacy campaigns change incrementally within their life span can help social justice advocates remain patient and realistic, a particularly important skill since often people want immediate change, especially when it has taken them a long time to raise enough interest and garner the necessary motivation to even gain social awareness that a problem exists. Recognizing the stages of evolution in any advocacy campaign can help stave off discouragement, and the temptation to give up prematurely.

Organizational Change

Change doesn't just occur within the attitudes and power structures of society though. Change occurs within the organizations advocating for the change as well, and if this change isn't understood or managed well, it can threaten the viability of the advocacy organization. The *organizational life cycle* theory describes the cycles an organization goes through in its own development. Often an organization will begin as a small grassroots movement initiated by a few passionate individuals who perhaps have been personally affected by a social issue. Mothers Against Drunk Drivers (MADD), and the Polly Klaas Foundation for Missing Children are two such examples.

Often these small grassroots organizations grow and evolve into larger and more powerful organizations, which can be a wonderful thing, since often there is strength is numbers and size. Yet, equally often such organizations will experience growing pains on the way toward becoming a more substantial entity. Sometimes these growth pains are so significant that they can threaten the viability of an organization, rendering it less effective in its quest to achieve social justice in its identified areas. Cohen et al. describe the typical agency growth cycle also using the lifespan approach,

Client-Related Values and Attitudes

Understanding and Mastery: Belief that individuals, service systems, and society change

Critical Thinking Question: Change theory, such as the lifespan development model and the organizational life cycle theory describe ways in which advocacy campaigns and advocacy organizations (respectively) develop and evolve. How can these theories help social justice advocates better understand how change impacts advocacy efforts?

identifying areas where change occurs, such as in the areas of leadership; organizational infrastructure; domains of skills and capacities; the nature of its relationships with its key constituents, the media, politicians, and even other advocacy organizations, and its level of experience indicated by its ability to learn from past mistakes; and take on new challenges.

Too often, advocacy efforts are hampered, not because of external forces and challenges but because of internal ones. Understanding the nature of organizational change can help social justice advocates recognize and then anticipate changes within their own advocacy organizations (as well as others), so that they can be better prepared to manage these changes.

Culturally Competent Generalist Advocacy on a Macro Level

Prior to any discussion of advocacy engagement, such as necessary skills and intervention strategies, the issue of cultural competence must be explored. Any student or professional working in the field of human services certainly has heard the term *cultural competence*—a term used to describe an awareness of and sensitivity to populations from different income levels, religions, physical and mental capacities, genders, and sexual orientations, as well as races. Yet despite the term being quite common now in human services circles, it remains an area that is often neglected in both education and practice. Cultural competence is a skill that while never completely attainable, is something that those working in the human services fields spend their entire careers attempting to master. The best place to start one's indoctrination into the world of cultural competence is with the recognition of the uniqueness of every individual. Increased sensitivity and acceptance of difference and diversity is the foundation human rights work where every individual, regardless of their uniqueness, is believed to have the right to respect and equal treatment, as set forth in the Universal Declaration of Human Rights.

Rothman (2008) argues that each individual in the world is a unique being comprised holistically of biological, psychological, social, and spiritual elements, as well having unique "experiences, influences, perspectives, and world view" (p. 7). He cautions against the common practice of stereotyping, where those who are different than the majority culture (or mainstream society) are perceived as a homogeneous population and viewed (as a whole) in a negative light. Rothman notes the importance of challenging stereotyping, recognizing that

> … not all Chinese people like Chinese food, not all African-Americans are good athletes, not all Jews are good students, not all Muslims wear head coverings, not all gays are "out", not all developmentally disabled people seek sexual encounters, and not all Latinos are macho. (p. 7)

Rather than celebrating uniqueness, stereotyping (whether positive or negative) can significantly harm one's self-esteem and hamper creativity leading to negative bias, oppression, and discrimination (Rothman, 2008).

Differences in people occur on a continuum, with some differences being elevated in society and attributed to the elite (e.g., perceived intelligence, education, and income levels), and other differences being relegated to marginalized populations (e.g., racial background, migration status, and lower incomes). Uniqueness can occur in a variety

Many within the Muslim community are subject to negative stereotyping commonly called Islamaphobia.

PETER SCHNEIDER/epa/Corbis

of domains but typically include differences with regard to gender, race, ethnicity, and culture, religion, physical and mental ability, language proficiency, sexual orientation, age, social class, and citizen or migration status.

Human services professionals working in the area of macro-advocacy practice for social justice must be diligent in working on their cultural competency skills so that they do not internalize the negative stereotypes held by many people within the majority culture. Biases are often subtle, and we are not always aware that they exist. For instance, believing that women must remain at home and raise children, or that all kids must go to college, or that most black men are violent, or that those who rely on public assistance just don't want to work, may seem like commonsense realities to some in the United States. Yet, these four beliefs involve stereotyping, and embracing these beliefs may lead to holding a bias against members of a group who do not share your experiences with majority cultural beliefs and attitudes. Human service professionals must challenge their own preconceived notions of right and wrong. This does not mean that advocates must throw out all notions of morality—quite the opposite in fact. What it does mean though is that we may need to redefine our sense of right and wrong so that we are not unconsciously biased against those members of diverse cultures, who often do not enjoy the same social benefits experienced by the majority culture, thus may experience challenges you or I simply cannot imagine. In other words, when one is starving the moral imperative not to steal may seem to be a bit of a luxury.

Throughout this book advocacy for social justice is explored within a context of cultural competence, with the goal of recognizing how and when difference and

Administration

Understanding and Mastery: The worth and uniqueness of individuals including ethnicity, culture, gender, sexual orientation, and other expressions of diversity

Critical Thinking Question: How can developing cultural competence help social justice advocates avoid stereotyping people just because they're different than the majority culture?

uniqueness is used as a justification for exploitation and oppression. Globalization, a concept that I addressed in Chapter 2, has made it possible for people to be exposed to a wide range of cultures that are quite different than their own. While this can certainly be good, it can also create challenges, primarily due to the human tendency to resist change, including new perspectives and new traditions. When confronted with significant differences, a natural response is to become fearful and feel discomfort. A common defense to fear and discomfort can include the gravitation toward *ethnocentrism*—"the tendency to perceive one's own background and associated values as being superior, or more 'normal' than others" (Martin, 2013, p. 61).

I challenge preconceived notions of morality throughout this book, not because I want students to enter the human services profession with a completely morally relativistic perspective, but because so many of our Western notions of rightness and wrongness are really quite culturally bound and can serve as veiled forms of discrimination and prejudice. Students' biases will be challenged, but no ultimate conclusions will be argued because I want new human service professionals to come to their own conclusions, based on the critical analysis of new information.

Levels of Advocacy Intervention Practice

Throughout this book advocacy efforts are explored on a variety of levels. Advocacy can occur on a *micro level*—involving work with individuals on a one-on-one basis, or on a *macro level*—involving work on a collective or community level. Advocacy on a micro level is a very common activity and can include any intervention that involves acting in the best interest of their clients or behalf of their clients, such as defending your client's right to leave an abusive marriage, or encouraging your clients to have a voice with regard to their children who aren't getting their educational needs met within the public school system. Human service professionals who work with individuals often engage in advocacy as a part of the counseling and case management process.

Advocacy for social justice is typically an activity that occurs on the macro level. Netting, Kettner, McMurtry, and Thomas (2012) define macro practice as "professionally guided intervention designed to bring about planned change in organizations and communities" (p. 6). Macro-level activities involve interventions in organizations and communities (Netting et al., 2012), as well as within the political arena where laws and policies that are perceived as being unjust are challenged, or socially just laws and policies are lobbied for (Gilbert & Terrell, 2013; Haynes & Mickelson, 2010). Human service workers who are advocating for and against certain laws and policies within the political arena will often work side-by-side with advocates from other professions such as policy analysts and community organizers, as well as professionals advocating within their own industry when a particular law or policy is relevant to their practice (Netting et al., 2012). Throughout this book the focus is on macro interventions, where broad change is effected at a collective level, much like the type of work in which Jane Addams engaged.

Advocacy Skills and Intervention Strategies

The skills relied on for macro-advocacy work are immensely varied, and often context specific, meaning that different skills are required depending on the issue being advocated for, the type of change sought, and the environment or venue the change will occur within (e.g., changes within a local school district, passing federal domestic violence legislation, increasing worldwide awareness of the plight of vulnerable women in the Congo). Certainly any social justice issue can be advocated for in a variety of ways, requiring a wide range of skill sets, such as the ability to work with a variety of people, to manage budgets, the ability to write well, as well as organizational skills, public speaking skills, and the ability to think strategically. Yet, not every advocate will need to possess all of these skills, particularly since it is rare to find one individual who is so well rounded! Advocacy organizations often employ human rights advocates, researchers, attorneys, humanitarian aid workers, crisis counselors, political lobbyists, accountants, media specialists, and so forth, thus as a team, the necessary skill sets are attained. Within this section, I attempt to identify some key skill sets that those working within the human services field in social justice advocacy will likely need; yet again it is important to recognize that what these skills look like and how they are utilized will change significantly depending on the actual issues, the victims involved, the source of the problem(s), and the environment.

In the most general sense (without considering actual problems and their environmental contexts), advocacy skills can best be understood within the context of steps in the change process. Often the first step in advocating for an issue is *identifying the problem*. This involves several substeps, each encompassing a particular skill set. Identifying the problem to be advocated for will require the advocate to thoroughly analyze the social problem, including determining who is affected and how.

ANALYZING THE SOCIAL PROBLEM Far too often advocates jump to conclusions about the nature of the social problem, including its causes and consequences without knowing all of the facts. We all have opinions about why a condition may be occurring, but if we do not take the time and make the effort to analyze a social problem by exploring its various components, and related variables (such as its causes and consequences), then we are likely to jump to the wrong conclusion, based on our own anecdotal experiences. In fact, in describing the importance of analyzing a social problem thoroughly, Netting et al. (2012) state that "leaping to quick solutions without adequate study is the antithesis of professional practice" (p. 86).

FRAMING THE SOCIAL PROBLEM One of the first steps in gaining information about a social problem is to hit the academic databases and conduct a literature review. Although social problems will be influenced by the unique context within which they occur, there is often very valuable information to be gained by reviewing national, and even international studies on a particular issue. Such an endeavor can give an advocate a broader perspective: What this social problem looks like in other contexts, what patterns exist locally, nationally, and globally (e.g., demographic patterns, whether the problem effects people differently, what other variables may be at play), and ultimately a literature review can shed light on possible solutions that can then be advocated for from an "evidence-based" perspective.

OPERATIONALIZING CONCEPTS AND TERMS A more technical aspect of problem definition include operationalizing definitions of concepts and issues, which refers to the process of clearly articulating how a researcher is defining various concepts. This is important in order to reduce confusion in how various terms are being used, and provide further clarity on how various concepts and issues may be defined. For instance, how is homelessness defined? Individuals who reside in shelters or only those who live on the streets? Is someone who lives in a motel, or who "couch surfs" considered homeless? Or, how is mental illness defined? Does the definition include only severe and chronic mental illness, such as schizophrenia? Or does it involve clinical depression and anxiety as well? How is "older adult" defined? Over 55? Over 60? Operationalizing concepts and issues pertaining to the social problem being advocated for requires critical thinking skills, the ability to think "outside of the box," and to anticipate various ways that certain terms might be defined by various groups, such as how cultural perspectives influence definitions. While there may not be one right way of defining a concept, having transparency in the way *you*, the advocate, is defining a concept will help increase clarity and ultimately lead to being able to more clearly articulate action steps in the advocating process.

DETERMINING THE DEMOGRAPHICS OF AFFECTED POPULATION   In addition to defining terms, advocates must determine who is being affected by the social problem. This involves exploring the *demographics of the target population*. Demographics can include the age (or age range), gender, socioeconomic status, race and cultural group, immigrant status, mental and physical ability, intellectual status, and any other descriptive information that describes the population affected by the social problem. Gaining information about the nature of the problem including who is affected leads to the next step, engaging those who are being affected by the problem, often referred to as key stakeholders.

ENGAGING KEY STAKEHOLDERS   Once it is determined who is affected by a particular social problem, the advocate must then evaluate the social problem from the perspectives of as wide a range of affected individuals as possible. Chambers and Wedel (2013) state that to "understand a social problem is to understand how and what another person (or group) thinks and believes about the social events being defined as a problem" (p. 8). Engaging key stakeholders in framing the problem will not only help to ensure that the problem has been comprehensively evaluated, but it will also ensure that a variety of perspectives will be included in the problem definition, since various individuals and groups will frame the problem differently depending on how they are being affected (Netting et al., 2012). Such information will not only give clues to potential solutions but will also provide important contextual information that can inform future action steps, such as how the problem has been perceived in the past, what vulnerable groups have been affected in the past and present (Netting et al., 2012), types of intersectionality that may increase vulnerability to the social problem (e.g., gender, ethnicity, education level, and history of domestic violence), what social or personal precursors tend to make the social problem worse (e.g., intergenerational poverty, a bad economy, a poor education, and a childhood filled with violence), and what solutions have already been tried. Finally, engaging key stakeholders in the framing of the problem increases the likelihood that those affected by the problem will be more committed to the solution process since they have been engaged throughout the entire advocacy process.

EXPLORING CAUSES AND CONSEQUENCES   A part of analyzing the social problem involves identifying its potential causes and consequences, including exploring what people believe causes a social problem and its consequences. When exploring causes of social problems, it's important to remember the complex nature of serious social problems, which often renders finding solutions particularly challenging. In fact, identifying specific causes of social problems is controversial in the sense that rarely is there a consensus, even among experts, on what causes a particular social problem or issue. For instance, what causes poverty? Conservative political economic policies that favor the rich? Big government that spends too liberally on social welfare programs? What causes domestic violence? A violent childhood? Weak domestic violence laws? Mental illness? A patriarchal culture that does not value the rights of women? As you can see, not only is identifying specific causes of social problems not an exact science, the process can be quite controversial and is influenced by one's personal, political, and cultural ideological stance (Chambers & Wedel, 2013).

It is thus more helpful to consider risk factors of social problems, rather than attempting to isolate distinct causes. Risk factors include certain conditions or characteristics that will increase the likelihood that an individual or a population will experience a social problem. For instance, research has shown that a significant number of homeless and runaway youth cited sexual abuse in their childhood homes as a chief reason they chose to run away and live on the streets (Yoder, Whitbeck, & Hoyt, 2001). While we may not be able to say with any certainty that childhood sexual abuse will always cause youth homelessness, we can assert that child sexual abuse is a risk factor for youth homelessness. Research also indicates that risk factors for suicide include depression; a prior suicide attempt; a family history of mental disorders; substance abuse; violence; and physical and sexual abuse (Miller, Azrael, Hepburn, Hemenway, & Lippmann, 2006), as well as firearms in the home (Moscicki, 2001). It is helpful to identify risk factors before developing an advocacy campaign designed to reduce teen suicide, since a prevention campaign will need to focus on dealing with risk factors early, with the goal of addressing the roots of the social problem before it has an opportunity to blossom. Risk factors for many of the issues social justice advocates are dealing with are static and cannot be changed. Consider how a person's risk of poverty (which is a risk factor for various social problems, in and of itself), is often increased based on what country they're born in, the caste of their family, or being born a particular gender. Clearly these are risk factors that cannot be altered, but advocates can direct their efforts toward focusing on systemic issues such as empowerment, equality, and poverty alleviation.

Identifying the consequences of a social problem is an equally important aspect of the social problem analysis because it is the consequences that result from a social problem that will also be the focus of advocacy efforts. In fact, Chambers and Wedel (2013) note one of the most important aspects of a social problem analysis is distinguishing between the cause (or antecedents) of a social problem and its consequences. While this can be very challenging due to the complex and often reciprocal nature of most social problems, they recommend the use of a *causal chain*—a graph that reflects a time sequence showing the social problem evolution, starting with risk factors, and other antecedents, the problem itself, and the consequences. It's important to remember though that a causal chain will never reflect the definitive chain of events, but rather the *beliefs of those who are queried*, since as stated earlier, there will always be numerous ways to conceptualize these factors, in a "chicken-and-the egg" sort of manner.

> ### Administration

Understanding and Mastery: Constituency building and other advocacy techniques such as lobbying, grassroots movements, and community development and organizing

Critical Thinking Question: Advocacy practice on a macro level involves many skills. Why is it important to engage key stakeholders in the advocacy process?

Understanding the importance of first analyzing the social problem comprehensively before jumping ahead to developing coalitions and action plans is best understood by seeing this process in action. Consider the following two fictionalized vignettes—the first involving a local social problem in need of advocacy, and the second a global one.

Assess your comprehension of <u>Culturally Competent Generalist Advocacy on a Macro Level</u> by taking this quiz.

The Case of the Truant Students

Consider that you are working as a school counselor in an urban school with high rates of truancy. You are charged with the responsibility for developing a program to address the problem of school absenteeism. Because of the negative experiences you have with parents (difficulty reaching them, ensuring that their kids will be at school, only to have them be absent again the next day, moving without any discussion with the school), you automatically conclude that the cause of the truancy problem is neglectful parents. Certain you are correct, you set about to establish a program that punishes parents for their children's truancy. The program you design requires that parents accompany their child to school for each day that the student has an unexcused absence. In addition, you also conclude that a financial penalty may help in motivating lazy parents as well, thus you add a $25 per day fee, for each day their child is absent. Now let's assume that on implementation, a group of parents file a complaint with the school board, and the superintendent asks for information from you on the basis on which you came to your conclusions. What is your evidence base? You then have to admit that your only evidence was your assumptions, based on personal experience.

Now let's assume that you have taken a different path. Prior to coming to any conclusions, you set aside what you think you know and do some academic research on the social problem by conducting a literature review. You then conduct a survey of affected parties, and perhaps even a *needs assessment*, asking parents how they perceive the problem. Why do they believe their children are struggling to attend school? What barriers—personal or otherwise—exist that makes regular attendance impossible? You then interview collateral key stakeholders, including teachers, school administrators, neighborhood communities, social service agencies in the area, religious leaders, and those working at after-school programs. After obtaining all of this data, you then review the information and synthesize it. What you find shocks you. Although there is clearly variation in the ways that stakeholders are framing the problem of school truancy, consistent themes emerge:

- Parents, particularly single parents living in low-income/high-crime areas care very much about their children but are very overwhelmed.
- The parents very much want their children to attend school.
- Students who are living in a high-crime neighborhood often miss school due to fear of gang violence.
- Many students are working to help support their parent(s).
- An exceptionally high percentage of children are in relative foster care with grand-parents who are overwhelmed and in need of outreach assistance.

- Many single parents are working two jobs, rendering children having to fend for themselves in the morning before school.
- Many children come to school without having had breakfast.
- A lack of a school bus system forces students to rely on the public transportation system, which experienced recent cutbacks, resulting in the normal 40-minute commute increasing to over two hours.
- A national trend has shown increases in school truancy among students living in homeless shelters.
- A national trend has shown increases in school truancy among lesbians, gays, bisexual, and transgendered individuals (LGBT) students due to bullying on campus.

This information yields a picture of school truancy that is far more complex than originally thought. The information also reveals that any solution will potentially need to be just as complex, addressing multiple problems. No longer are you imagining parental neglect as the sole problem, but you now conceptualize the problem, and potential advocacy in response, from a systemic perspective. Advocacy efforts can target a reduction in neighborhood crime and gang activity, increased support to custodial grandparents, scholarship programs for single-parent families, increased funding for a district school bus system, advocacy to reestablish cut public transit lines, development of an antibullying campaign, development of coalition to examine bullying against the LGBT population, and so on.

Now let us consider an example of a social problem analysis with global implications:

The Case of the Reluctant Refugee

Consider that you are a caseworker working for a refugee resettlement agency contracted by the U.S. state department to resettle refugees from refugee camps operated by the United Nations High Commissioner for Refugees (UNHCR). Your agency is provided with a limited amount of money allocated per refugee, which provides approximately three months of housing, one year of medical case management, and two years of general case management. The expectation though is that the majority of agency resources will be focused on assisting new refugees in gaining self-sufficiency. Newly arrived refugees are provided with an apartment, basic staples (food, household items, and clothing), assistance with tapping into basic social services, a school liaison for children, and a medical card for six months. The restructuring of the primary social welfare system in the United States, Temporary Assistance for Needy Families (TANF), did away with entitlement programs, and replaced them with a "welfare to work" program where benefits are tied to a recipient's compliance with various requirements—virtually all aimed at obtaining employment and gaining self-sufficiency.

You are currently working with Burundi refugees who are being resettled by the UNHCR from a camp in Tanzania. Your client is a 35-year old woman named Claire, and her three young children, one of whom is still nursing. You begin your work by taking Claire to the U.S. Social Security office, as well as the local public aid office so that she can apply for Medicaid for herself and her children, as well as Temporary Assistance to Needy Families (TANF). You coordinate services with another caseworker who is responsible for ensuring that her eldest child is registered at the local elementary school and receives the appropriate assistance, with language and tutoring. Claire speaks her native language, Kirundi, as well as French, but does not speak English, so you enroll her in your agency's English as a Second Language (ESL) classes. After allowing Claire a few weeks to adjust to her apartment and her new surroundings, you let Claire know that it is time for her to attend your agency's job readiness courses. Between ESL classes, job training and a weekly coed "adjustment" support group, Claire is at the agency approximately three days a week, with the goal that she will be self-sufficient in three to six months. It is a part of your responsibility, as a refugee resettlement caseworker, to create within Claire a sense of urgency with regard to getting a job and assimilating into mainstream American society, since funds are limited and you are only able to provide financial assistance (such as rent subsidy, etc.) for about six months. Additionally, within nine months of relocation, you are aware that Claire will have to start repaying the travel loan all refugees receive to relocate to the United States. The loan is for airline tickets from Tanzania for Claire and her three children, thus the amount will be approximately $10,000.

Despite the considerable amount of assistance being provided to Claire—both financial and human services—you are becoming increasingly concerned because she does not seem to be progressing at the same rate as other refugees. She has not learned much English, often misses the job readiness classes, and is increasingly absent for the adjustment support group meetings. You are aware that Claire grew up in a refugee camp, and you begin to wonder if the problem isn't a matter of "learned helplessness" and taught dependence. While you're not completely familiar with life in a refugee camp, you are aware that the UNHCR provided the basic necessities for refugees, such as housing, food, clothing, basic medical care, and education for the children. You've also heard that adults are not allowed to work, thus you assume that the refugees spend the majority of their days just hanging out. During a team meeting, you address your concerns about Claire's lack of progress, stating that Claire does not seem interested in becoming self-sufficient, often calls you three to four times per week asking for assistance with minor tasks, such as making telephone calls to her children's school, and has, in general, resisted your efforts to assist her in becoming more proactive and independent in managing her life and the lives of her children. The employment caseworker chimes in sharing his concerns as well. He states that Claire is "nonresponsive" and "uncooperative," often either missing class, or coming to class without having done her homework. She has apparently neglected to research potential jobs in the area and has done no work on finding resources for childcare. The counselor who facilitates the adjustment support group shares that Claire is very quiet in the group sessions, does not engage in group discussions, and recently has been failing to attend altogether. The team concludes that Claire suffers from dependency, a normal response to growing up in a refugee camp, but unlike refugees from other countries, Claire appears to be rejecting attempts to help her gain self-sufficiency. Your supervisor determines, somewhat reluctantly, that Claire must be notified that if she does not comply with all agency program requirements and fails to become more proactive in her own cultural adjustment, that you will have no choice but to exercise your right to report her to the TANF caseworker for noncompliance. This action will result in punitive measures, which could include anything from a temporary suspension of one or more benefits, to the permanent termination of all benefits.

During your next meeting with Claire, you share your concerns and tell her the team's decision. To ensure that Claire understands the seriousness of what you are telling her, you ask the translator to make sure she understands. You note Claire saying "yes" and nodding her head, which you record in your notes as an indication of her understanding and agreement. You leave the meeting with Claire confident that you have framed the problem correctly—poor refugee resettlement adjustment, and you are equally confident that your team has developed a solution that will "spur" Claire on and motivate her to become more proactive, taking responsibility for her life and the future of her children. You feel a tinge of guilt—wondering what will happen to Claire and her children if she is not able to pull this off, but you also feel a bit angry. Claire should be thrilled that she has the opportunity to live in the United States—Land of Plenty—people all over the world would give their right arm to live here, and yet from your perspective Claire is throwing away the opportunity of a lifetime because she doesn't want to take responsibility for herself and her family and wants others to continue to take care of her. You tell yourself that perhaps she needs to experience a few hard lessons before she can appreciate how fortunate she is.

Now let's assume that you have taken a different path. Prior to coming to any conclusions you set aside what you think you know and do some academic research on the social problem by conducting a literature review. You then conduct a survey of affected parties, and perhaps even a *needs assessment*, asking key stakeholders–refugees, trauma counselors, refugee experts–how they perceive the problem. What is the reason why Burundis ended up in refugee camps? What was life in the camps really like, particularly for women? What choice did Claire, and others like her have in deciding whether they would be able to return home, be resettled to a second host country, or remain in the camp? What does Claire think about her experiences of displacement? After obtaining all of this information, you then review the information and synthesize it. What you find shocks you. Although there is clearly variation in the ways that stakeholders are framing the problem of refugee resettlement and adjustment, consistent themes emerge:

- In the last three decades, there have been 16 to 22 civil wars, primarily in Africa and southern Asia, most conflicts having roots in colonialism.
- Many civil conflicts in Africa and Asia have resulted in mass forced migration where hundreds of thousands of residents flee either within the country, becoming internally displaced persons (IDPs), or across international borders, rendering them refugees.
- The UNHCR is currently responsible for approximately 44 million refugees worldwide, with several million refugees remaining in UNHCR refugee camps, in a protracted situation without a durable solution. Some refugees have been in campus for three or more decades.
- The Burundi refugees in the camp in Tanzania that is currently being resettled resulted from a violent conflict in Burundi in 1972.
- Refugee camps are a dismal place with most refugees experiencing significant mental and physical trauma. Refugees are not permitted to work and are not allowed out of the camp. Camps are dangerous. Recently there has been a spike in witchcraft-related crimes where many children have been killed.
- Refugees in the camp Claire lived in have been moved several times. They were originally located in the Democratic Republic of the Congo but were displaced due to numerous cycles of violence, including two civil wars.
- Humanitarian workers presume that the majority of women living in this camp have been victims of sexual assault (particularly while in the DRC) and have

experienced significant loss, including the loss of immediate family members in civil war, including children, yet received no counseling.

- Refugees who are victims of forced migration and who live in protracted situations in camps are at significantly higher risk of violence and trauma, such as sexual violence and other types of serious victimization. Women who have been raped are often rejected by their husbands and families.
- Recently, several rebel groups have been going into the camps and kidnapping and conscripting children into armed service. Male child soldiers are often forced to fight on the front lines and are used as human shields and female child soldiers are often used as "wives" of soldiers, or are forcibly raped by numerous men. Some of the boys and girls who are kidnapped are as young as nine. Many children who are fortunate enough to escape have been rejected by their families.
- In the camps, refugees are discouraged from acting independently. They are not permitted to work and are completely dependent on the UNHCR. In fact, proactive behavior could be perceived as insolence, punishable by imprisonment.
- UNHCR made an error when processing Claire's application for resettlement. Her first husband (and father of her two older children) was killed, and the marriage to her second husband (the father of her youngest child) was not registered properly due to an error in paperwork; thus, when she was processed for resettlement, she was accidentally placed on the relocation card with her father. Thus her husband remains in the camp, with very few prospects of rejoining his family.
- In Burundi culture, most women do not work outside the home and are responsible for taking care of the home and the children. Most traditional Burundi women could not fathom a scenario where they were required to work outside the home and have strangers care for their children. Culturally, this would be very inappropriate.

This information yields a picture much different than you originally conceptualized. A thorough and comprehensive analysis of the social problem reveals numerous social, systemic, and structural dynamics that have created barriers to Claire's difficulty in adjusting to life in the United States." to "successful adjustment to life in the United States. Most notably, the severe trauma Claire has likely endured, which has not been addressed. Additionally, cultural bridges have not been addressed, leaving Claire confused about gender roles in the United States regarding gender roles. In fact, it is likely that Claire is still waiting for her husband to join her, as he promised her he would. Claire was a victim of a violent civil conflict before she was born, had no choice regarding where she lived and whether or not she migrated to another country. Further, she lived in an environment and a culture where being "proactive" could have been proved fatal, and self-sufficiency was consistently discouraged.

You now realize that what you and the team perceived as Claire's (and other refugees') "resistance" was nothing of the sort. Claire's behavior was reflective of untreated posttraumatic stress disorder (PTSD), depression, conflicting cultural values, and numerous systemic problems, including protracted refugee situations, where individuals get loss in a maze of UNHCR red tape and a lack of political will of the international community to intervene appropriately in situations involving mass forced migration. What you've learned from your social problem analysis has directed you to a completely different set of solutions, focusing less on problems with individuals and more on problems within various social systems. You decide that you are not prepared at this point to take on the entire UNHCR, but you are ready to take initial steps in exploring the possibility of establishing a mental health and trauma center within your agency that focuses on refugees, particularly those who are victims of civil war and forced migration, who have lived in refugee camps. You are also determined to establish a stronger connection with the UNHCR, and the Office of International Migration (OIM) to develop stronger cultural competency in your staff, so that caseworkers have a much better idea of what refugees experience (physically, emotionally, and culturally) prior to their resettlement.

BRINGING IT ALL TOGETHER   Each step in the social problem analysis helps advocates become more clear about the nature of the social problem, who is involved, the history of the problems, and the perspectives of the those affected by the problem. These steps can also limit the possibility of misunderstanding the nature of the problem, which can lead to poor policy-making, and ineffective or even damaging action that may end up causing more harm to the affected population, and key stakeholders, than good.

Social Justice Advocacy within Communities: Partnering to Effect Change

Advocates do not work alone. To be most effective, advocates work with other advocates and professionals—sometimes side-by-side as direct partners, and at other times coordinating services with other advocacy or related organizations in what are called *coalitions*. Advocacy coalition members work together as a team to effect change in many different ways and on various levels, but always within some type of community, which is the primary arena where change is most likely to occur (Netting et al., 2012).

Communities have been conceptualized in a variety of ways with most conceptualizations viewing the purpose of community as being related to the functions they serve, which can include production, distribution, and consumption of goods; social control through the establishment and enforcement of norms and values; and providing opportunities for social interaction and social support (Warren, 1978). While these functions can change depending on the size, location, political structure, and level of organization and cohesion of the community, one thing that all communities have in common is that they are social systems. Thus, in order to effect change within any community, on any level, an advocate must approach the community members using a social systems theory approach, acknowledging how systems behave, affect other systems, and ultimately yield to pressures to change (see Figure 3.2).

Although communities are often conceptualized within a local context, there are actually several levels of communities spanning from the local community to the global community. Advocates then must choose the level at which advocacy efforts will be primarily focused, with some advocacy interventions being on a local level within neighborhoods, villages, or cities (e.g., working with local leaders to educate the community about HIV transmission), on a broader level that might include statewide or national campaigns (e.g., advocating for new legislation that would increase state or federal funds for HIV clinics on Native American reservations), or a global level (e.g., advocating for the ratification of a UN human rights treaty). Ideally, broad-based social

FIGURE 3.2
Social Problems Are
Best Addressed When
Community Agencies
Join Forces

problems should be advocated for all of these levels, but realistically there are very few social justice campaigns that have the benefit of having such broad-based and well-coordinated advocacy. Additionally, a particular social problem will likely manifest quite differently depending on its context, thus the strategies and skills used, even the analysis of the social problem would vary significantly depending on where the social problem is manifesting.

Most of the time, advocacy efforts have a tendency to be rather ad hoc, relatively disconnected and somewhat disorganized with regard to what's happening on the ground versus on national or global levels. Advocacy efforts resulting in interventions occurring on a broad level (state, national, and global) are often referred to as *top-down*, indicating that the intervention is being imposed on the local community, whereas advocacy efforts resulting in interventions occurring at the local or grass-roots level are often referred to as *bottom-up*, implying that change at the local level can work its way up effecting broader change. The risk of any top-down approach is that often what seems viable on a policy level faces unanticipated challenges in real life. For instance, UN Human Rights Treaties, discussed in Chapter 1, set forth standards for the treatment of all humans, yet often these treaties directly conflict with cultural mores, norms, and values within specific cultures. A country that has a long-standing tradition of using children in labor, such as Bangladesh, may resist attempts to implement the UN Convention on the Rights of the Child, which prohibits child labor, because child labor is so integrated into its society and economic systems (Hindman, 2009). The risk of a bottom-up approach is that what works within the local community may not be viable on a broader level, or in other local communities, even within the same culture.

Regardless of the level at which the advocacy occurs, all change can be said to occur within communities. Again, the community might consist of a neighborhood, a village, a city, state, country, or even a global village, but no matter how big (or small) the community, advocates for social justice working within coalitions must develop skills necessary to work within communities and among community members.

Advocacy partners in the form of a coalition will then work together to effect change within communities of various sizes, at the desired levels and points of intervention. What this coalition will look like and how it will be comprised will depend, in large part, on the nature of the problem, its extent, and the level of the advocacy campaign (i.e., local, national, and global). The coalition might be informal and grassroots, or it might involve an international network of advocates from a variety of advocacy organizations, but regardless of the level of intervention or nature of the social problem, working in a coalition requires a wide range of generalist skills. Generalist skills must be general enough to be applied to a variety of situations and problems, yet specific enough that they can be applied in a very particular way within unique contexts. The generalist skills most often used by social justice advocates working in coalitions often include:

- *Networking skills:* the ability to identify and draw together multiple partners with similar goals, as well navigating various systems such as educational, political, media, and other advocacy organizations.
- *People skills:* the ability to work with a wide range of people often with different personality and working styles, drawing them together, coordinating working groups and tasks, and overcoming competing goals, and differences of opinions.
- *Writing skills:* the ability to write letters and other materials to different audiences, including key constituents, professionals, politicians, consumers, academics, and a lay audience, each requiring excellent grammar, clarity, the ability to reach different audiences (who will have different knowledge levels), on an emotional as well as intellectual level.
- *Researching skills:* the ability to research various sources (such as academic and other informational databases, government databases and websites, and research archives).
- *Technical skills:* the ability to access and utilize various computer software packages, as well as the ability to identify, access and navigate social media, such as listservs, Facebook, Skype, Twitter, websites, online newsgroups, and blogs. In fact, social media has recently become one of the primary platforms for social justice advocacy.

> ## Planning and Evaluating
>
> *Understanding and Mastery: Skills to evaluate the outcomes of the plan and the impact on the client or client group*
>
> **Critical Thinking Question:** How do the generalist skills explored in this chapter impact the human service professional's ability to engage in effective social justice advocacy?

As I have mentioned in the beginning of this chapter, the social justice advocate must, to a certain extent, be a "jack of all trades" to be truly effective. This does not mean that an advocate does not specialize, or does not have specialized skills. Certainly some advocates will be far more proficient with one set of skills, such as writing or researching, and others may feel far more comfortable with public speaking, and organizing public awareness campaigns and events. Yet to be effective and a good coalition member, advocates must be able to engage a variety of systems, working effectively with a wide range of people, in varying capacities. It is important to keep Schatz et al.'s (1990) definition of generalist practice in mind as having as its primary goal, "social justice, humanizing systems and improving the well-being of people" (p. 220), since it reminds us of that even in the seemingly mundane tasks, advocacy for social justice is involved.

Concluding Thoughts on Human Services Advocacy Interventions

In Chapters 1 through 3, I have laid a foundation for moving forward and exploring advocacy for social justice and the role of the advocate within the context of particular social justice issues. In subsequent chapters, specific human rights violations are explored with regard to their histories, the nature of the social problem, who is affected, the dynamics involved, past and current advocacy efforts, and the role and functions of the human services professional advocating for social justice on behalf of a particular population and/or social problem. Within each of these chapters, theories of change and power applicable to specific human rights violations are examined, as well as how generalist advocacy skills can be applied within specific areas of advocacy work.

Assess your analysis and evaluation of this chapter's content by completing the Chapter Review.

CHAPTER 4

Patricia Phillips/Alamy

Advocacy Women and Girls

. . . .

The Fight for Gender Equality

The first act of violence that patriarchy demands of males is not violence toward women. Instead patriarchy demands of all males that they engage in acts of psychic self-mutilation, that they kill off the emotional parts of themselves. If an individual is not successful in emotionally crippling himself, he can count on patriarchal men to enact rituals of power that will assault his self-esteem.

—bell hooks

History of Social Injustice against Women

It's tempting to begin a section on the history of social injustice of women and girls with some global statement about how women and girls have always been oppressed and exploited within all societies by all men, yet that would be a mistake—not because gender oppression hasn't existed throughout history, but because it is vitally important when exploring is sues such as gender oppression to avoid painting with a broad brush, due to the vast complexities involved. Historians have traced gender oppression, particularly involving violence against women and girls through early civilization, but not all females within a given society were oppressed, not all men oppressed females, and not all societies condoned, or sanctioned gender oppression.

So what is the history of gender oppression of women, and what has changed in the last several centuries? How have women and girls historically been viewed and treated, and how does gaining a better understanding of a historical context help us to better understand modern-day gender oppression, exploitation, and social injustice of women and girls?

The majority of historic societies were patriarchal in nature and involved hierarchical political and social systems that privileged males giving them power over women, both within social institutions as well as within cultural norms and practices (Hunnicutt, 2009). In most historic cultures, women were perceived as the property of men—first of their fathers, and then of their husbands. In fact, in ancient Babylonia, the rape of a woman was considered property damage and the rapist, if caught, would often be forced to pay a fine to the owner of the "property," the father or husband of the woman who was raped (Meier Tetlow, 2004).

Historical writings also indicate the prevailing belief (at least among men) that women were defective, both emotionally and physically. During the Victorian era, women were often diagnosed with *hysteria*, and women who behaved in a manner that was perceived as immoral were often diagnosed as nymphomaniacs—a medical disorder that would often warrant involuntary institutionalization (Ussher, 1992). Women were also frequently perceived as having the ability to put men under their spell, and men were cautioned to avoid their influence at all costs (Karlsen, 1989).

These historic views of women as physically and morally defective, emotionally unstable and mysteriously evil served as the precursor for "witchcraft hysteria" in Europe and North America during colonial times. Witchcraft hysteria involved the practice of accusing women considered "aberrant" of being witches embodied by Satan (despite the fact that the true practice of Wiccan has no relationship whatsoever with Satan worship). Such women were then imprisoned, and executed by a public burning or hanging. Although some men were convicted of witchcraft and condemned to death, the great majority of victims of witchcraft hysteria were older women who were married, and

DEA/E. LESSING Universal Images Group/Newscom

A demonstration of a female patient diagnosed with "hysteria".

women who behaved in ways that were threatening to the male-dominated puritanical and patriarchal society (Karlsen, 1989).

When exploring historical patterns of gender oppression and women's empowerment, intersectionality (explored in Chapter 1) must be considered in order to understand ways in which race, socioeconomic level, marital status, age, sexual orientation (including perceived orientation), and behavior have intersected with gender, influencing the perception and treatment of women throughout the course of history. Women of color, women of lower socioeconomic status, women who were single, or married but behaved in a manner perceived as too independent, women who lived lives that were not socially sanctioned, women who struggled with mental illness or other diseases and disabilities were treated differently in patriarchal societies; thus, while white women were certainly oppressed, women who possessed unique characteristics that increased their vulnerability experienced increased oppression within most patriarchal societies (bell hooks, 2000).

For instance, Smith (2005) explores the relationship between colonization of Native Americans and the rape of Native women, describing how Native American bodies were considered so filthy, and their culture marked by such sexual perversion and sexual sin that they were considered "unrapeable," meaning that if they were sexually violated by European or early American colonists (as happened quite frequently), the assault could not legally be considered rape. Smith explains that in patriarchal culture only those with "pure" bodies could be violated, and any other type of rape wasn't considered "rape" in a legal sense since an impure body wasn't deserving of that type of legal respect.

Smith describes how Native American women were a particular threat to English colonizers of America because of their empowered status within their tribal culture, which rendered them able to speak their mind freely. The freedoms they enjoyed in their nonpatriarchal native culture increased their vulnerability to being sexually assaulted by colonizers who wished to silence them. In describing this dynamic, Smith explains how in Native culture, women were highly respected and had a voice in society. Additionally, they were not forced to conform to puritanical expectations that women be subservient to men. Rather, Native American women were free to be independent, to express their sexuality in comparable ways as men, and did not see themselves as fallen or condemned in a biblical sense. Smith describes how the colonizers were outraged by the freedom Native women had, and set about to stifle them, or in reality, stamp them out completely through cultural and physical genocide. For instance, Native women were not merely raped—they were frequently sexually mutilated. For instance, their private parts were often cut off by colonists and used as bridals for their horses (among other things). These acts represented an attempt to completely annihilate an indigenous population through the genocide of their women, the Native population's most prized possession and the representation of hope of their continued survival in the face of genocide, through the women's reproductive capabilities (Smith, 2005).

Many cultures have become more egalitarian through the years and increasing attention has been paid to domestic violence as a social evil as well as a personal one, through the advocacy efforts of women (and some progressively thinking men). Yet, many of these same atrocities continue to occur today across various societies, both in Western cultures as well as in developing countries, leaving one to wonder what we have learned from history, and why history must constantly repeat itself.

Assess your comprehension of History of Social Injustice against Women by taking this quiz.

Theories of Gender Oppression and Exploitation

Perhaps you have attempted to advocate for gender equality only to have someone counter your argument with claims that gender differences are innate, thus cannot be changed, and men are just hardwired to be aggressive, to "spread their seed," and to be protective of women. Is there empirical evidence in support of this perspective? Are men more naturally aggressive than women? Are women naturally more nurturing than men? And relevant to our discussion, are women the weaker sex in need of physical and emotional protection from men? And if so, why? Do hormones or our DNA determine gender roles? Are gender roles the response of how we emotionally respond to our mother and father? Or do we learn what it means to be feminine and masculine through the media, our teachers, and our respective religions? Before exploring theories that attempt to explain why women are more often the victims of violence and oppressive conditions, it is important to explore the nature of gender roles and gender differentiation (how and why are men and women are different), and what causes these differences. Advocates can then better challenge theories that are deterministic and dichotomous in nature—those theories that render bad behavior the natural order of things, despite little empirical evidence.

Gender Role Determinants: "Boys Will Be Boys"—They Can't Help It, or Can They?

There are several theories that have been put forth in an attempt to describe the nature of gender, including what forms and influences the traits and behaviors of the genders (to be distinguished from sex—a term used to describe the functional differences between the genders), and explain the differing characteristics between men and women. Theories that attempt to explain the nature of *masculinity* and *femininity*, particularly in regard to our response to our biological sex, fall into three general categories: biological theories, psychological theories, and sociocultural theories.

BIOLOGICAL THEORIES OF GENDER Biologically based theories, sometimes referred to as genetics determinism, have dominated the field of gender theory for years. Such theories posit that gender is determined biologically, thus men behave like men, and women behave like women because of genetic differences (this is of course the "short" version of the theory) (Rowe, 1994). Such theories often describe gender roles in terms of reproductive necessities or gender-based behaviors that guarantee the continuance of the species (Buss & Schmitt, 1993), and attempt to explain male aggression in biological terms, suggesting environmental (and evolutionary) protective factors (Archer, 2004).

Early biological theories regarding masculinity and femininity consistently highlighted the inferiority of women and the superiority of men, and often used biology as proof of these differences. These theories have extended well into areas of morality as well, specifically the domain of women's sexuality. For instance, in ancient writings during the time of Aristotle, men were often described as being the active initiators of the sex with women, with women being passive recipients. One of the first biological theories of procreation posited that only one "seed" was needed for procreation, and men possessed the seed in their seminal fluid. Women were only the incubator and did not have any genetic influence over the fetus. Claudius Galen, a prominent Roman physician who lived in the second century, was the first to propose that women actually did have some biological part to play in procreation. In Galen's "two-seed" theory, he postulated that women released seminal fluid as well during sexual intercourse, which then commingled with the male seminal fluid producing a fetus. Yet consistent with patriarchal belief, Galen's theory stated that the women's "seed" was significantly thinner and weaker than that of a man's (Schaus, 2006).

Feminists in particular have taken a hard line against the notion that gender roles and characteristics are biologically determined thus immutable. In her best-selling book, *Myth of Gender*, Anne Fausto-Sterling (1992) confronts the contention that gender roles are determined solely by biological or genetic forces, arguing that such perspectives can be used to justify gender-based inequity. For instance, in reference to the relationship between female poverty and gender income inequity, she challenges the position that men are more natural leaders than women, thus are more successful in their careers than women. She cites Gilder's (1981) theory on gender income disparity as an example of a false theory of gender inequality based on perceived biological differences.

Gilder explains away the income gap between men and women as a natural and avoidable phenomenon, which he refers to as the "biological factor." Arguing that men are more aggressive by nature than women, and they had an innate desire to dominate (evidenced by their larger stature), they were more natural leaders than women. Gilder relies on both biological and evolutionary theories in making these assertions, citing how in prehistoric times men did all of the hunting and women waited at home with the children for their husbands to arrive home with the meat. Gilder asserts that this practice, which he argued is innate and instinctual, served as a precursor to "modern-day" gender roles, where men go out into the workforce due to some innate need to provide, and women, having no real desire or instinctual abilities to work, wanted nothing more than to stay at home raising children and wait for the man to come home. In support of gender-based income disparity, Gilder cites the innate nature of the genders, arguing that because of these instinctual dispositions, women are just not able to invest the same level of effort as men into the workforce, outside the home (Fausto-Sterling, 1992). Fausto-Sterling cautions that these and other biological explanations for what she argues are social phenomena suggest that advocacy efforts to challenge the status quo are vitally important.

> ### Human Systems
>
> *Understanding and Mastery: Theories of Human Development*
>
> ---
>
> **Critical Thinking Question:** What concerns have feminists expressed with regard to biological theories of gender development?
>
> •

Similar criticism of the genetic determinist perspective argue that such biological theories of gender role differences are too dichotomous, meaning that if gender-related traits and behaviors are determined solely by genetics, then there are only two options: male behavior or female behavior. Not only can this perspective lead to stereotyping, but as Lippert-Rasmussen (2010) argues, it invalidates the lived experience of anyone who does not fit into these two categories, and it can also reinforce limiting perspectives of the appropriate or "normal" role for males and females within society. Lippert-Rasmussen challenges genetic/biological theories of gender pointing to the effect that such deterministic (and fatalistic) theories has on women, cautioning that if socially constructed notions of femininity are presumed to be genetically determined, then women who deviate from socially prescribed gender roles will likely be viewed as biologically defective. Such theories also render gender-based behavior immutable and rigid. After all, if a women's soft, caregiving, passive nature is biologically determined then gender roles cannot evolve to a more egalitarian state, and those women who do not fit the "feminine" stereotype are social misfits and deviants.

Further, empirical support for genetic determinates of gender behavioral differences is limited. For instance, research on genetic factors influencing gender differences, such as studies conducted on identical twins who were raised apart and evaluated for differences in cognitive abilities and personality traits, found little support for the theory that genetic factors significantly influence intellectual and personality attributes (Bouchard, Lykken, McGue, Segal, & Tellegen, 1990; Plomin, Chipuer, & Neiderhiser, 1994; Plomin & Daniels, 2011; Scarr, 1992 as cited in Bussey & Bandura, 1999).

PSYCHOLOGICAL THEORIES OF GENDER Psychological theories of gender tend to emphasize the intrapsychic influences of gendered experiences, gender development, and gender expression. Famous developmental theorists such as Sigmund Freud (1905/1930) and Lawrence Kohlberg (1966) theorized that masculinity and femininity were formed and influenced through the early childhood developmental process, such as in the early identification with the same-sex parent, emotional responses to psychological development in childhood, and/or cognitive development. Such theories, while having some merit, for the most part lack empirical support (Bussey & Bandura, 1999).

SOCIOCULTURAL THEORIES OF GENDER The third category of theories suggests that gender-based behaviors (what it means to be masculine and what it means to be feminine) are formed and influenced by social and cultural forces experienced in one's environment. For instance, social constructivist theories posit that what society considers gender-based behaviors are primarily formed and influenced by cultural mores and social expectations (Bussey & Bandura, 1999; Lippert-Rasmussen, 2010). So, boys learn what it means to be masculine, and girls learn what it means to be feminine by watching others in their environment and by watching how others (both peers and elders) respond to their behaviors. Most contemporary theorists tend to embrace a social constructivist perspective, but a newer perspective, referred to as the biopsychosocial approach, is gaining popularity as well. The biopsychosocial approach theorizes that gender-based behaviors are formed through an intricate and complex combination of biological, psychological, and social influences, including cultural and environmental factors, which manifest uniquely depending on a variety of circumstances.

Image Courtesy of The Advertising Archives

Patriarchy: It's a Man's World

Traditional gender-based theories are often used to support patriarchy within societies, defined earlier in this chapter as a hierarchical political and social system that privileges males both in a structural sense as well as in an ideological sense (Hunnicutt, 2009). The roots of patriarchy extend much further than is reasonable to explore in an advocacy textbook, but suffice it to say that the system has been in place for a very long time (some might say since the beginning of recorded history!). In agrarian society, from the Middle Ages through the Industrial Era, patriarchal systems placed the father as the head of the household, in charge of his wife, children, and servants. And while the wife may have had considerable responsibility and played an important role within the household and broader community, women were generally perceived as being the weaker sex, ungifted in most senses requiring men to maintain complete control over of the household. Social laws existed to support male dominance over females, and religious systems served to ordain this social structure by God (Dahlström & Liljeström, 1983; Rowland, 2004).

Legislation supported this patriarchal system with inheritance laws guaranteeing that property and leadership roles passed down from father to son, guaranteeing complete control over women (since women were considered property by law). Social laws as well as religious traditions (particularly Catholicism and then later Protestantism) controlled the activities of women by controlling marriage, kinship relationships, and morality. For instance, English common law passed from the twelfth century onward stipulated that any property held by the wife became the possession of her husband on marriage (Dahlström & Liljeström, 1983; Westerkamp, 1999).

It wasn't until the 1800s that a feminist movement began to take root challenging these laws and demanding gender equality, culminating with the women's suffrage movement that demanded a woman's right to vote. With the dawning of the Industrial

At the 1920 Republican Convention in Chicago, Abby Scott Baker, Florence Taylor Marsh, Sue Shelton White, Elsie Hill, and Betty Gram accused the Republican Party of blocking ratification in Vermont and Connecticut. International Film Service Co., Inc. June 1920.

Everett Collection/Alamy

Era, precapitalist patriarchy ultimately faded away, only to be replaced with what some scholars call "man rule" (versus "father rule"). In fact, some scholars note that the patriarchal system justified by the false theories of male biological dominance has now been replaced by a male-dominated system based on the belief that men are more superior in science and technology, two domains that warrant significantly higher earnings in modern society (Dahlström & Liljeström, 1983; Gilder, 1981).

In the last few decades, many scholars have discouraged the use of the term *patriarchy* due to a historic tendency to oversimplify the concept (Hunnicutt, 2009; Kandiyoti, 1988). Traditionally patriarchy was viewed in a relatively uniform manner, where all men were privileged and all women oppressed. Patriarchal systems do not exist in a vacuum, though, and are actually quite complex and contextually driven. Patriarchy is often embedded in other social systems, many of which are systems of dominance, including racism and classism. Thus, within a patriarchal system, some women will experience more oppression and some will experience more privilege. In recognition of the true complexity of patriarchal systems, more contemporary scholarship has begun to challenge the notion of uniformity, noting that while white women may have led feminist movements demanding gender equality, white women in general have experienced far less oppression than black women, particularly in the United States.

> ### Client-Related Values and Attitudes
>
> *Understanding and Mastery: The worth and uniqueness of individuals including ethnicity, culture, gender, sexual orientation, and other expressions of diversity*
>
> **Critical Thinking Question:** What are some ways in which patriarchy is embedded in societal systems within the United States and other Western countries?

Black feminist and author bell hooks has written extensively on this topic, challenging the virtually all white modern feminist movement of the 1970s and 1980s, as having failed to recognize the intersectionality involved in patriarchal systems, particularly as it relates to race. She challenges the notion that all women are oppressed arguing that such assertions negate differences with regard to social class, race, religion, and sexual orientation, thus negating the diversity in experiences that women with increasing levels of stigmatizing characteristics experience (hooks, 2000). In other words, according to hooks, a black woman, who struggles financially, who is a member of a minority religion (or no religion at all), and who is a lesbian, will be far more oppressed in American society than an upper-income Caucasian heterosexual woman who is married and attends a Protestant church (for instance).

Yet, abandoning the term *patriarchy* due to its ambiguity did not appear to help in furthering the development of a more comprehensive and solid theoretical framework of gender oppression, exploitation, and violence against women. In light of this theoretical deficit, Hunnicutt (2009) advocates for a resurrection of the term *patriarchy*, but with a more contemporary definition to capture the various forms and degrees of patriarchy that can exist within a given society. Such a theoretical framework, according to Hunnicutt would acknowledge the role intersectionality plays in both male privilege and female oppression highlighting how in patriarchal systems, women experience "degrees of vulnerability." Hunnicutt argues that a simplistic definition of patriarchy obscures the varied nature of women's experiences, whereas a more complex understanding of patriarchy includes variations of gendered norms based on secondary characteristics such as social class and race, while highlighting different types of male domination. Ultimately, he cites the importance of viewing patriarchy in more flexible ways enabling the complexity of this social phenomenon to be better understood.

Regardless of the term used, patriarchal social and political systems where men are privileged, and thus receive preferential treatment in society based on the rationale that they are superior to women (biologically or otherwise), still exist in many societies around the world. There are patriarchal macro systems operating within various institutions in society, including governments, the legal system, the economic market, and religious traditions, as well as at the micro level, within families, friendships and romantic partnerships, including marriage (at the micro level). Exploring the nature of gender oppression and social injustice experienced by women in the world today is more effectively done when evaluated through a theoretical lens that recognizes the long-standing role of patriarchy within the overlapping systems in the majority of societies and cultures.

Assess your comprehension
of <u>Theories of Gender
Oppression</u> by taking
this quiz.

Engaging in Culturally Competent Gender Equity Advocacy

There are several ethical considerations that must be taken into account when working with vulnerable and oppressed women, a few of which I touch on in this section. The first relates to ensuring the use of a culturally competent approach, with increased sensitivity to issues involving race, socioeconomic level, education level, and historic treatment of vulnerable subgroups within the female population.

Another ethical consideration relates to global advocacy, where advocates from Western cultures provide advocacy for women living in developing countries in a culturally competent manner. This ethical dynamic is similar to that of working with different cultures within the United States, but the level of sensitivity required when advocating for issues across borders is much higher. This issue is particularly relevant when advocates have never even visited the region for which they are advocating; in this instance, a considerable amount of cultural preparation and study is required to ensure that the advocate has a comprehensive understanding of the dynamics involved, particularly when using a Western template in framing social issues affecting women. The ultimate goal in culturally competent global advocacy practice is to ensure that advocates do not do more damage to the community they are advocating for with their advocacy efforts thus potentially making a situation worse for the women they are intending to help.

There are several models of cultural competent practice, but essentially when we refer to cultural competence within the human services field we are talking about developing the skills necessary to work effectively in cross-cultural situations, reflecting values and attitudes of respect and understanding, as well as attributes of cultural humility and receptivity (Whitaker et al., 2007). The three primary components of becoming a culturally competent human services provider are

1. an awareness of one's own cultural values and biases,
2. an awareness of one's clients' worldview, and
3. the use of culturally appropriate intervention strategies (Arredondo et al., 1996).

These values are important to keep in mind whether advocates are working in their countries of origin or in a different country with divergent cultures. For instance, the issue of gender oppression and exploitation occur globally, but definitions of oppression and exploitation may differ significant from culture to culture. Thus any time an advocate is from a different culture than the primary target population, cultural competence and cultural sensitivity are paramount to effective practice.

Cultural competent advocacy practice requires that advocates ensure that their goals are the same as the goals of those for whom they are advocating. It is also important to ensure that cultural perceptions do not lead to a situation where ethnocentrism—the tendency to perceive one's own culture as superior—influences how pertinent issues are perceived. In addition, in the same way that counselors learn early in their educational training that effective counselors begin where their clients are, not where the counselor believes the client should be, the same is true for advocates for social justice. For instance, advocates focusing on gender oppression and exploitation are often feminists, but it is vital for them to recognize that in many places in the world (even in the United States), feminism is not embraced, or is embraced only marginally, and it may very well be that the women in a particular culture are the strongest advocates for keeping the status quo. Thus time must be taken to learn about a different culture, recognize that various perceptions of cultural values and lifestyles will exist, and that clients are the best judges of whether or not they want change within their lives.

Having increased cultural sensitivity and cultural humility will help the social justice advocate ensure that they are not imposing a Western agenda on non-Western cultures, either within the United States, or abroad. Additionally, cultural competence helps advocates better understand how women from different cultural backgrounds define and experience violence, oppression and exploitation, historic and existing barriers to receiving assistance, what cultural ties exist that keep women in abusive and oppressive situations, and what women within racial/ethnic minority groups actually consider to be helpful (i.e., ensuring that the goals of the target group and the advocate are aligned).

Self-Development

Understanding and Mastery: Awareness of Diversity

Critical Thinking Question: Lipson discusses the importance of human service professionals developing self-awareness that includes an understanding of one's cultural characteristics, influences, and biases. What are some common influences and biases that members of the majority culture (Caucasian "Western" culture) are most likely to experience that could potentially create challenges to the development of cultural competence?

In the last few decades, globalization has blurred the lines between domestic and global advocacy, and while there are still marked differences between gender advocacy work within the Western countries (such as the United States), and advocacy occurring in a non-Western country, many of the issues addressed in this section, particularly with regard to cultural competence and ethical issues can be applied to both situations. For instance, Latinas have unique experiences with oppression and exploitation compared to other cultural groups living in the United States, and differences exist even within the Latina population, depending on many factors, including whether Latina women remain in their country of origin or have migrated to a more economically developed country. In fact, research indicates that recently arrived, as well as undocumented Latinas living in the United States are at significantly higher risk of intimate partner violence (IPV) than Latinas who remain in their country of origin. Specifically, research has found that for those Latinas living in English-speaking countries, language can act as a barrier to receiving services (Whitaker et al., 2007). Cultural perceptions of IPV though may be similar between Latinas who remain in their country of origin and those who have migrated, but the circumstances they find themselves in will be different.

Another example of blurred lines between domestic and global advocacy relates to working with resettled refugee populations. Increases in civil conflict and forced migration have resulted in the transport of large migrant groups (many of whom have been living in protracted refugee camps in developing countries for years) into Western countries. Many of these refugees once resettled, reside within their own

Refugees from the Democratic Republic of the Congo in a UNHCR camp in Rwanda.

cultural groups (as a subcultural group within the host country), so while the environmental or political context has changed, many of the cultural issues refugees are dealing with are similar to those they may have dealt with in their country of origin. For instance, most advocates working on gender issues with recently arrived refugee populations understand that certain cultural groups may have come from countries where violence against women is not only legal, but actually seen as a necessary component of a healthy marriage. Advocates working with migrant groups within the United States will work within cultural and political systems that are more supportive of gender equality, but will be dealing with many of the very same cultural and ethical dynamics as the advocate working with similar populations in their countries of origin.

Thus while I have delineated differences between domestic and global issues with regard to practice considerations, the discussion of cultural competence and ethical values can be applied to a variety of advocacy situations and settings with blurred lines between "domestic" and "global."

Global Gender Empowerment Programs: A Clash of Cultures

Another aspect of globalization as it pertains to advocacy for gender equality pertains to the internationalization of women's rights. The process of internationalizing women's rights began in around the mid-1970s when gender empowerment increasingly became the focus of several UN conferences on gender equality. This journey has not been without its challenges though, and introducing the concept of gender equality to a worldwide audience has been wrought with claims of Western dominance, cultural insensitivity, and various other ethical dilemmas related to the implementation of gender empowerment programs or agendas.

For instance, many women's advocates may struggle to recognize that not all women living within patriarchal cultures feel oppressed or want to be rescued by Western feminists who are determined to set them free. Women's advocates must then learn to manage the conflict between their commitment to valuing other cultures and their commitment to gender equality, which at times might mean compromising their feminist values, and at other times might mean trampling a bit on cultural values to advocate for gender equality (see the discussion on female genital mutilation in Chapter 5 as an example). Striking a balance between a commitment to respecting differing cultural values and advocating for gender equality becomes particularly contentious when religion is involved. The most notable example of this would be in the case of Western advocates working toward the goal of a Western perspective of feminism within a Muslim context, or Christians (particularly fundamentalists) advocating for issues perceived as moral, in a country without a human rights structure (see the discussion in Chapter 7 on U.S. Evangelical influences in Central African laws on homosexuality).

Most international development programs facilitated by the UN or by nongovernmental organizations (NGOs) are based on Western secular models, thus program goals are at times perceived by target countries with anything from suspiciousness to outright scorn, particularly within cultures where conservative religious practices are sanctioned by the government, as is the case in many Islamic countries (De Cordier, 2010). The same is true for the international human rights treaties, including the *Convention on the Elimination of all forms of Discrimination against Women* (UN General Assembly, 1979), the *Beijing Declaration and Platform for Action* (a UN agenda for women's empowerment worldwide) (Beijing Declaration, 1995), and the UN *Millennium Development Goals* (MDGs) (a UN-sponsored action plan to eliminate poverty that includes a gender equality goal) (UNDP, 2000), each of which are based on Western values and embedded in principles of gender equality and gender mainstreaming as a component of development aid programs (De Cordier, 2010).

Values of gender equality are sometimes not embraced to the same extent (if at all) in many developing or least developed countries. This becomes problematic when gender equity policies are implemented using a *top-down approach*, a management style in which decisions are made by top leadership without consideration of local realities (as discussed in previous chapters). In fact, a significant portion of international aid money is now tied to gender equality goals. This policy can create resistance on the part of more traditional societies based on patriarchal values, which are forced to embrace Western versions of gender equity to receive assistance. For instance, the Organization for Economic and Co-operation and Development (OECD), which coordinates much of the international aid from Western countries, increasingly ties gender equality and women's empowerment to aid money within four different contexts, including aid to support women's economic empowerment, aid in support of gender equality in education and health, aid in support of gender equality in fragile and conflicted-affected states, and aid in support of gender equality in humanitarian contexts (OECD, 2011). For countries to qualify for aid money from donor countries, recipient countries must meet eligibility criteria where gender equality is explicitly promoted in activity documentation through specific measures which

- reduce social, economic, or political power inequalities between women and men, girls and boys, ensure that women benefit equally with men from the activity, or compensate for past discrimination; or
- develop or strengthen gender equality or antidiscrimination policies, legislation, or institutions.

Between 2006 and 2007, approximately 23 billion dollars in international aid money was spent on programs that included gender equality and women's empowerment as a primary activity, representing over 30% of all OECD international aid money (OECD, 2011). The trend toward tying gender equality to aid monies can sometimes lead to what De Cordier refers to as a "clash of civilizations."

In Chapter 1, I explored neoliberal economic policies and how these are often used by international lending organizations such as the World Bank and the International Monetary Fund (IMF), as well as international aid and development programs to manage recipient government's economic behavior. When gender empowerment values are embedded within the policies of aid and development programs, a cultural backlash can occur, both because a particular society may not be ready to embrace gender egalitarianism to such a great extent, but also because the gender equity goals embedded in these programs are often ensconced in a web of other Western programmatic policies that may be antithetical to more collectivist and/or traditional cultures. This "clash of civilizations" can lead to a general mistrust on the part of recipient countries, that may perceive such donor policies as being based upon Western dogmatism (De Cordier, 2010; Roy, 2008).

De Cordier cautions against this type of ethnocentric thinking, citing several studies and surveys where women in Islamic countries have shared their desire for

---

| **Box 4.1** | **The Minangkabau: A Matriarchal Society** |

Despite common belief that virtually all societies are patriarchal to some extent, some societies are actually matriarchal. Matriarchal societies are those that have "cultural symbols and practices associating the maternal with the origin and center of growth processes necessary for social and individual life" (Sanday, 2002, p. 237). In true matriarchal societies, women are the head of household in most respects, and have greater level of privilege compared to men, such as having inheritance rights and more control over the children.

The Minangkabau tribe is a cultural group of approximately 4 million people who live in West Sumatra, Indonesia. The Minangkabau are matriarchal society, or a matriarchaat, as the Minangkabau prefer to refer to themselves. The Minangkabau practice an ancient nature-based philosophy called Adat, which emphasizes nurturance and growth within nature. Anthropologist Peggy Reeves Sanday, who has spent over 20 years studying the Minangkabau tribe, wrote a book about her experiences called *Women at the Center: Life in a Modern Matriarchy*. Sanday explains how the tribe actually embraces gender egalitarian principles with a governance based on consensus. In her book, Sanday shares what a member of the tribe, and an Adat expert state that in virtually all ways, men and women are considered the same in the Minangkabau society, with most privileges that are typically granted to men in traditional patriarchal societies being granted to women in Minangkabau society. For instance, Sanday describes how women have inheritance rights that supersede that of men, and also have control over the community's economic structures. Sanday describes that the premise on which these matriarchal customs are based is the belief that women ensure the continuation of the lineage, thus should be granted more privileges and power within society.

greater freedom and autonomy but do not necessarily have a desire to become more Western. For instance, a Gallup poll conducted between 2001 and 2007 found that while Muslim women admire aspects of life in the West, they do not necessarily embrace all Western values, and in fact, view feminism with a large measure of suspicion (Esposito & Mogahed, 2007, as cited in De Cordier, 2010). Since gender is so inextricably linked to culture, including religion, it is difficult to address gender equality in a culturally competent manner without addressing larger cultural dynamics related to Western cultural values. Not only are concepts defined differently, at least to a certain extent (one woman's "oppression" is another woman's "social safety net"), but often the individuals who are on the ground implementing gender equity programs in non-Westernized countries are often perceived to be Western elites who do not have much respect for those they are attempting to assist, and who have lifestyles and a mentality that are remote if not outright disconnected from the majority of their supposed beneficiaries. De Cordier points out that since many of the gender empowerment programs are funded by foreign countries, they are often perceived by those living in the recipient country as having a "foreign agenda," which then ultimately undermines the program, regardless of its actual worth or good intentions.

Human Services Delivery Systems

Understanding and Mastery: Political and ideological aspects of human services

Critical Thinking Question: What does De Cordier mean when he references the "clash of civilizations" in relation to gender roles within society?

• •

A possible solution to the issue of Western dominance in humanitarian and advocacy intervention programs in both Western countries as well as in non-Western countries is to use a *bottom-up* approach where the values of the target population are recognized and valued, and solutions to local problems are explored from a local perspective. What this means is that advocates—whether working with culturally marginalized populations in the United States, or in other cultures abroad—utilize a culturally sensitive approach in honoring all cultures, even those that embrace values antithetical to Western values. It also means that advocates do not jump to conclusions about the goodness or badness of certain cultural practices (particularly when these practices are rooted in the context of collectivist cultures) without thoroughly exploring the nature and effect of those practices. This also means that Western advocates make sure that they are using the same critical lens with their own culture, as they do when evaluating another culture. In other words, when social justice advocates from the United States feel compelled to criticize divorce laws in a developing nation in Asia or Africa, they should make sure to evaluate the U.S. family law policies with the same level of scrutiny to avoid the ethnocentric tendency to perceive that Western countries always manage such sensitive issues well.

Finally, some scholars have suggested that the best opportunity for change, particularly with regard to gender equity resides with local agencies that have the social capital necessary to gain the trust and cooperation of members of the local community. Such organizations may be well known to the local community, thus they likely have a common investment in confronting harmful cultural practices, which will then benefit the entire community (De Cordier, 2010). Essentially what this approach is suggesting is that social justice advocates working in cultures other than their own partner with local organizations so that solutions to social problems are "homegrown."

Assess your comprehension of Culturally Competent Gender Equity Advocacy by taking this quiz.

•
•
•
•
•
•
•
•

Women from a rural area in India that practices patriarchy.

Xander Martin

Concluding Thoughts on Advocating for Gender Equity

Advocating on behalf of women and girls, whether in one's home community, or in a completely different culture thousands of miles away, is challenging but vitally important, particularly in light of the many risks women face worldwide. With increased sensitivity to unintended effects of advocacy efforts and with diligent efforts to recognize and respect divergent values, advocacy efforts can be managed in a way that respect the rights of others, value cultural differences, and engage local efforts to create sustainable and long-lasting positive change.

Assess your analysis and evaluation of this chapter's contents by completing the **Chapter Review**.

CHAPTER 5

Violence against Women and Girls

. . . .

Advocacy Intervention Strategies on a Local and Global Level

Bjanka Kadic/Alamy

Violence against Women and Girls in the Global North

Domestic violence, also referred to as family violence and intimate partner violence (IPV), involves physical and emotional abuse acted out between intimates. This may include violence between husbands and wives or boyfriends and girlfriends, violence within gay and lesbian relationships, or violence between siblings. IPV can include hitting, punching, slapping, pinching, shoving, and throwing objects at or near the victim. IPV is also typically associated with verbal and emotional abuse including name-calling, harassment, taunting, put-downs, and ridiculing. Emotional and verbal abuse can occur without physical abuse, but rarely does physical abuse occur without emotional or verbal abuse (DiLillo, Giuffre, Tremblay, & Peterson, 2001; Martin, 2014; Tjaden, & Thoennes, 2000).

Statistics on the incidence of domestic violence in the United States alone are alarming. The Centers for Disease Control and Prevention (CDC) estimates that one in three women (36%) and one in four men (29%) of the U.S. population report having been a victim of some form of IPV in 2010, with one in four women (24%) and one is seven men (14%) having experienced severe IPV. Both men and women are survivors of IPV report significantly higher rates of physical and mental health problems compared to the general population. According to a CDC survey conducted in 2010, although both men and women are survivors of IPV, women are survivors far more often of multiple forms of violence,

Ermolaev Alexander/Shutterstock

Many female survivors of IPV believe they must endure the abuse by their partners in silence

such as physical, sexual, and emotional violence, than men, who are far more often survivors of solely physical violence. IPV has resulted in 1.3 million injuries each year, and 2,340 deaths in 2007, with the majority of victims being women (Black et al., 2011).

Nearly 325,000 women are survivors of IPV while pregnant, and research suggests that pregnancy can actually render women more vulnerable to abuse. Once considered a personal family matter, IPV in recent generations is recognized to affect entire communities, both fiscally and socially. Women who have a history of IPV report having significantly higher rates of physical health problems. For instance, women who have a history of IPV report having significantly higher rates of physical problems, such as those caused by assaults, partner rape, stress, chronic pain, gynecological problems, HIV/AIDS and other sexually transmitted diseases, and gastrointestinal problems. The estimated health costs related to IPV is close to $6 million per year and $1.8 billion in lost productivity, including lost time from work, unemployment, and increased dependence on public assistance programs (CDC, 2008). Additionally, IPV costs the U.S. economy about $8.3 billion per year in health costs, and another 727 million in lost productivity and lost revenue due in large part to survivors of IPV missing collectively about 8 million days from work (CDC, 2008; Max, Rice, Finkelstein, Bardwell, & Leadbetter, 2004).

IPV does not just affect the abused partner. The children living in an abusive home are IPV survivors as well, even if the violence is not aimed directly toward them. For instance, boys who witness IPV are twice as likely to commit violence against their partners when they reach adulthood, whereas girls who grow up in homes where IPV is practiced are at increased risk of partnering with an abuser (NCADV, 2007). Clearly, IPV is not a private family matter. The cost to society, both in injured members and in lost revenue, is far too high to ever allow this issue to be ignored again (Martin, 2014).

Advocacy Efforts in Response to IPV in the Global North

The Nature of Domestic Violence: The Cycle of Violence

Lenore Walker (1979) was the first to coin the phrase *the cycle of violence* in describing the pattern of interpersonal violence in intimate relationships. The cycle consists of repeating patterns of good times—called the *honeymoon phase*—then tense times—called the *tension-building phase*—and then violence—called the *rage* or *explosion phase*. It is

Cycle of Violence

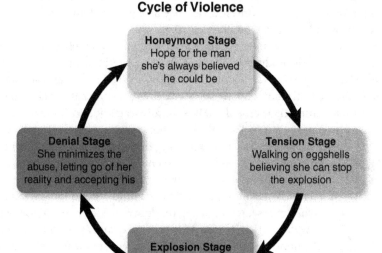

FIGURE 5.1
Cycle of Violence
Source: Michelle Martin

this cyclical nature of interpersonal dynamics that makes leaving an abusive relationship so challenging. A woman is most likely to leave after the explosion stage, yet quite quickly most batterers begin the cycle again by honeymooning the victim, making her think that he has finally learned his lesson and will become the man of her dreams (Martin, 2014).

Victims are not controlled just by violence either, but through control of their financial resources, through isolating them from other support systems, including close family and friends, and through long-term denial of the victim's reality and perceptions of the relationship, leading most victims to feel the need to deny the extent and severity of the abuse. Research also indicates that women who remain in violent relationships have certain personality characteristics that make them more vulnerable, such being inclined to forgive easily and quickly (Gordon, Burton, & Porter, 2004). Research on IPV, including studies on why men batter and why women stay, can provide advocates with points of intervention in both macro and micro advocacy efforts.

As was discussed in Chapter 1, the first step in social justice advocacy is to ensure that the issue being advocated for is in fact considered a problem within the society. According to Blumer (1971), a social problem becomes legitimized within society through a sequential process of development. In order for a society to respond effectively to a social problem, the problem must first be recognized and then legitimized. Blumer argues that in the early stages of an issue becoming recognized as a social problem, there must be public discussion and debate as well as media attention. Once an issue becomes recognized and legitimized by power groups within a society, mobilization and social advocacy will then follow as attempts are made to develop an action plan to address the problem.

The recognition of IPV as a social problem within North America (and consequently throughout the Global North) has been a process whereby powerful groups within society have identified it as a valid social problem, and acknowledged its damaging ripple effects within society, including individual and collective costs to public health, child welfare, police enforcement efforts, lost productivity for victims, and so on. The legitimization of domestic violence as a social problem emerged in the 1970s coinciding with the feminist movement, as well as other social forces that compelled mainstream U.S. society to no longer perceive domestic violence as a private family matter, and "wife beating" as a husband's legal right (Schuyler, 1976).

A key component in each stage of this legitimizing process involves advocacy efforts, and the key for social justice advocates is to engage in the legitimizing process in a way that best utilizes what Schuyler (1976) describes as the "snowball effect," where each stage of development in the legitimization of domestic violence as a significant social problem leads to increased momentum. In a sense then, it is the advocates' job to "jump on this bandwagon" and keep the momentum of social recognition, awareness, and attention going.

The process of legitimizing domestic violence as a social problem has been evolving in the Global North. Yet research reflects a snowball effect similar to what Schulyer describes. For instance, a relatively recent literature review found a trend that reflected an increase in research focusing on domestic violence and an increase in new domestic violence advocacy programs, particularly in the area of public health (Schow, 2006). Advocates who make themselves aware of the literature on this topic can avail themselves to these trends, and thus be better prepared to "jump on the bandwagon."

Advocacy in the area of gender-based violence and IPV can involve many different activities including raising public awareness of the nature, breadth, and seriousness of the problem through public awareness campaigns, developing prevention strategies, policy practice involving advocating for the passage of laws that provide greater protection for women, stricter legal enforcement of existing laws, and advocacy for increased funding for social services for victims and perpetrators.

In the United States, domestic violence advocacy organizations and coalitions often engage in a variety of services and advocacy efforts, including providing shelter for victims, public awareness and education campaigns, legal advocacy, case management, counseling, and public policy advocacy (Schow, 2006). *The National Domestic Violence Hotline* publishes a list of the network of domestic violence advocacy coalitions from all 50 states. These services are provided in compliance with domestic violence legislation, principally, the *Violence Against Women Act* (VAWA) discussed later in this chapter.

Prevention Strategies and Public Awareness Campaigns

Prevention strategies are intervention strategies that are designed to intervene before violence begins, but focusing on risk factors and warning signs. Prevention strategies require some level of knowledge about the nature of risk factors and warning signs of IPV, which is another reason why it is vital that advocates avail themselves to research being conducted in the field.

Prevention strategies are often separated into different levels. Primary prevention strategies focus on preventing problems within a population before they begin, secondary prevention strategies focus on reducing problems in the early stages, and tertiary prevention strategies focus on reducing the incidence of a problem during its course. The most common gender-based violence prevention strategy used in the United States is at the tertiary level where prevention efforts target victims and batterers currently engaged in IPV relationships (e.g., batterers intervention programs, victims advocacy programs), yet often such efforts do not have a good track record of success due to the very complex nature of IPV and its cyclical nature, particularly once physical violence has manifested in the relationship (Wolfe & Jaffe, 1999).

There are numerous primary and secondary prevention strategies employed in the United States and other countries in the Global North, such as Great Britain. For instance, a school-based conflict resolution program is an example of a primary prevention strategy, and an early intervention program focusing on adolescents who have experienced violence in the home and exhibit early signs of anger management problems is an example of a secondary prevention program. Both programs can be found across the United States and Europe in a number of different advocacy campaigns.

Public awareness campaigns are strategies that focus on increasing awareness of IPV and its effect on abuse survivors (including children), and society as a whole. Such campaigns can include:

- The dissemination of posters targeting victims and friends/families of victims in public places detailing the cycle of violence and where to get help,
- An educational campaign targeting a specific population, such as teachers or law enforcement, or the specification of a particular month as domestic violence month targeting the general population and drawing attention to the nature of domestic violence.

For instance, the *Domestic Violence Awareness Project* (DVAP) is the result of a partnership between several advocacy organizations that came together and worked collectively to develop an awareness campaign through the designation of October as *Domestic Violence Awareness Month* (DVAM). This project has now evolved far beyond its initial mandate and now involves a partnership between numerous national domestic violence organizations and coalitions, tribal advocacy groups, and local grassroots organizations that work together to "… collect, develop and distribute resources and ideas relevant to advocates' ongoing public and prevention awareness and education efforts not only in preparation for DVAM, but also throughout the year" (DVAP, 2011).

Victim Advocacy: Advocating for Policy and Systematic Change

Victim advocacy is another type of advocacy effort that is designed to intervene in situations involving ongoing violence. Victim advocacy can include activities on a micro or macro level, with the boundaries between these two levels of practice often being blurred. Victim advocacy on the micro level includes direct service with and on behalf of victims helping them to navigate the court systems (such as obtaining orders of protection), providing medical advocacy (accompanying victims at the hospital or other medical facility), and helping victims obtain necessary services within the community, including housing, financial assistance, information referral, counseling, and case management services (Bennet, Riger, Schewe, Howard, & Wasco, 2004; Shepard, 1999).

Victim advocacy on a macro level often ventures into the area of policy practice and systems advocacy, which involves effecting institutional change, chiefly in governmental bodies and agencies. This type of advocacy can include advocating for legislative changes that empowers women, advocating for increased funding for government-sponsored programs focusing on violence against women, or advocating for gender-empowering policies within government agencies and bodies such as the Department of Health and Human Services, child welfare agencies, Veterans' Affairs, and the military.

An example of advocating for policy change includes confronting the genderization and racialization of poverty, involving economic injustice against female racial

/ethnic minorities. Despite research that indicates that poverty is caused by structural causes, such as domestic violence and economic policies that favor white males, the majority of people in the United States surveyed in the past few decades cited personal moral failings, such as promiscuity and having children out of wedlock as the chief causes of poverty (Feagin, 1975; Martin, 2012; Weaver, Shapiro, & Jacobs, 1995; Wright, 2000). These surveys reflect misunderstandings among mainstream populations and a tendency to scapegoat poor women for their "lot" in life.

Policies concerning poverty are often predicated on these negative stereotypes of female welfare recipients being morally deficient. For instance, the creation of the stereotype of the "welfare queen" by Ronal Reagan discussed in Chapter 1 is an example of manipulating the broad-based negativity toward and suspiciousness of welfare recipients (particularly female ethnic minorities), which then led to sweeping welfare reform measures and the ultimate passage of the Personal Responsibility and Work Opportunity Act of 1996 (PRWORA), and the implementation of the Temporary Assistance for Needy Families (TANF) program (replacing Aid to Families with Dependent Children [AFDC]) (Martin, 2012).

Domestic violence advocates are particularly concerned about the punitive nature of TANF and its affect on victims of domestic violence, particularly since research indicates that the majority of women struggling with poverty either have or are experiencing domestic violence. For instance, approximately three-quarters of all homeless single mothers who were married prior to becoming homeless cited domestic violence as the primary reason for leaving their marital home and moving into a shelter with their children (Nunez & Fox, 1999).

Yet, PRWORA and the TANF program often negate the underlying causes of female poverty, such as domestic violence, and instead base policies on the presumption that the causes of poverty lie with the individual woman whose behavior is immoral (too much promiscuous sex with too many men, outside of the protection of marriage, resulting in too many out-of-wedlock births). Advocates point to TANF's strict time limits for benefits (ranging between three to five years depending upon the state), stringent work requirements (often regardless of circumstances), and promotion of marriage, as well as other measures designed to control the behavior of female recipients, as examples of how this social welfare legislation and resulting program are based upon false stereotypes and thus scapegoat women (El-Bassel, Caldeira, Ruglass, & Gilbert, 2009; Hudson & Coukos, 2005; Martin, 2012; Siegel & Williams, 2003).

Human Services Delivery Systems

Understanding and Mastery: Skills to effect and influence social policy

Critical Thinking Question: What are some ways that social justice advocates can advocate for women of color who experience stigmatization due to the genderization and racialization of poverty?

Women's advocates continue to lobby for legislative change, including tracking what happens to recipients once they leave the TANF program. Since PRWORA does not require states to track what happens to TANF recipients once they time out of the program, declining welfare utilization is sometimes framed as the success of the program. Advocates can more effectively push for reforms in the social welfare system once more information is known about the impact of TANF on women struggling with poverty, particularly those women who are survivors of domestic violence (Hildebrandt & Stevens, 2009).

Legislation Empowering Women and Addressing Domestic Violence

Policy and systems advocacy can include lobbying for the passage of laws that empower women or against laws that disempowered them. Such legislation might be within the civil arena, such as the advocacy of better child support laws and increases in civil rights protections for women of color and indigenous populations, or within the criminal justice arena with the passage of domestic violence laws.

An example of legislative lobbying for issues affecting women on a local level is the successful advocacy of new legislation in Washington, D.C., designed to address the issue of TANF failing to effectively meet the needs of recipients. Advocates developed a bill called the *Temporary Assistance for Needy Families Educational Opportunities and Accountability Act of 2010* (Sec. 2. Title 4, chapter 205.19d), which increases government accountability for assessing, monitoring, and tracking TANF recipients to ensure that they are receiving the benefits they need to become economically self-sufficient. The bill addresses domestic violence specifically, specifying that TANF recipients must be assessed for domestic violence, and be given a work waiver in order to receive domestic violence services.

Advocacy for domestic violence legislation on a national level has occurred as well. In fact, it was through the tireless work of women's advocates that the first comprehensive federal domestic violence legislation, VAWA was passed in 1994 and reauthorized in 2000, and 2005 (which expired in 2011), and was most recently reauthorized in 2013. VAWA, an amendment to the Violent Crime Control and Law Enforcement Act of 1994 (Pub. L. No. 103-322), established policies and mandates for how states were to handle domestic violence cases. This was seen as particularly important since prior to VAWA passing, there was significant inconsistency in how domestic violence cases were handled from state to state.

VAWA is comprised of nine titles, each focusing on a different aspect in the efforts to combat violence against women:

Title I: Enhancing judicial and law enforcement tools to combat violence
    against women
Title II: Improving services for victims
Title III: Services, protection, and justice for young victims of violence
Title IV: Strengthening America's families by preventing violence
Title V: Strengthening the health care system's response
Title VI: Housing opportunities and safety for battered women and children
Title VII: Providing economic security for victims
Title VIII: Protection of battered and trafficked immigrants
Title IX: Safety for Indian women

Additionally, VAWA includes such stipulations as mandatory arrests for offenders, interstate enforcement of domestic violence laws, and maintaining state databases on incidences of domestic violence incidents. It also provides for numerous grants for educational purposes (e.g., the education of police officers and judges), a domestic violence hotline, and funding for battered women's shelters and for improvement in safety of public areas such as public transportation and parks where women are at increased risk of harm. Despite the broad-based nature of VAWA though, its primary focus is on victim safety and perpetrator accountability with the goal of empowering the victim and punishing the abuser (McDermott & Garofalo, 2004).

The act itself is a form of advocacy in that it has significant influence over state policies. For instance, in order to receive funding states must comply with stipulations regarding mandatory arrest policies and mandatory orders of protection when warranted (Part U, SEC. 2101). It is important to note that unlike a civil case where a plaintiff brings an action and thus has the right to subsequently drop the case, in criminal cases the plaintiff is the state and the victims are witnesses, so theoretically the only party with

Advocates demonstrate in Washington, D.C. for the reauthorization of VAWA, which was delayed from 2011 to 2013 due to increased and controversial protections for vulnerable populations of women.

the power to drop charges is the state. Yet in the past criminal prosecutors have allowed domestic violence victims to drop charges (sometimes at the urgings of the batterer). Domestic violence legislation has for the most part put a stop to this practice. Currently, in order to remain in compliance with VAWA, domestic violence is typically treated as any other crime where the victim is called as a witness and must appear at the trial to testify on behalf of the state. Not only does VAWA mandate arrests if there is probable cause (since charges cannot be dropped), but victims are often compelled to cooperate with law enforcement officials in the prosecution of the case. VAWA also mandates victim safety checks, which can be done either by the arresting police department, or the local battered women's shelter, which receives a referral from the arresting agency.

VAWA was recently reauthorized after a fierce political battle. The 2005 reauthorization expired in 2011, and it took proponents until March of 2013 for the reauthorization act to be signed into law. The core of the controversy over the newest version of the law relates essentially to two new provisions to the existing legislation. The first new provision provides legal protection to Native American women by enabling tribal courts to try non-Native perpetrators of IPV if the victim is Native and registered with a tribe. The second provision extends VAWA to the lesbians, gays, bisexual, and transgendered (LGBT) population. Many Republicans in the House of Representatives refused their initial support due to these new provisions, but ultimately the reauthorization passed with 286 yays to 138 nays.

Despite overwhelming support for VAWA among women's advocates, there are some who criticize VAWA because it uses a criminal justice approach to domestic violence management with mandatory arrest and "no-drop" policies. McDermott and Garofalo (2004) discuss the possible unintended effects of VAWA, asserting that it can actually take power away from the domestic violence victim who might not want services, might not wish to pursue the criminal prosecution of her partner, and who might find safety checks intrusive and unwelcome. Thus while VAWA has advanced our understanding of the domestic violence syndrome and process, and demonstrates an increased commitment to take this social problem very seriously, its goal of empowering women by using the criminal justice system as a frontline response may lead to the unintended effect of disempowerment. The recognition that domestic violence takes a toll on society in the areas of public health, child welfare, and lost productivity is what led to the passage of federal domestic violence legislation in the first place, yet this cost must be weighed against a victim's right to self-determination. Ultimately decisions must be made about how to balance the right of society to be free of violence, and the right of victims to have a say in how they manage their lives.

Assess your comprehension of Prevention Strategies and Public Awareness Campaigns by taking this quiz.

Advocacy Efforts in Response to Sexual Assault in the Global North

Another form of gender-based violence that is of a similar nature to domestic violence is the act of rape, or sexual assault against women. Sexual assault involves forcing some form of sexual act on another person without his or her consent. Determining the rate of sexual assault in the United States is difficult due to dramatic variations in the way sexual assault is defined (Martin, 2014). In 2012 the Federal Bureau of Investigation (FBI) changed its legal definition of forcible rape, which is the first time the definition had been updated since 1927. The previous definition reflected in the Uniform Crime Reports (UCR) was "the carnal knowledge of a female, forcibly and against her will." That definition was far too narrow, limiting rape to penile penetration of a female vagina. Thus, not only did the former definition exclude the wide range of ways that sexual assaults can occur, but it also excluded the rape of males. The new UCR definition of rape is "[t]he penetration, no matter how slight, of the vagina or anus with any body part or object, or oral penetration by a sex organ of another person, without the consent of the victim." Expanding the definition of rape to include a range of assault types, as well as including male victims, is an important victory for advocates because it provides law enforcement more tools to fight sexual assault, as they can now report sexual assaults more accurately (U.S. Department of Justice, 2012).

Although both men and women can be raped, women are victims of rape far more often than men, with 91% of rape victims being female and 9% being male. Additionally, about 99% of rapists are male (U.S. Department of Justice, 1997). Approximately 243,800 women, 12 years and older were raped or sexually assaulted in 2012 (Truman & Planty, 2012). About 75% of all women who were raped were assaulted by a perpetrator they knew, and about 25% were assaulted by strangers. Of these to Among the latter, the FBI reports that 83,425 cases of forcible rape were reported. Black women are raped at a higher rate (relative to the population) than white or Hispanic women. The actual incidence of forcible rape is presumed to be much higher though due to underreporting. In fact, only half of all rapes and sexual assaults in 2010 were reported to police

Women's advocates demonstrate against prevailing stereotypes that blame women for their own rapes.

(Catalano, Smith, Snyder, & Rand, 2009; Federal Bureau of Investigation, 2011; Turner & Planty, 2012). According to the CDC, rape and sexual assaults typically fall into four categories (Basile & Saltzman, 2002):

1. Completed sexual acts such as sexual penetration but may also include any act of sexual nature attempted or otherwise such as contact been a sexual organ and another part of the body
2. Attempted sexual assault such as the use of physical force or restraint with the clear intent of sexual assault
3. Abusive sexual contact such as intentional touching even through clothing
4. Noncontact sexual abuse such as intentional exposure and exhibitionism ("flashing") and voyeurism ("Peeping Tom")

Why Men Commit Rape

Social justice advocates who work on behalf of survivors of sexual assault must understand the psychological dynamics of rape in order to advocate effectively (Martin, 2014). One of the more common myths of why rape occurs includes blaming the victim by asserting that the victim wanted it, liked it, or in some way deserved the sexual assault because she provoked the assailant (by dressing or acting provocatively, etc.). Myths about rapists include assertions that only truly evil or insane men rape and that men just cannot control their sexual desires, thus are not responsible for sexually assaulting women (Burt, 1991). The damage done by the proliferation of these rape myths is plentiful because they blame the victim while exonerating the perpetrator, which undermines societal prohibition against sexual violence (Martin, 2014).

In fact, a 1998 study at University of Mannheim in Germany (Bohner et al., 1998) found that such myths actually encourage sexual assault by giving rapists a way of rationalizing their antisocial behavior. In other words, although Western social customs may claim to abhor rape, popular rape myths provide rapists a way around such social mores by convincing themselves that the women in some way *asked for it* and that men simply *cannot control themselves*, thus they really haven't done anything wrong, or at least nothing that many other men don't do (Martin, 2014).

The Psychological Impact of Sexual Assault

It is also important for the social justice advocate to understand the physical and psychological impact of sexual assault since a considerable amount of advocacy work centers on the consequences of rape that the victims endure (Martin, 2014). Such consequences are serious and long-lasting and may include posttraumatic stress disorder (PTSD), depression, increased anxiety, fear of risk-taking, development of trust issues, increased physical problems including exposure to sexually transmitted diseases such as HIV/AIDS, chronic pelvic pain, gastrointestinal disorders, and unwanted pregnancy (CDC, 2005).

In 1975 Lynda Holmstrom and Ann Burgess coined the term *rape trauma syndrome* (RTS), a collection of emotions similar to PTSD, commonly experienced in response to being a survivor of a forced violent sexual assault. RTS includes an immediate phase where the survivor experiences both psychological and physical symptoms such as feeling extreme fear, chronic crying and sleep disturbances, and other reactions to the actual assault as well as the common fear of being killed during the assault. Survivors in subsequent phases of recovery include avoidance of social interactions, particularly those that remind them of the rape, experiencing a loss of self-esteem, inappropriate guilt, and clinical depression. Many survivors deny the effects of the sexual assault because they do not want to be subject to the negative stigma associated with being a rape victim. In fact, one of the primary reasons most rape crisis advocates refer to clients as *survivors* rather than as *victims* is to reduce this stigma by focusing on the strength it takes to survive a sexual assault (Martin, 2014).

Sexual Assault Advocacy Efforts

Many of the same advocacy efforts used in response to IPV are used with sexual assault and in fact often times these efforts are combined, focusing on both types of assaults against women. In fact, the reauthorization of VAWA includes the implementation of the Safer Act, which is an enhancement to the Debbie Smith Act, and allows for the creation of a national registry of forensic evidence for sexual assault cases. The registry will allow the public, including victims to log on and check the status of the DNA testing (rape kit), which by design will reduce the backlog of rape kits awaiting DNA testing.

Advocacy efforts on behalf of survivors of sexual assault are often in the form of prevention and awareness campaigns, focusing on increasing general awareness about the problem of sexual assault—as a component of domestic violence, date rape, or stranger rape with the goal of confronting myths and increasing safety. Policy practice in this area includes a range of activities from advocating for increased funding for government-sponsored programs for victims and perpetrators, passage of legislation that strengthens the prosecution efforts of perpetrators and protects victims from revictimization. For instance, many sexual assault advocates have advocated for the passage of *rape shield laws,* which are designed to protect rape victims from retraumatization through abusive cross-examination during court trials (in an attempt to blame the victim), disclosing the identity of a rape victim in the media, or using the past sexual behavior of a rape victim against her in the trial of the offender.

An example of an effective public awareness campaign focusing on removing the stigma of sexual assault and other forms of violence against women is called *Take Back the Night*, and includes public marches that occur at night and involve speaking out against what has historically been the silent and stigmatized crime of rape. The first Take Back the Night event was held in Philadelphia in 1975 in response to the murder of a young woman one block away from her home as she was walking home at night. This public awareness campaign evolved to represent a collective fight against all forms of violence against women, with a particular focus on sexual assault. Currently there are numerous events that occur throughout the year all over the world as a very public way of taking a stand against sexual violence, particularly against women. With the tagline of "Shatter the Silence," Take Back the Night events typically involve men, women, and children marching through their community holding banners and posters and chanting antirape slogans, a keynote speaker (a celebrity, survivor or expert on sexual violence against women), a rally, candle-lighting ceremony, and featured exhibits designed to educate, create awareness, and inspire survivors and allies (for more information visit the official website at http://www.takebackthenight.org).

Assess your comprehension of Advocacy Efforts in Response to Sexual Assault in the Global North by taking this quiz.

Violence against Women and Girls in the Global South

Many of the same human rights violations against women that occur in the United States and other countries in the Global North also occur in the Global South. In this section, I explore social issues and human rights violations on an international level, primarily violations occurring in developing countries, including what is called *least developed countries* (LDCs), such as countries in South Asia and Sub-Saharan Africa. Yet, while similar human rights violations occur against women and girls everywhere in the world, when they occur in certain parts of the world the consequences are often qualitatively different. For instance, domestic violence occurs worldwide, but violence against women in countries that do not have laws protecting women and girls, or countries with institutionalized gender oppression is significantly different than the nature of IPV committed in the Global North (e.g., countries that permit honor killings of women, child marriages, or government-sanctioned life imprisonment of women who allegedly commit adultery).

Women in many developing countries and LDCs face abject poverty with little to no hope of upward or social mobility, a risk factor for commercial sexual exploitation (also known as human sex trafficking), and various other forms of gender-based oppression. They often do not have the right to make choices about their bodies and may be forced to endure an unwanted pregnancy and bear children they cannot sustain, or have an abortion they do not want. Many women in African and some Asian countries are subject to forced circumcision (also known as female genital mutilation [FGM]) in an attempt to control their sexual behavior. They often bear the burden of health crises, such as the AIDS pandemic, and they are most often employed in unstable and unsafe working conditions in the agricultural sector or in factories with sweatshop conditions in order to provide for their families.

In this section, I explore many of these crimes against women, and the conditions in which women find themselves, yet it is important to note that what is explored in this section is certainly not an exhaustive list of conditions and human rights abuses against women and girls. Rather, what is included in this section is meant to give readers a sense of the different types of gender-based oppression and human rights violations women and girls experience, and some of the ways in which advocates work to combat these injustices.

International Protection of Women: UN Treaty Bodies

Since advocacy cannot occur without some sort of framework with definitions, goals, and objectives, it is often useful to use relevant UN Human Rights treaties and conventions (many of which were explored in Chapter 1) as a good starting point for finding common definitions, goals, and realistic benchmarks for achieving social justice. In Chapter 4, I touched on the UN *Convention on the Elimination of all Forms of Discrimination against Women* (CEDAW), passed in December of 1979, noting some of the criticisms of this and other UN conventions because of their top-down policy approach and Western values template. In this section, I explore the positive aspects of this and similar conventions, most notably how they have laid a foundation for universal goal-setting in the area of gender equity on a global scale. Since the majority of countries in the Global North have incorporated gender equity language in their constitutions, and other governmental policies, the CEDAW will be explored within the context of global human rights violations against women in developing countries and LDCs as a framework for understanding gender oppression and exploitation within this global context.

The reason behind the development of the CEDAW was that despite the ratification of other human rights conventions designed to put an end to discrimination of any kind, discrimination against women persisted globally on a vast scale. These reasons were detailed in the CEDAW's preamble, which states (in part) that the convention is necessary because discrimination against women:

- Violates the principles of equality of rights and respect for human dignity,
- Is an obstacle to the participation of women, on equal terms with men, in the political, social, economic, and cultural life of their countries,
- Hampers the growth of the prosperity of society and the family, and makes more difficult the full development of the potentialities of women in the service of their countries and of humanity. (UN CEDAW, 1979)

The preamble further specifies that the state parties who developed the CEDAW were:

- Concerned that in situations of poverty women have the least access to food, health, education, training, and opportunities for employment and other needs,
- Convinced that the establishment of the new international economic order based on equity and justice will contribute significantly towards the promotion of equality between men and women,
- Convinced that the full and complete development of a country, the welfare of the world, and the cause of peace require the maximum participation of women on equal terms with men in all fields. (UN CEDAW, 1979)

The CEDAW consists of six parts and a total of 30 articles. Article 1 of the CEDAW defines "discrimination against women" as:

Any distinction, exclusion or restriction made on the basis of sex which has the effect or purpose of impairing or nullifying the recognition, enjoyment or exercise by women, irrespective of their marital status, on a basis of equality of men and women, of human rights and fundamental freedoms in the political, economic, social, cultural, civil or any other field.

Article 2 sets forth the policy objectives of the CEDAW, which includes:

(a) To embody the principle of the equality of men and women in their national constitutions or other appropriate legislation if not yet incorporated therein and to ensure, through law and other appropriate means, the practical realization of this principle;

(b) To adopt appropriate legislative and other measures, including sanctions where appropriate, prohibiting all discrimination against women;

(c) To establish legal protection of the rights of women on an equal basis with men and to ensure through competent national tribunals and other public institutions the effective protection of women against any act of discrimination;

(d) To refrain from engaging in any act or practice of discrimination against women and to ensure that public authorities and institutions shall act in conformity with this obligation;

(e) To take all appropriate measures to eliminate discrimination against women by any person, organization or enterprise;

(f) To take all appropriate measures, including legislation, to modify or abolish existing laws, regulations, customs, and practices which constitute discrimination against women;

(g) To repeal all national penal provisions which constitute discrimination against women.

The CEDAW outlines expectations of country leaders to ensure equal participation and protection of women in all aspects of life, including egalitarian roles in parenting (Article 5), the suppression of trafficking (Article 6), equality in opportunities for women in education (Article 10) and free choice in employment with safe working conditions (Article 11), equal access to health care, including family planning (Article 12), equality in economic opportunities (Article 13), equality in the legal system (Article 15), and equality in marriage (Article 16). Article 14 outlines the expectations of equality for rural women in light of the unique and considerable problems they often face related to community isolation, lack of resources, and the nature of their employment, which often consists of work they are paid very little for, or for which they are not paid at all. This article is particularly important since over 70% of women in LDCs live in rural areas (UN Women, 2011).

Every country in the world has ratified the CEDAW, except seven—three Islamic countries (Sudan, Somalia, and Iran), three small Pacific Island nations (Nauru, Palau, and Tonga), and the United States. As with other UN conventions, this treaty is non-enforceable, but those countries that have signed and ratified the CEDAW engage in a voluntary process of implementation with assistance from other member countries, and intermittent monitoring of progress through the submission of reports to the Secretary-General of the United Nations. Again, while there is some criticism of the CEDAWs top-down approach and Western orientation, this convention provides a detailed and concrete framework for government leaders to work within in order to achieve universally accepted objectives related to gender-based equality and the elimination of discrimination and disparate treatment of women. The CEDAW also provides advocates with a concrete list of objectives and universally agreed-upon definitions and goals they can target when advocating for gender equality and the end to discrimination and exploitation of women globally.

The *Beijing Declaration and Platform of Action* is another advocacy tool representing the work of thousands of women and men who came together in 1995 and developed a plan and framework for addressing several key human rights violations affecting women (United Nations, 1995). The platform's name references the location of the *UN's Fourth World Conference on Women* held in Beijing, China. The *Platform for Action* built on earlier platforms (i.e., the Nairobi Conference) and is based on the belief that for a society to function optimally, men and women must share power equally in all facets of life. The mission statement of the Beijing Declaration and Platform for Action cites women's empowerment as the chief goal, accomplished by "… removing all the obstacles to women's active participation in all spheres of public and private life through a full and equal share in economic, social, cultural and political decision-making" (United Nations, 1995).

The Beijing Declaration and Platform for Action provides a comprehensive policy framework for governments and nongovernmental organizations (NGOs) to develop a strategic action plan addressing 12 critical areas affecting women worldwide, including:

- The persistent and increasing burden of poverty on women
- Inequalities and inadequacies in and unequal access to education and training
- Inequalities and inadequacies in and unequal access to health care and related services
- Violence against women
- The effects of armed or other kinds of conflict on women, including those living under foreign occupation
- Inequality in economic structures and policies, in all forms of productive activities, and in access to resources
- Inequality between men and women in the sharing of power and decision-making at all levels
- Insufficient mechanisms at all levels to promote the advancement of women
- Lack of respect for and inadequate promotion and protection of the human rights of women
- Stereotyping of women and inequality in women's access to and participation in all communication systems, especially in the media
- Gender inequalities in the management of natural resources and in the safeguarding of the environment
- Persistent discrimination against and violation of the rights of the girl child

The implementation of the Platform for Action is the responsibility of individual governments, but responsibility is also placed upon the entire international community, including civil societies everywhere to ensure:

[t]he full and equal participation of women in political, civil, economic, social and cultural life at the national, regional and international levels, and the eradication of all forms of discrimination on the grounds of sex are priority objectives of the international community. (United Nations, 1995)

One hundred and eighty nine countries were signatories of the Platform for Action, including the United States. Since its implementation, there have been three reviews and appraisals conducted by the Commission on the Status of Women (CSW) noting areas of progress of signatory countries and areas in need of improvement, with the most recent review occurring in 2010. The most recent CSW report, referred to as *Beijing +15*, evaluated progress (and areas of continued struggle) toward the goals in the Platform for Action within the context of the UN Millennium Development Goals (MDGs).

Some international human rights treaties are binding and some are not, but all provide governments with goals, frameworks, and steps for addressing areas of inequality affecting women. Women's advocates can use these treaties as tools when working on local, national, or international levels advocating for women's empowerment in all facets of society.

> **Administration**
>
> *Understanding and Mastery: Constituency building and other advocacy techniques such as lobbying, grassroots movements, and community development and organizing*
>
> **Critical Thinking Question:** As a comprehensive policy platform, what tools does the Beijing Platform for Action provide social justice advocates who are advocating on behalf of women in a global context?

Assess your comprehension of <u>International Protection of Women: UN Treaty Bodies</u> by taking this quiz.

Advocacy Efforts to Confront Crimes against Women and Girls

Gender-Based Economic Injustice and Labor Abuse

According to United Nations Women, women bear the brunt of global poverty, primarily due to discrimination they face in multiple sectors of society, including in the labor market, education, the health care sector, and in the ability to own and maintain control of their assets. Poverty, particularly extreme poverty, is often considered a human rights issue because it intersects with other social problems that make it difficult, if not impossible, for women to remain safe and live optimal lives. Women living in extreme poverty often do not have access to clean drinking water, sufficient food, adequate health care (including family planning), education, suitable and sustainable employment, and often cannot protect themselves and their children from violence and other forms of exploitation. Thus as referenced in Chapter 1, poverty tends to be an underlying issue in many of the human rights violations explored in subsequent sections of this chapter.

Women living in LDCs are also at increased risk of poverty because the majority of them live in rural areas and are dependent upon agriculture for their livelihood. There are approximately 48 countries that are considered LDCs many of which are located in Africa and Asia. Over 70% of the populations in all LDCs live in rural areas, where agriculture is the main source of employment, and food insecurity is a daily event (UN Women, 2011). What this means is that about 300 million people alone in Africa are living in rural areas and are not getting nearly enough food to eat. While both men and women experience food shortages in rural areas, women who work in agriculture in an LDC are particularly vulnerable because they have less access than men to economic opportunities and resources, get paid less than men, are often excluded from the lending and credit market, and work in informal or undocumented work such as domestic work, which can be unstable and insecure, as well as in factories, which typically involves long hours, harsh working conditions, and low pay (UN Women, n.d.).

Xander Martin

Women in LDCs are most vulnerable to extreme poverty.

Many economic policies in LDCs are not designed with women in mind, and whether intended or unintended women are often the most significantly affected by policies that are economically unjust. Global lending practices are an example of economic policies that can hit women hard. Polack (2004) discusses the impact of hundreds of billions of dollars in loans made to countries in the Global South (South America, South Asia, and Sub-Saharan Africa) by countries in the Global North (UK, Spain, France, the United States, etc.). Polack argues that the cumulative impact of these loans to some of the poorest countries in the world has been devastating to the most economically vulnerable members, many of whom are women. Very little if any of this loan money has benefited women in these countries; rather, it has harmed them, and in fact continues to harm them by increasing the poverty within these already devastatingly poor regions. In an attempt to repay this debt, many countries of the Global South exploit their own workers, many of whom are women, to make loan payments.

One of the most devastating effects of what has now evolved into trillions of dollars of debt for countries in the Global South is the proliferation of the sweatshop industry consisting of large-scale factories that develop goods exported to the North for a very low price. Some of the poorest people in the world, again, primarily women, work in sweatshops throughout Asia, India, and many Latin American countries where horrific abuses abound. This occurs legally in many of these countries because in a desperate attempt to attract export contracts, many countries in Asia and Latin America have created Free Trade Agreements or free-trade zones for Western corporations allowing them to circumvent local trade regulations such as minimum wage, working hour limits, and child labor laws, if the corporations would open factories serving the Global North in their impoverished countries (Martin, 2014; Polack, 2004).

Polack (2004) suggests that literally every major retail supplier in the United States benefits from these sweatshop conditions that pay extremely low wages, have extremely poor working conditions including physical and sexual exploitation without retribution, excessively long working hours (sometimes in excess of 12 hours per day with no days off for weeks at a time), and immediate termination or physical attacks in response to requests for better working conditions. In many sweatshops, adolescent girls and young women are preferred as employees over men because they tend to be more compliant thus are more easily exploited (Martin, 2014).

Although local and international human rights advocates work diligently to change these working conditions, at the root of the problem of female labor exploitation is economic injustice (often gender-based) rooted in generations of inter-country exploitation. Thus, there is significant complexity involved that is not easily confronted without government involvement, which is often slow in coming when large corporations are making billions of dollars with the system as it currently operates. For instance, as labor unions have become the norm in the United States, many companies such as Nike and Wal-Mart moved their factories to Asia and Central and South America, where billions of dollars can be saved in wages and benefits cuts (Phanor-Faury, 2012).

Primarily female garment workers sewing jeans in a factory in China to be sold in major retail stores in the United States

Rob Crandall/SCPhotos/Alamy

There are several different ways that advocates can effect change in the areas of economic injustice and labor abuse of women. One of the most frequently used methods is to draw attention to the abuses using the media. Social justice advocates often work with the media to bring injustices to the attention of the public with the hope that this will influence the public's consumer purchasing choices, which is hoped will change the way companies do business.

Advocacy organizations focused on labor abuses often utilize technology to get their message out, including having *interactive websites* that inform the public of various types of abuses, and what the public can do to help. *Action alerts* are emailed to subscribers to draw attention to urgent situations enabling advocacy organizations to mobilize thousands of people to advocate in unison, such as sending letters or emails to their legislators.

The next tactic might seem somewhat inconsistent with a human services strengths-based approach, but many advocacy organizations believe strongly that a strategy with the greatest chance of success is one involving calling out bad behavior through public humiliation. By humiliating a company, a political party, or a country leader and shining a flashlight on their bad behavior, many advocates believe that their behavior will be forced to change. This approach is based on the belief that when billions of dollars in revenue are at stake, voluntary change based on ethics and honesty are unlikely. It was the National Labor Committee (now the Institute for Global Labour and Human Rights [IGLHR]) that publically humiliated television personality Kathy Lee Gifford by going public with the information that her clothing line, sold in a popular retail store, was made in foreign sweatshops by impoverished young girls. While some criticized this strategy as having been unfair to Gifford who did not appear to know this information, advocates rationalized that once Gifford's reputation was on the line, she actually became an advocate for gender-based labor abuses herself (Institute for Global Labour and Human Rights, 1996). This advocacy method has been repeated numerous times with the hope that companies will stop abusive labor practices if their activities (or perceived activities) are brought to the attention of the public.

Najlah Feanny/CORBIS SABA

A demonstration against the GAP accused of using factories in developing countries with sweatshop conditions.

IGLHR employs several other advocacy strategies as well, including engaging in public awareness campaigns by developing documentaries that are then sold on their website or posted on the online film site YouTube (www.youtube.com), and engaging in on-site mobilization efforts by assisting the exploited workers in foreign sweatshops to advocate for themselves by forming unions or using their own voices to effect change. For example, IGLHR has brought exploited female workers to the United States to testify before Congress so that legislators can be educated about their plight, and on what steps the U.S. government can take to stop contributing to this type of labor abuse.

It is important to keep in mind Cohen, de la Vega, and Watson's (2001) cautions that advocacy work such as this is not without risk, and advocates must be aware that when they go up against multimillion dollar conglomerates (particularly those in foreign countries) that have so much to gain by keeping the status quo, they not only put themselves in harm's way but may also be jeopardizing the safety of those for whom they are advocating. In an IGLHR documentary entitled "The Hidden Face of Globalization," IGLHR's director Charles Kernaghan explains how it is a common practice of U.S. companies to use factories in developing countries, such as Bangladesh and Haiti, to produce their goods, such as clothing, shoes, and other products sold for a multifold profit. I Kernaghan explains that among all garment workers, 80% are women between the ages of 16 and 23, explaining that the factory owners prefer to hire young women rather than adult males, because of the belief that they will be less likely to mobilize and advocate for themselves. Shifts are often 20 hours (per day), with most women working about 107 hours per week—even more during August when clothing production increases for the holiday season. Garment workers are often cursed at and beaten, are given birth control pills against their will, and are often forced to sleep on the floor of the factory between shifts. The working conditions are extremely unsafe; the factories can become very hot, with temperatures in the summer time exceeding 100 degrees Fahrenheit. With no proper ventilation, the women are forced to breath in the dust from the cut fabric, causing respiratory illness. The women are paid approximately $3 to $6 per week, which is what IGLHR refers to as "starvation wages." If women are seen talking to union leaders they are often beaten and put in prison on trumped up charges.

In IGLHR's documentary "Mickey Mouse goes to Haiti" about Disney's exploitation of workers in one of the poorest nations in the world. IGLHR advocates went to Haiti and interviewed several workers in an attempt to mobilize them to request that Disney increase their wages modestly to 58 cents an hour—what they consider a living wage. The workers implored Disney not to close the plant in response to their request, but to consider their life of misery and respond with compassion. After the making of this documentary, IGLHR reported that the workers who spoke with advocates were fired and Disney never responded to their request for dialogue.

Despite these tragic stories, IGLHR has been successful in creating greater awareness of the plight of the sweatshop worker. Their primary goal is to encourage the American shopper to become a conscious buyer, and boycott brands they know are produced by companies that exploit foreign workers.

Human Trafficking of Women and Girls

The U.S. State Department defines trafficking as:

1. Sex trafficking in which a commercial sex act is induced by force, fraud, or coercion, or in which the person induced to perform such an act has not attained 18 years of age; or

2. The recruitment, harboring, transportation, provision, or obtaining of a person for labor or services, through the use of force, fraud, or coercion for the purpose of subjection to involuntary servitude, peonage, debt bondage, or slavery (U.S. Department of State, 2013, p. 8).

Trafficking can include forced labor, sex trafficking, bonded labor, debt bondage among migrants, involuntary domestic servitude, and forced child labor. As of 2013 there were an estimated 27 million individuals who were victims of human trafficking worldwide at any given time, the majority of whom are young females (U.S. Department of State, 2013). In fact, young women and girls are the most sought after targets of large criminal organizations that are in the business of trafficking human beings. Human sex trafficking comprises a smaller portion of all trafficking incidences per year, but its consequences are severe and long-lasting. Human sex trafficking involves forced sexual slavery, where young women and girls are forced to become prostitutes. Women and girls are sold into sex slavery by family members in need of money, are kidnapped, or are lured into the sex trade with promises of modeling contracts or domestic work in other countries. Many of these girls are kept in inhumane living conditions where they are forced to have sex with between 10 and 25 men a day. Many contract the HIV/AIDS virus and are cast out onto the street once they become too sick to be useful (Martin, 2014; U.S. Department of State, 2013).

Human rights reports are replete with firsthand accounts of trafficking incidences from both traffickers and victims. Stories of women and girls being manipulated, coerced, drugged, and kidnapped into prostitution abound. The stories have a similar theme—vulnerable women who accept offers of help for a better life never to be experienced, women who accept jobs in foreign countries only to realize later that they were sold to a brothel, girls who are on their way to school, meet a stranger, and are never seen again. Dhalia was a young girl who lived in Bangladesh, born to a very poor

Stephen Barnes/Public Protests/Alamy

An anti-human trafficking demonstration in Belfast, Ireland sponsored by Soroptimist International, s eomrn's advocacy organization.

family in Dhaka. When she was 11, her aunt approached her parents with an offer of a job for Dhalia in Pakistan. The job was as a domestic helper, but the aunt promised that she would be able to attend school. Dhalia's parents agreed, trusting that their daughter would have a better life in Pakistan than they could provide her. Yet once they were on their way, Dhalia knew something was very wrong. Her aunt became angry and abusive. They arrived at the border and Dhalia's aunt gave her a cigarette to smoke. Dhalia initially refused, but her aunt insisted so she took a few puffs. The next thing she remembers she was in a hotel in Pakistan with two men. She tried to run, but they held her by her arms until a larger man came and escorted her to a van. She fell asleep and when she awoke she was in a large but crowded room with several other girls her age. It was then that she was told that she had been sold to a brothel. Each time she attempted to run away, she was beaten and told she would be killed before she would be allowed to escape. She was forced to have sex with 10 to 20 men per day and was rarely allowed outside of the compound where she was kept. She was forced to endure three abortions by the time she was 17. Between the ages of 15 and 24, she was arrested 14 times. The first few times she told the police that she had been kidnapped when she was 11. Each time she was charged with adultery or other moral charges, and released back into the care of the brothel owner, but with a new debt she was told she needed to pay off. When she was 25, she became very ill and learned that she had contracted HIV/AIDS. When she was too ill to perform her "duties," the brothel owner dragged her outside and left her in an alleyway. A counselor for a local social service agency found her and brought her to a shelter where she received modest medical care. She never returned home, never saw her parents or siblings again, and died at the age of 26. Unfortunately, Dhalia's story is not unique—repeated thousands of times, throughout the world. Throwaway women and girls who are rarely rescued, and ever more rarely, vindicated.

In the year 2000, both the United States and the United Nations passed legal instruments in response to what was now recognized as the serious problem of trafficking. The *United Nations Protocol to Prevent, Suppress, and Punish Trafficking in Persons, Especially Women and Children*, also known as the Palermo Protocol, is an international treaty that calls for a three-pronged approach to combating trafficking: prevention, criminal prosecution, and victim protection. Thus it is not enough that countries pass legislation and prosecute traffickers, but they should also work to address conditions that lead to trafficking in the first place, as well as providing vital services to victims of trafficking.

In this same year, the U.S. government passed federal legislation designed to confront and combat trafficking as well, both at home and abroad. The *Trafficking Victims and Protection Act* (TVPA) provides a comprehensive definition of trafficking, including human sex trafficking, and sets forth guidelines for how trafficking should be confronted on a global scale. In compliance with the TVPA, the U.S. State Department releases a report annually entitled the *Trafficking in Persons Report* (TIP), which provides an analysis and update on the status of trafficking conditions worldwide, as well as a ranking of each country based on actions taken by the respective government's attempts to combat trafficking.

The ranking systems—what is called the Watch List—consists of three tiers, with Tier 1 being the highest and reserved for those countries that are in compliance with the minimum standards set forth in the TVPA. Countries that are not in compliance with TVPA but are making significant strides toward compliance are placed in Tier 2, and Tier 3 countries do not meet the TVPA's minimum standards and are not making significant efforts to do so. Within the report, summaries are included on each country, including the country's tier, its annual accomplishments, and areas in need of further improvement. Countries are challenged to not only increase prosecution of traffickers but also to extend services to victims as well.

Human Rights Watch (HRW) is an international human rights organization that uses many means to advocate for victims of all human rights violations. One method that has proven quite successful is the preparation and dissemination of human rights reports, which are then relied on by various governmental bodies, the press, and other organizations in making decisions about granting aid, disseminating resources, and taking punitive or corrective action. In a 2004 *Global Report on Human Rights*, HRW cited numerous examples of women and girls being trafficked across international boundary lines after being abducted and drugged. Often these young girls were sold to traffickers by neighbors or even family members, sometimes for as little as $1,000. Human trafficking is particularly rampant in South Asian countries, such as Nepal, India, Bangladesh, and Pakistan. In these countries, it is not uncommon for girls to be held in brothels, seeing 20 to 25 clients a day to pay off their "loan," which includes bribe money to pay off local officials, including police (Aronowitz, 2009).

> **Client-Related Values and Attitudes**
>
> *Understanding and Mastery: The worth and uniqueness of individuals including ethnicity, culture, gender, sexual orientation, and other expressions of diversity*
>
> Critical Thinking Question: What are some of the underlying risk factors of human sex trafficking in LDCs?
> •

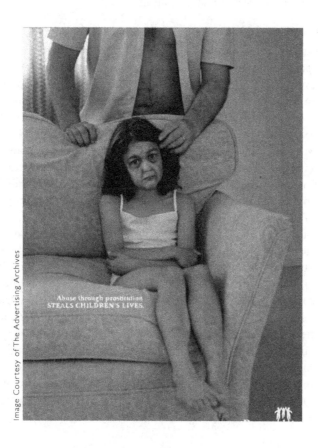

Image Courtesy of The Advertising Archives

Abuse through prostitution STEALS CHILDREN'S LIVES.

In some countries, children as young as five are forced into sex slavery

Despite international trafficking laws, local trafficking laws appear to have done little to protect trafficking victims from being sold into the sex trade. Police in Nepal for instance were either paid off by brothel owners, or did not see sex trafficking as a criminal justice problem (some reported that this problem was something NGOs should solve, and others claimed that an effective solution might be to arrest the victims) (Aronowitz, 2009). Police in Pakistan and Bangladesh often detain victims, charge them with adultery-related crimes for having sex with men who were not their husbands, or charge them with immigration violations.

While advocacy has increased public awareness, it has also increased the covert nature of trafficking and brought the entire process even further into the shadows. For example, in the 1990s law enforcement in Nepal began to enforce existing trafficking laws in response to pressure from advocacy organizations. In response, traffickers resorted to marrying victims off to buyers or brothel owners, and calling the payment a dowry (HRW, 1995a).

Other advocacy efforts include micro practice where advocates reach out to victims individually, offering residential services, counseling, and legal advocacy. Engaging the general public is vital as well, since far too often victims of trafficking garner little sympathy because they are often perceived and treated as prostitutes and presumed to be working in the sex trade voluntarily. Although the international community has made significant progress in combating the trafficking of women and girls into the sex trade, advocates have much farther to go and must work collectively to achieve the goals set forth in the international treaties and legislation.

Rape as a Weapon of War

The sexual assault of women occurs on a global level, in a variety of contexts. One context that is particularly egregious and is receiving increased attention is rape that occurs as a weapon of war. According to HRW, rape of women has long been used as a method for humiliating the other side in war, terrorizing communities, destroying families (since rape often brings cultural shame onto a family and community), and even as a form of ethnic cleansing. During the 1994 genocide in Rwanda and the 1990s Balkan wars, rape was used as a way of ensuring the end of an ethnic group, since in these cultures ethnicity is passed down to the next generation through the father. Thus, forcing women to endure giving birth to a child of a different ethnic group and changing the ethnic of the next generation is a form of genocide (UN Department of Public Education, 2007).

Advocates argue that rape within the context of war should be seen as a weapon used against a community, where sexual assault of the opposition's female members is used as a strategic and tactical weapon to break down the other side (HRW, 1995b, 2002, 2009). In many countries in sub-Saharan Africa, such as the Democratic Republic of the Congo (DRC), armed rebel groups hiding in the jungles consistently rape women collecting wood. In fact, many advocacy organizations cite the DRC as having the highest number of rapes committed as a weapon of war. Rape is committed by soldiers fighting on all sides in this complex conflict, with many rapes being committed by former Hutu Interahamwe soldiers (responsible for the Rwanda genocide) now hiding out in the jungles in Eastern Congo. It is difficult to determine who is raping though since several survivors reported to HRW that the soldiers either attempted to mislead them regarding their identities (by speaking with an accent or in a different language) or told the women and girls to report that they were raped by soldiers from the opposition (HRW, 2002, 2009).

Estimates of the number of women raped during war are difficult to determine, but research indicates that in many recent wars, particularly civil wars in LDCs, approximately 90% of all women are raped during conflicts. UN agencies estimates that between 250,000 and 500,000 women were raped during the Rwanda genocide, and in Liberia, a country that experienced civil war for 13 years, a government survey of 1,600 women found that 92% admitted to having been sexually assaulted (Global Justice Center, 2010; UNIFEM, 2007). A recent United Nations report estimates that approximately 200,000 women had been raped in the DRC since 1998, and in 2008 alone at least 16,000 women were raped in relation to the Congo's bloody civil wars (UNIFEM, 2007).

When rape is used as a weapon of war, it is particularly egregious not only because of its violent nature, but also because it is committed with impunity. Women are often raped in public while their families and/or community members are forced to watch. They are often tortured as well, and sometimes left to die. Romeo Dallaire, head of the UN Peacekeeping Mission in Rwanda wrote about the vast numbers of rapes committed against Tutsi women by the Hutu army and Interahamwe during the 1994 genocide. In his book *Shake Hands with the Devil: The Failure of Humanity in Rwanda*, Dallaire wrote about coming upon scenes where Tutsi women had been viciously raped and then killed. Dallaire and his team found many women with knives plunged into their vaginas, women whose uteruses were cut from their bodies, and women with their nipples cut off. In describing the atrocities he and his team members witnessed during the genocide he states:

> Early on I seemed to develop a screen between me and the sights and sounds to allow me to stay focused on the work to be done. For a long time I completely wiped the death masks of raped and sexually mutilated girls and women from my mind as if what had been done to them was the last thing that would send me over the edge. But if you looked, you could see the evidence, even in the whitened skeletons. The legs bent and apart. A broken bottle, a rough branch, even a knife between them. Where the bodies were fresh, we saw what must have been semen pooled on and near the dead women and girls. There was always a lot of blood. Some male corpses had their genitals cut off, but many women and young girls had their breasts chopped off and their genitals crudely cut apart. They died in a position of total vulnerability, flat on their backs, with their legs bent and knees wide apart. It was the expressions on their dead faces that assaulted me the most, a frieze of shock, pain and humiliation. (Dallaire, 2003, p. 430)

Dallaire's testimony illustrates the savage nature of rape when used as a weapon of war. Rape is always violent and intended to harm and humiliate the victim, but when rape is used as a weapon of war, all aspects of this assault become more violent—more egregious.

Advocates long complained that the international community ignored the vast number of rapes that occurred during war, despite the fact that rape committed as a weapon of war violates international humanitarian law and human rights laws, which governs both inter- and intracountry conflict (HRW, 1995b). The Geneva Conventions of 1949 include four treaties that constitute the core of humanitarian law governing the rules of war as they pertain to the protection and treatment of people, such as wounded and sick soldiers (first and second treaties), prisoners of war (third treaties), and the fourth treaty that provides for the protection of civilians. Article 27 of the Geneva Convention states that

> [W]omen shall be especially protected against any attack on their honor, in particular against rape, enforced prostitution, or any form of indecent assault ... willfully causing great suffering or serious injury to body or health, "torture," and "inhuman treatment" as war crimes and as grave breaches of the conventions (Fourth Geneva Convention, 1949)

Both HRW and the International Committee of the Red Cross (ICRC) have cited in human rights reports that Protocol II of the Geneva Conventions, which pertains to governments in the midst of a civil conflict fighting opposition forces or rebel groups within its own borders, must prohibit any humiliating and degrading attacks including rape (HRW, 1995b; ICRC, 1987).

The mass sexual assaults committed by soldiers during the Balkan wars of the 1990s (occurring in former Yugoslavia), and the Rwanda genocide of 1994 garnered the attention of the United Nations as well as the general public and rape was finally allowed to be prosecuted by the UN tribunals trying crimes against humanity occurring in both regions. This was a very important step in ending the climate of impunity of soldiers committing rape, and governments turning their proverbial heads, but advocacy efforts do not stop at the prosecution of perpetrators. HRW lists several ways in which it advocates for victims of rape in war, and combats this horrific crime, including documenting incidents of rape, coordinating efforts with other organizations and advocacy efforts, working within the policy arena lobbying for change, and coordinating with journalists. HRW has cited recent improvements in the cooperation of governments in combating rape as a weapon of war, in particular DRC President Joseph Kabila's willingness to meet with HRW staff to collaborate on ways to end the mass sexual assaults occurring throughout the country (HRW, 2009), but all advocates working on this issue acknowledge that much more needs to be done.

Female Genital Mutilation

Another issue often confronting women's advocates in many parts of the world including many countries in Africa and Asia is FGM, or "female circumcision." FGM is defined by the World Health Organization (WHO) as the cutting away of part or all of the external female genitalia for non-medical purposes (WHO, 2013).

FGM is a culturally rooted "rite of passage" that is performed on young girls signaling their transition to womanhood. The prevailing belief in cultures that practice FGM is that female circumcision is necessary to ensure a woman's purity and to control her sexual behavior. Depending on the country and specific cultural traditions, FGM is typically performed on girls 10 and older, but in some countries it may be performed on girls much younger, and in some cases, even during infancy (WHO, 2013).

The WHO (2013) estimates that between 100 and 140 million girls and women worldwide have had their female genitalia mutilated or cut as a rite of passage cultural tradition. FGM is categorized into four levels of increasing severity.

Type 1: Clitoridectomy: the partial or total removal of the clitoris and, in very rare cases, only the prepuce (the fold of skin surrounding the clitoris).

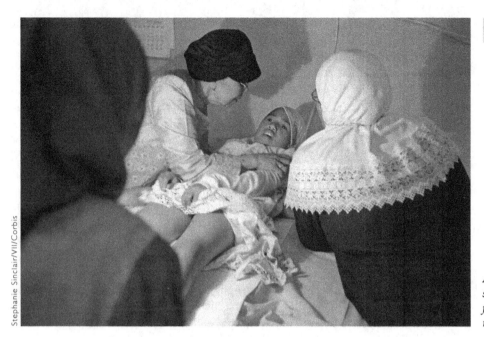

A young girl is restrained and prepared for circumcision by a midwife.

Type 2: Excision: partial or total removal of the clitoris and the labia minora, with or without excision of the labia majora.

Type 3: Infibulation: this procedure involves the scraping away of the inner labia (labia minora). The outer labia (labia majora) is then sewn together to cover the wound and create a vaginal "seal" leaving only a small opening for the passage of menstrual blood and urine. This "seal" is intended to keep the girl or woman from having sex prior to marriage. It is often torn open when the woman has sex with her husband the first time. In some cultures, the torn pieces of labia are then sewn back together and must be torn open again for childbirth.

Type 4: Other: all other harmful procedures to the female genitalia for nonmedical purposes such as pricking, piercing, stretching, incising, scraping, and cauterizing the genital area.

Clitorectomies are most common in African countries with infibulation being most popular in Islamic cultures, although most Muslim countries do not practice FGM (Lightfoot-Klein, 1991).

The historical origins of FGM are difficult to trace, but there are some indications that this practice can be traced back to Arab and Ethiopian cultures in the fifth century BC, or perhaps even earlier. There are indications that it was practiced in ancient Rome and Egypt as well (Lightfoot-Klein, 1991). The reasons for FGM are similar, but vary somewhat. Most cultures practicing FGM connect female circumcision to purity, cleanliness, modesty, and sexual restraint. Currently, FGM is practiced in several Central, Eastern, and Northern African countries including Benin, Cameroon, Central African Republic, Chad, Cote d'Ivoire, Democratic Republic of the Congo, Djibouti, Egypt, Ethiopia, Eritrea, Gambia, Ghana, Guinea, Kenya, Liberia, Mali, Mauritania, Niger,

Nigeria, Senegal, Sierra Leone, Somalia, Sudan, Tanzania, Togo, and Uganda. Some Muslim cultures within Indonesia also practice FGM, as well as Iraqi Kurdistan, Yemen, and Oman. Although FGM is believed to be primarily culturally rooted, some people in Muslim countries cite the practice as a religious one (UNFPA, 2009).

In general, the practice has its origin in the cultural or religious belief that the clitoris is dirty, dangerous and will lead to sexual promiscuity. Girls who refuse to undergo FGM are not considered marriageable and often look forward to a life of scorn and social isolation. In a 2010 report on FGM prepared by HRW detailing the extent of FGM in Iraqi Kurdistan, advocates emphasized that most girls are forced to endure FGM by loving mothers and aunts who believe this is the only way to ensure that their daughters or loved ones are marriageable, and in a culture where there are few other options for girls, turning away from this long-practiced cultural tradition is not easy (HRW, 2010).

Lightfoot-Klein, a noted expert on the practice of FGM, conducted field research in Sudan, Kenya, and Egypt and wrote four books based on her years of research within each of these countries. In her first book published in 1989, she describes some common perceptions in Sudan of the woman's clitoris, which make it clear why changing attitudes in traditional cultures is so challenging. She cites a prevalent belief in Sudan that if the clitoris is not cut, it will continue to grow to the point where it rivals the man's penis in size. Men are so anxious about this possibility that most would never marry a woman who wasn't circumcised, and those girls who refuse to undergo the procedure for whatever reason are considered "unclean" and are shunned from society.

The procedure is typically conducted by a community or tribal healer, such as a midwife, in a nonmedical setting. The instruments are commonly nonsterile razors or scalpels, and ashes are often used as a healing agent. No anesthetics or medications are given during or after the procedure, even though the pain is severe, and the chance of infection is significant. Women and girls who have undergone FGM share stories of being told they are going to see a friend, then being held down, and beaten if they resist. With legs forced open they are forced to endure this extremely painful procedure without pain medication. Many girls shared stories of being in immense pain, sometimes for more than a month (HRW, 2011).

There are numerous health risks associated with FGM, including intense pain, some women reported not being given any pain medication and being immobile for up to a month, infection, scar tissue that interferes with sexual intercourse and childbirth, urinary problems, infertility, cysts, and reinjury. When women undergo infibulation and have sex the first time, their vaginas are torn open, and must be kept open so that the wound does not heal, thus closing the vagina again. This practice is particularly painful as the raw and bleeding remnants of the labia may take months to heal (WHO, 2013).

There has been a strong international response to the practice of FGM, starting in the early 1990s with numerous UN international treaties referencing FGM, calling it a human rights violation against women and girls, and identifying this practice as a gender-based discriminatory practice. For instance, in 1990 the Committee for the UN Treaty, CEDAW, adopted a general recommendation calling on all state parties to develop health policies that incorporate measures to eradicate the practice of FGM.

In 1997 WHO, United Nations Children's Fund (UNICEF), and United Nations Population Fund (UNFPA) issued a joint statement condemning the practice of FGM acknowledging the cultural nature of FGM, but asserting that culture is not static and is always evolving, particularly in response to increased awareness about the harm caused by some cultural practices. The statement serves as a reminder that the meaning of a ritual need not be lost, even though the ritual itself changes or diminishes over time (WHO, 1997).

In 2002, the United Nations General Assembly (UNGA) passed a resolution urging all nation states to enact national legislation to abolish FGM. In 2008 numerous UN agencies, such as WHO, UNICEF, UNFPA, UNAIDS, UNHCR (to name a few), issued a joint statement on FGM in a report that included increased information about the extent of the practice as well as the severity of the consequences (WHO, 2008). Three of the United Nations MDGs also directly address FGM by focusing on women's health.

HRW engages in advocacy on a variety of levels, including issuing annual reports that provide comprehensive information on current conditions in at-risk countries, as well as making recommendations to their governments. For instance, in a 2010 report focusing on FGM in Iraqi Kurdistan, HRW made numerous recommendations such as complying with all relevant UN treaties, putting in place a comprehensive legal and policy framework to eradicate FGM, coordinating with relevant ministries and government agencies to develop a community task force to address FGM on a community level, developing services for women and girls who have undergone FGM, and developing preventative and protective mechanisms to protect women and girls to the Kurdish Regional Government (KRG). HRW also works with willing governments to assist them in implementing all recommendations (HRW, 2010).

In order for advocacy efforts to be successful in eradicating FGM, interventions must not be solely top-down, but must be bottom-up as well to ensure community acceptance, ownership, and involvement. Community-based approaches that can build upon international pressure will have the greatest likelihood of success (Lexow, Berggrav, & Taraldsen, 2009). There has been a recent surge in grassroots efforts to eradicate FGM in response to a backlash among local women, particularly in several African countries. Such grassroots organizations are discouraging FGM in their communities by addressing this issue from multiple perspectives, including training tribal leaders about the true origins of FGM highlighting the physical risks as well as the effect on self-esteem, and helping men in the community to better understand the female anatomy, explaining how their marital relationships would likely improve if their wives experienced increased sexual pleasure.

Many of the women interviewed in various human rights reports referenced how they sensed a shift in attitudes about FGM, including beliefs that some people in their communities are turning away from this practice. While this is certainly a positive sign, significant work remains to be done since long-practiced historical traditions tend to be enduring. One successful approach that can be pursued quite easily in this era of globalization involves an increased focus on international and local partnerships. Such partnerships would allow the international community to provide information and resources to local efforts with the recognition that it is the members of local grassroots organizations who know best how to effect change within their own communities.

Health Injustice: Reproductive Choice and Sexual Health

In the Global North, reproductive rights often refer to the right to have an abortion. Yet in reality, the area of reproductive rights is much broader, particularly for women living in developing countries. Reproductive choice and sexual health includes the right to have control and autonomy over one's body (being neither forced to become pregnant and carry a child to term nor being forced to terminate a pregnancy), access to quality health care in relation to a woman's reproductive system, and access to accurate information about family planning, pregnancy, and pregnancy termination. Reproductive health also encompasses maternal health and infant mortality, protection and treatment of sexually transmitted diseases, including issues related to the HIV/AIDS pandemic, particularly since the greatest burden of this pandemic currently rests upon women. Most of these areas are intertwined, which can be good if progress made in one area, such as maternal health, means progress made in another area, such as infant mortality. Yet, this also means that one aspect of reproductive health can slow progress in another area, such as the HIV/AIDS pandemic slowing progress made internationally in reducing maternal deaths (Hogan et al., 2010).

According to the UNFPA website, "reproductive health problems remain the leading cause of ill health and death for women of childbearing age worldwide." While reproductive health affects women in all countries, women in developing countries are disproportionately affected by unwanted pregnancies, poor maternal health, maternal death, infant mortality, sexually transmitted diseases, and HIV/AIDS. In fact, reproductive health is such an important issue it has been added as a target goal of the MDGs.

Reproductive rights are referenced in several UN human rights instruments, including the CEDAW and the Beijing Declaration and Platform for Action discussed earlier in this chapter. The right to family planning was first referenced in a UN Human Rights conference held in Tehran, Iran, in 1968 (commonly referred to as the *Tehran Human Rights Conference*). Proclamation 16 of the *Final Act of the International Conference on Human Rights* report states:

> The protection of the family and of the child remains the concern of the international community. Parents have the basic human right to determine freely and responsibly the number and the spacing of their children. (United Nations, 1968)

To be truly empowered, women must be able to control their own fertility, which includes deciding when (or whether) to get pregnant and how often. Research indicates that in cultures where women's status is low, family size tends to be larger (UNFPA, 2011). While this relationship is correlational only, it does point to the noted problem of women having more children than they desire when they do not have the power and freedom to decline sex and do not have access to contraceptives and other family planning services.

The area of reproductive rights tends to be wrought with controversy, particularly among religious groups and conservative organizations espousing traditional family values. The majority of the controversy tends to center on whether a woman has the right to terminate an unwanted pregnancy, and whether birth control is moral and ethical. For instance, many pro-life groups actively put pressure on governments, international organizations, such as the United Nations, as well as funding organizations to take whatever actions necessary to prohibit abortion. For instance, at the end of each session meeting of the UNCSW, the Agreed Conclusions are proclaimed, and member countries agree or lodge disclaimers. Under the George W. Bush administration, the United States consistently added a disclaimer that its agreement did not constitute an endorsement of abortion. The Obama administration did not add such a disclaimer, which outraged pro-life and conservative religious organizations such as Family Research Council, which cited the actions of the Obama administration as a "clear signal" that it was promoting abortion throughout the world (Saunders & Fragoso, 2009).

Antiabortion groups also work on limiting funding for any agency that provides services interpreted as support for abortions, even if that agency provides other vital services related to reproductive health. The Helms Amendment of 1973, which banned U.S. funding of abortion services overseas, is often considered the genesis of the U.S. antiabortion movement on a political level. In 1984, former president Ronald Reagan instituted what was called the Global Gag Rule (also referred to as the "Mexico City Policy" since this is the location where Reagan announced the new policy), which significantly increased restrictions placed on NGOs providing comprehensive family planning services. Under the Global Gag Rule, foreign NGOs could not use funding from the U.S. Agency for International Development (USAID) for any services relating to abortion. Critics complained that not only was the definition of what constituted "services relating to abortion" far too liberally defined, but the Global Gag Rule did not lower the incidence of abortion, but in fact increased them because it failed to address the problem of unwanted pregnancy (a very complex issue particularly in developing countries) (International Women's Health Coalition, 2009).

Former president Bill Clinton lifted these restrictions, but former president George W. Bush fully reinstated the Global Gag Rule on his first day of office, instituting even more restrictions on NGOs, including prohibiting NGOs from performing abortions, recommending abortions as an option, lobbying for abortion services or providing information on where abortion services could be obtained. Bush did not just limit NGOs from receiving USAID funding though; rather, he asserted that NGOs could not only not use USAID funding for such services, but stipulated that if they used other funding, including private funding for such services, they would no longer be eligible for USAID money (Bogecho & Upreti, 2006).

Women's advocates decried this policy as a culturally incompetent and dangerous importing of American values to foreign countries without consideration of context. For instance, most women in the United States have access to accurate information about family planning and access to birth control. The United States has laws that prohibit the sexual assault of women, U.S. women do not have to fear being raped as a weapon of war, nor does the United States have laws that make it legal for children to be married, or force women to endure unwanted sexual advances of their husbands. U.S. women can see their medical doctors at will and utilize contraception without the permission of their husbands. Further, despite the lack of fully funded and open-access universal health-care system in the United States, even impoverished women have access to some level of maternal health care.

Yet women in other countries, particularly developing countries, are often forced to endure conditions that most people in the United States simply cannot fathom, as many of these countries have neither the legal framework nor the cultural mores that support women's rights. Thus to force the values of a conservative coalition within the United States onto NGOs providing valuable services in foreign countries by limiting not only U.S. funding of these contested services, but also limiting an NGO's ability to utilize private funding sources negates the reality of women living in very desperate circumstances. Most importantly though, the Global Gag Rule did not save the lives of unborn babies, but actually resulted in significant loss of life since in the absence of safe abortion alternatives, desperate women sought out unsafe abortions, which often resulted in the loss of life of both, the mother and the fetus.

The NGOs that were most affected by this policy provided vital comprehensive services related to family planning and birth control, treatment of sexually transmitted diseases, maternal health services, and treatment and/or counseling for HIV/AIDS. NGOs reported that the loss of funding not only drastically reduced their ability to provide these services but also resulted in an increase in unsafe abortions, resulting in unnecessary loss of life (International Planned Parenthood Federation, 2007).

Although President Obama lifted the Global Gag Rule a few days after his inauguration in January 2009, the impact of the Global Gag Rule continues. The advocacy group the Center for Reproductive Rights cites numerous ways in which this U.S. policy has eroded not only family planning services but other health-related services for women as well. The following information is included on the Center for Reproductive Rights website:

- By 2002, the global gag rule resulted in an end to all shipments of USAID-donated contraceptives to 16 countries, and to leading family planning agencies in another 13 countries.
- In Ethiopia and Lesotho, some NGOs are no longer able to offer comprehensive and integrated health-care services to patients suffering from HIV/AIDS.
- In Kenya, the gag rule forced two leading family planning NGOs to close five clinics, cut up to one-third of their staff and reduce services in remaining clinics. One of the shuttered clinics had served a crowded slum neighborhood of Nairobi since 1984, providing sexually transmissible infection (STI) screening and treatment, family planning, pre- and post-natal obstetric services, and well-baby care.
- In Peru, USAID officials pressured an organization to withdraw from a campaign supporting emergency contraception (EC), even though EC helps prevent unwanted pregnancies and is not an abortifacient (a substance that induces miscarriage).
- In Uganda, the global gag rule led to the cancellation of an EC program as well as community education programs for post-abortion care services, which USAID has identified as a priority.
- In Zambia, the nation's leading family planning organization lost 24% of its funding because of the gag rule and had to reduce its programs, clinic-based services and community outreach to underserved rural areas. It can no longer provide much-needed contraceptive supplies to smaller NGOs and government health centers. (Center for Reproductive Rights, 2003)

Reproductive rights extend far beyond abortion and must be considered within the context of non-Western realities. While it might be tempting for some to argue that foreign NGOs should just not accept U.S. funding if they want to advocate abortion, this line of reasoning is illogical since these restrictive policies extend far beyond the targeted goal of limiting abortions and most importantly, not only do such policies not limit abortions, they increase them.

Assess your comprehension of Advocacy Efforts to Confront Crimes against Women and Girls by taking this quiz.

Advocates working in the area of reproductive rights and women's health work with a broad range of issues, extending into many other areas of human rights abuses against women. Many advocates believe that reproductive rights goes to the heart of women's empowerment mirroring Dr. Nafis Sadik's (former Executive Director of UNFPA) assertion that women's ability to reproduce is used to trap them in many cultures, making them subordinate to men, and it is the UNPF's goal to liberate women by enabling them to control their own bodies (UNFPA, 1997).

Concluding Thoughts on Violence against Women and Girls

Crimes against women and girls are vast and complex. This chapter provides an overview of some common human rights abuses endured by women in both Western and non-Western contexts, providing an overview of some effective advocacy interventions used both domestically and globally. Although no international treaty can successfully eradicate human rights violations against women (or any vulnerable group), such instruments can provide a legal and policy framework outlining and defining the nature of women's rights, as well as providing concrete action steps for effecting long-lasting change in the direction of greater equality between the sexes. Advocates working in the area of women's rights must be able to work effectively using top-down and bottom-up approaches in a manner that engages the local community. This will involve challenging long-standing cultural traditions that are resistant to change. A comprehensive approach that involves increased international awareness and support with culturally competent interventions that respect local knowledge will have the greatest likelihood of success.

Assess your analysis and evaluation of this chapter's content by completing the Chapter Review.

CHAPTER 6

Xander Martin

Advocacy for Children

Protection of Child Welfare
at Home and Abroad

"Children are the world's most valuable resource and its best hope for the future," July 19, 1963, John F. Kennedy, the 35th President of the United States

Does the above-referenced quotation accurately reflect how children are perceived and treated in American culture? Many would likely say that it does—children should be treasured because they are the leaders of the next generation. Children should be cherished because they are vulnerable. All conventional wisdom suggests this—all children deserve unconditional love and nurturing from their parents and caring concern and protection of society. This must be why an Internet search on "parenting advice" using Google results in 42.2 million hits! A search on *Amazon.com* for books on childhood development reveals 91,241 books dealing with some aspect of how children develop psychologically, socially, physically, intellectually, biologically, and even spiritually.

So at least on the surface, it appears as though society as a whole really does value children, recognizing their fragile nature, the importance of nurturing them into adulthood, and the importance of sacrificing as a culture in order to see them succeed. In fact, in many places in the world, a significant portion of public resources are reserved for the care and nurturing of children, including the allocation of public funds for public education, child welfare, child care, and even child-centered parks and recreation programs. But has society in general, and the United States in particular always treated children so well? Do we feel this protective of all children? Are there some children, from certain groups, who are not treated with such love, care, nurturing, and protection? Are there some children who society does not believe are "the world's most valuable resource and its best hope for the future"?

It might come as a surprise to many reading this book that children were not always considered to be a "valuable resource," or "the best hope for our future" in many places in the world, including the United States. There was a time in U.S. history where children, in general, and certain groups of children, in particular, were seen not as vulnerable beings whose healthy development required nurturance and protection but as potential threats who must be treated with a stern hand lest they turn toward vice and debauchery. In the United States and Europe, attitudes toward children in general were far harsher 100 years ago than they are today, in large part due to ignorance about child development but also because of the prevailing philosophical and religious theories popular during earlier times, such as some aspects of Reformed Theology and social Darwinism, which posited that immutable traits such as ethnic origin, immigration status, and socioeconomic status determined the inherent worth of a person, even a child. In fact, early theories about children were based upon the belief that children were born evil because they were born of original sin, thus were in need of firm discipline (versus nurturing). Modern theories of child development did not begin to emerge until the early part of the twentieth century. For instance, developmental theorist pioneer Jean Piaget published his first book *The Language and Thought of a Child* in 1926.

Prior to the advent of child psychology, the United States had in many respects a dismal record of child protection, particularly with regard to certain groups of children, such as child migrants, disabled children, and children who were African American and Native American. African Americans, in general, were completely excluded from government-sponsored child welfare programs, and Native American children were a specific target of interest and as a consequence were forcibly removed from their homes (particularly if they lived on Indian reservations) and placed in government-run or religious boarding schools, where they were barred from practicing their ethnic and cultural traditions (Adams, 1995). Thousands of migrant children who were orphaned and neglected roamed the New York City streets in search of food and shelter and were often arrested and treated as adults, while others were put on trains and shipped out West to farms in need of helping hands to work the land (O'Conner, 2004).

While our understanding of child development and our treatment of children in general have improved considerably in the last 100 years, historical trauma has been passed down from generation to generation within certain ethnic minority groups that were disproportionately affected by society's harsh treatment of its children, deeply affecting many ethnic communities across the United States even to this day. Unfortunately, it's often these same communities that continue to need the greatest amount of advocacy for their children, in response to various types of maltreatment and disparities in treatment. In this chapter, I explore both historical and contemporary problems facing children in Western societies, as well as ways in which advocates are working to confront these issues to protect the welfare of all children.

Children in developing countries are currently facing many of the same issues children faced in historically in many countries in the Global North. Many of the problems children in the Global South are currently experiencing are economically driven and some are driven by cultural values that are not particularly child-centered. This chapter also explores the history of child welfare leading up to contemporary times, particularly in the Global North, and also explores major human rights violations against children in many developing or least developed countries in the Global South, with a focus on domestic and international remedies for protecting child welfare on a global level.

Advocacy for Children in Western Society

Historical Treatment of Children and Efforts of Early Child Advocates

There are many ways in which children were mistreated historically in the Global North, but in this section, I explore primarily two areas of mistreatment of children in England and Colonial America. These two areas include the use of children in the labor market, otherwise known as *child labor*, and the treatment of children who were, for whatever reason, without parents, thus considered *orphaned*. Of course there are many other ways in which children were mistreated as well—without federal laws protecting children, there was rampant sexual abuse, physical abuse, and various other forms of maltreatment such as physical and emotional neglect. Thus, by exploring primarily child labor and the treatment of orphans and street children, readers should not presume that other forms of maltreatment were not prevalent in early America's and England's past. The rationale for exploring these two areas of maltreatment (child labor and the treatment of orphans and street children) is based upon the fact that they represent a significant departure from how children are treated today and also highlight key areas of activism among early child welfare activists.

Child Labor in England and Early America

INDENTURED SERVITUDE AND APPRENTICESHIPS During colonial America all children were expected to work, whether bonded or not. In fact, children as young as six often worked alongside their parents, and children as young as 12 were expected to work in an adult capacity, often working in apprenticed positions outside of their homes and away from their families. Children from poor families, particularly immigrants, were often forced to work alongside their parents in either indentured servitude or as slaves. During the many waves of early immigration, individuals, families, and minor children as young as 10 or 11 years old often paid for their passage to the Colonial America through a process called indentured service. Indentured service contracts required that the servant—most often a poor individual, or families hoping for a better life in America—worked off the cost of their travel by working for a master in some capacity once they arrived in America. If a family immigrated to Colonial America States in this manner, then their children, regardless of age, were required to work as well (Galenson, 1984; Hindman, 2002; Marten & Greven, 2007; Morgan, 2001).

The economic system of indentured servitude was extremely exploitative. Research indicates that it was the ship owners who would often recruit unsuspecting, yet desperate individuals from other countries, with stories of abundant life in America (Marten & Greven, 2007; Morgan, 2001). Many individuals and entire families accepted the call, believing that they could make a better life for themselves in colonial America. They were often told that the terms of their service would last for three years, and then they would be free—free to buy land and to make a life for themselves that was not possible in many European countries (Hindman, 2002; Morgan, 2001). In reality, the cost of

North Wind Picture Archives

Children often worked alongside their parents in garment factories under indentured contracts.

their passage would be paid off in only one year, and the remaining years of service were considered free work. Further, masters often treated their bonded labor quite poorly. Servants received no cash wages but were supposed to be provided with basic necessities, which depending upon the nature and means of the master might include anything from sufficient sustenance to meager sustenance and substandard shelter. Thus, while indentured servants were not considered slaves, the treatment of them was quite similar (Marten & Greven, 2007).

Although most indentured servants were in their early 20s, children who immigrated with their families on bonded contracted were expected to work as well and were often treated no differently than their parents (Hindman, 2002; Marten & Greven, 2007). Children were not allowed to enter into bonded labor contracts without the permission of their parents, but very poor and orphaned children, particularly in London, were often kidnapped and sold to ship captains who then brought them to America and sold them as indentured servants, most often to masters who used them as house servants. Also, local governments that were responsible for the poor would "bind out" poor and orphaned children in early America as a form of poor relief (Hindman, 2002; Katz, 1996).

THE "CIVILIZATION" OF NATIVE AMERICAN CHILDREN   The treatment of Native American children during the colonial period is particularly noteworthy. Using Native children as indentured servants was initiated in large part by Christian missionaries in an attempt to "civilize" the children in a part of the grander scheme of converting Native Americans to Christianity, since it was believed that only the "civilized" could be Christian (Marten & Greven, 2007; Romero, 2007; Silverman, 2001). There were many contradictions between Native American and English values, which increased the motivation of Christian missionaries to transform Native children from what the colonists considered their immoral lifestyles and culture. For instance, in Native American culture children had far more freedom than Anglo-American children. They were not forced to work, were not physically disciplined, and their lives were free for the most part of institutional structure. How Native children were treated in their own cultures reflected Native American values. Yet, European colonists were highly critical of these more egalitarian and "democratic" parenting style because they did not understand them. In fact, they considered Native American parents ignorant and lazy, when in reality Native American parenting styles were used quite intentionally with the purpose of instilling pride, autonomy, and courage into their children, not fear or timidity, as was often the case with the more authoritarian Puritan-influenced parenting style used by colonial parents (Marten & Greven, 2007).

The colonists also objected to the freedom that Native women had within their culture and believed that the level of power they were granted within tribal society was far too great. Thus, the egalitarian nature of male–female relationships within Native culture was also perceived as immoral. The binding out of Native children served two purposes then—first, it enabled Christian missionaries in colonial America to Christianize Native populations through the conversion and the subsequent civilizing of their children—training boys to engage in "real work" (i.e., not fishing and hunting) and training girls to be good and submissive housewives (in accordance with the conservative Christian protocol of the time)—second, it served to address the significant shortfall of servants in seventeenth century colonial America (Marten & Greven, 2007; Romero, 2007).

CHILD LABOR IN THE SLAVERY ERA   Indentured servitude eventually waned during the seventeenth century in favor of slavery, but the binding out of children who were poor and orphaned continued well into the nineteenth century. During the 300 years of the Atlantic slave trade, over 15 million Africans were brought to the United States through the West Indies, or directly from Africa. Among these Africans were many children who were either forced or born into slavery along with their parents. In time masters realized that slaves who had once experienced freedom were far more difficult to control than those born into captivity, thus a market developed for children who could work for a slave owner and essentially grow up as captive slave and be trained to be a submissive servant. For the most part, younger children were sold with their mothers, but once the child was between the ages of 7 and 10, they could and often were sold off and separated from their families, particularly to fill the growing need for young "negro" slave children born into captivity (Fryer, 2007; Marten & Greven, 2007). Slavery was outlawed in 1865 with the passage of the Thirteenth Amendment to the U.S. Constitution, but the plight of African children did

Box 6.1	Infant Mortality in African-American Populations: Then and Now

There were not as many African slave children born into captivity as one might expect, due in large part to extremely high rates of infant mortality of African slave children because of disease and poor nutrition. In fact, the infant mortality of African slave children under the age of four was double than that of white children during the time when slavery was legal. Ironically, not only has this trend continued well into the twenty-first century, but it has gotten far worse with infant mortality among African-American infants being about three times than that of Caucasian infants (Rossen & Schoendorf, 2013).

• •

not improve significantly (and most advocates would argue that the legacy of slavery creates significant challenges for African-American children to this day).

Another form of work that children engaged in early America was apprenticeship. Apprenticeship involved the training of children in a craft. Essentially apprenticeship involved an artisan taking on an apprentice in early adolescence and teaching him a trade. The apprentice would move out of his family home, and live with the artisan serving as an assistant, sometimes for years (Schultz, 1985). Apprenticeships might involve learning to become a barber, making shoes or woodworking. Children were not paid, and in fact parents often had to pay to have their children apprenticed. While most apprenticeships did not involve overt exploitation, the practice did reflect a focus on work, rather than education. Apprenticeships eventually became less popular as industrialization began in the late eighteenth century as the advent of machinery ultimately replaced the need for craftsmen.

> **Professional History**
>
> *Understanding and Mastery: Skills to analyze and interpret historical data application in advocacy and social changes*
>
> Critical Thinking Question: It's important to identify historic influences of contemporary social problems. What are some ways in which historic treatment of vulnerable children, such as African-American and Native American children, has contributed to challenges children from these ethnic groups experience in contemporary society?
>
> •

CHILD LABOR DURING THE INDUSTRIAL ERA: CHILDREN AND FACTORIES   By the middle of the nineteenth century, virtually all apprenticeships and indentured contracts had disappeared, and the primary form of child labor, was factory work (Bender, 1975). Children were often recruited to work in factories, particularly orphans or those from poor families. By the early- to mid-nineteenth century, it is estimated that hundreds of thousands of children—some as young as six—were employed in the textile industry, including cotton mills. In fact, some scholars estimated that children were the bulk of the workforce in many factories throughout the nineteenth century, with some children working six days a week, 14 hours a day (Galenson, 1984). Excerpts of autobiographies written by people who worked in factories throughout their childhoods reference dismal conditions, with poor sanitation and air quality, repetitive work on machinery that left small hands bleeding, and very long days on their feet, which in many cases significantly shortened the life spans of these child workers (Hindman, 2002).

Mill factories and garment industry sweatshops began to spring up throughout New York and other large cities in the middle to latter part of the nineteenth century. Although sweatshops eventually occurred in factory-like settings, their origin involved what was called "outwork," where workers sewed garments and other textiles in their

A young girl working as a "spinner" at a New England cotton mill in 1913.

Paul usna/Alamy

homes. Women and children were primarily hired for these tasks because they could be paid a lower wage. Since they were paid by the piece, they often worked 14 or more hours per day, seven days a week. Children worked alongside their mothers, because their small fingers enabled them to engage in detail work, such as sewing on buttons that was challenging for adults.

CHILD LABOR IN ENGLAND   The plight of children in England from the late eighteenth century through the early part of the nineteenth century was in many respects a mirror image of what was occurring in the United States. Society greatly admired the notion of children working alongside their parents based upon the belief that idleness would most certainly lead to insolence or worse. It was considered prudent and morally upright to expect children to contribute to their own provision. Honeyman (2007) cites how several leaders of organizations in England charged with the responsibility of caring for poor and orphaned children cited idleness and laziness in children as the root of all evil, and as the path toward becoming a criminal (Honeyman, 2007).

In the decades prior to the Industrial Revolution, children in England, as in America, worked alongside their parents at home, often in sweatshop conditions. The centralization of labor did not occur until the beginning of the nineteenth century due to the development of manufacturing technologies in factory settings requiring a labor force congregated in one central location. Also similar to America, women and children were the preferred labor force in factories in England because it was believed that they would tolerate repetitive grinding work better than men. In both countries, government authorities compelled orphaned, neglected, and illegitimate children to work in the factories

Boy 'putters' moving coal in a narrow seam in England, 1848.

because it served as a solution to the problem of unsupervised children roaming the streets, but also because it served capitalist need (and greed). It wasn't until well into the early nineteenth century that a chorus of voices emerged in England, and then later in the United States, questioning the wisdom of allowing children to work long hours in factories, primarily because they were separated from their families for such long hours, yet often (Honeyman, 2007).

Early Advocacy Efforts to Confront Child Labor Abuses in America

Jane Addams and Child Labor Laws

Addams was appalled by the conditions of those living in poverty in urban communities, particularly the plight of recently arrived immigrants, who were forced to live in substandard tenement housing and work long hours in factories, often in very dangerous working conditions. In response, she and her friend, Ellen Gates Starr started the first settlement house in the United States, the Hull-House of Chicago, after visiting the Toynbee House in England. The Hull-House provided residential services, and what we would now call "wrap around" services for clients, as well as advocacy to marginalized populations (primarily immigrants) working in sweatshop conditions in Chicago.

Addams' and Gates' form of advocacy involved living among the residence of Hull-House. Hull-House offered several services for children and their widowed mothers, including after-school care for those children whose mothers worked long hours in factories. Providing comprehensive services to those in need and living among them in their own community were some of the ways in which Addams became aware of the plight of children forced to work in the factories. In her autobiography *Twenty Years at Hull House,* Addams wrote of her first encounter with child labor:

> Our very first Christmas as Hull-House, when we as yet knew nothing of child labor, a number of little girls refused the candy which was offered them as part of the Christmas good cheer, saying simply that they "worked in a candy factory and

could not bear the sight of it." We discovered that for six weeks they had worked from seven in the morning until nine at night, and they were exhausted as well as satiated ... During the same winter three boys from a Hull-House club were injured at one machine in a neighboring factory for a lack of a guard which would have cost but a few dollars. When the injury of one of these boys resulted in his death, we felt quite sure that the owners of the factory would share our horror and remorse, and that they would do everything possible to prevent the recurrence of such a tragedy. To our surprise they did nothing whatever, and I made my first acquaintance then with those pathetic documents signed by the parents of working children, that they will make no claim for damages resulting from "carelessness" (Addams, 2011, pp. 198–199).

Addams and her colleagues began an advocacy campaign against sweatshop conditions in Chicago factories early in the Hull-House's existence, advocating in particular for the women and children who were most often hired to work in them. Their activism seemed to pay off quickly when the Illinois legislature passed a law limiting the workday to just eight hours (from the typical 12 to 14 hour per day). Their excitement though was soon tempered when the law was quickly overturned by the Illinois Supreme Court as unconstitutional. In her autobiography, Addams discussed how the greatest opposition to child labor laws came from the business sector—businessmen from large corporations, such as Chicago's glass companies, who considered such legislation as "radicalism," arguing that their companies would not be able to survive without child labor (Addams, 2011).

Jane Addams reading to children at the Hull-House in Chicago

Addams and the Hull-House networked quite extensively joining efforts with trade unions and even the Democratic Party, which in 1892 adopted into its platform recommendations to prohibit children under the age of 15 years from working in factories. Addams and her Hull-House colleagues broadened their focus of activism to include the federal level with their support for the *Sulzer Bill*, which when passed allowed for the creation of the Department of Labor. In 1904 the National Child Labor Committee was formed, and Addams served as chairman for one term. In 1912, one of Addams' Hull-House colleagues, Julia Lathrop was appointed chief of a new federal agency created by President William Taft, focusing on child welfare, including child labor. As chief of the Children's Bureau, Lathrop was responsible for investigating and reporting on all relevant issues pertaining to the welfare of children from all classes and spent a considerable amount of time researching the dangers of child labor.

After several failed attempts, federal legislation barring child labor was finally passed in 1938 and signed into law by President Franklin D. Roosevelt, three years after Addams' death. The legislation, entitled the Fair Labor Standards Act is a comprehensive bill regulating various aspects of labor in the United States, including child labor. The act defined "oppressive child labor," set minimum ages of employment, and the maximum number of hours children were allowed to work. This act is still in existence and has been amended several times to address such issues as equal pay (Equal Pay Act of 1963), age discrimination (Age Discrimination in Employment Act of 1967), and low wages (federal minimum wage increases).

There were many other child rights advocates who I have not referenced in this section, but one of the most important points to emphasize when exploring the role of advocacy and activism in the area of child welfare is that there were two prevailing ideologies that emerged in response to the plight of children during early American history, and that is, who is to blame—the parents or society. Addams (and her colleagues) embraced the latter ideology—that society was to blame by permitting (and at times creating) the existence of harsh conditions for one segment of the population, because they benefited another, more privileged segment. Unfortunately, we see these competing ideologies at work not only throughout history with regard to child welfare issues, but also in response to a long list of other social injustices.

Child Welfare in Early America

THE U.S. ORPHAN PROBLEM During the eighteenth through the early- to mid-nineteenth centuries in particular, many orphaned or uncared for children roamed the streets, especially in growing urban areas such as New York. Since free public education was not yet available in the United States in the nineteenth century, children who were not working 14 hours a day in a factory, or whose parents were killed (often by a workplace accident or one of the many viral epidemics common during that era such as yellow fever), roamed the streets, often in search of something to steal, and then sell for sustenance.

These street children, many of whom were children of recent immigrants, were often treated as criminals, as if they were adults. In other words, the plight of the orphan did not appear to tug at the heartstrings of the average American because of the vast amount of abandoned and orphaned children and the lack of collective knowledge about child development. Despite the tremendous exploitation of the poor, including immigrants, women, and children, and the lack of free public education in the states, early advocacy efforts focused on the failure of parents, who were often perceived as lazy and undisciplined foreigners who did not care to supervise their children.

By the latter part of the nineteenth century, Charity House Organizations, religious leaders, and government officials were eager to address the problem of orphaned and abused children and the most commonly suggested solution was the creation of institutions designed solely for the care of orphaned and needy children, with a focus on the development of vocational skills in the orphans. Some orphanages, or orphan asylums, as they were often called, existed in the 1700s, but institutionalized care did not become the primary means for handling needy and orphaned children until the middle to late 1800s. By the latter part of the 1800s, there were more than 600 orphanages in existence in the United States (Trattner, 1998). As stated previously, child migrants were overrepresented in orphan asylums because there were often no extended family members on which to rely in cases of parental death or disability (Martin, 2014).

Orphan asylums also housed children whose parents were alive but could not economically afford to support them. Families who were for whatever reason suddenly unable to support their children could leave them in the temporary care of an orphanage for a small monthly fee, but if they fell behind in payments, the children would often quickly become wards of the state (which would then take over making monthly payments), and the parents would lose all legal rights to their children (Martin, 2014; Trattner, 1998).

The orphanage system was originally perceived as a significant improvement over placing children in almshouses and jails or forcing them into indentured servitude, yet these institutions were not without their share of trouble, and in time reports of harsh treatment and abuses, including labor abuses, were common in orphanages as well. Some orphanages were government-run, but most were privately run with governmental funding and had little, if any oversight or accountability. Because the government paid on a per child basis, there was a financial incentive to run large operations, with some orphanages housing as many as 2,000 children under one roof. Obedience was highly valued in these institutions out of sheer necessity, whereas individuality, play, and creativity were often discouraged (Martin, 2014; Trattner, 1998).

THE TREATMENT OF NATIVE AMERICANS IN THE U.S. CHILD WELFARE SYSTEM British colonization of North America involved an organized and methodical campaign to decimate the Native American population through invasion, trickery (such as trading land for alcohol), and ultimately the forced relocation of all reservations. Once Native Americans were relocated onto reservations, their assimilation into the majority culture because the primary goal of the U.S. government (Brown, 2001). The Native Americans who survived this genocide were broken physically, emotionally, and spiritually, suffering from alcoholism, rampant unemployment, and debilitating depression.

In the early part of the nineteenth century, the U.S. government assumed full responsibility for educating Native American children. It is estimated that from the early 1800s through the early part of the twentieth century virtually all Native American children were forcibly removed from their homes and reservations and placed in Indian boarding schools where they were not allowed to speak in their native tongues, practice their cultural religion, or wear traditional dress. During school breaks, many of these children were placed as servants in Caucasian homes rather than being allowed to return home for visits. The result of this forced assimilation amounted to cultural genocide where an entire generation of Native Americans was institutionalized, deprived of a relationship with their biological families, and robbed of their cultural heritage.

This ongoing campaign to assimilate the Native Americans into European American culture became even more aggressive between 1950 and 1970, when social workers with governmental backing removed thousands of Native American children from their homes on reservations for alleged maltreatment, placing them in adoptive Caucasian homes. In reality, many of the problems on the reservations were the product of years of governmental oppression resulting in extreme poverty and other commonly associated social ills, and the U.S. government response to this was to tear Native American families apart rather than intervene with mental health services.

Between 1941 and 1978, approximately 70% of all Native America children were removed from their homes and placed either in orphanages or with Caucasian families, many of whom later adopted them (First Nations Orphan Association, n.d.). In truth, few of these children were removed from their homes due to maltreatment as it is currently defined. Rather, approximately 99% of these children were removed because social workers believed that the children were victims of social deprivation due to the extreme poverty common on most Indian reservations (U.S. Senate, 1974).

The result of this government action has been nothing short of devastating. Native Americans have one of the highest suicide rates in the nation, with Native American youth, particularly those who have spent time in U.S. boarding schools, having on average five to six times the rate of suicide compared to the non–Native American population. When these children graduated from high school, they were adults without a culture—no longer feeling comfortable on the reservation after years of being negatively indoctrinated against their cultural heritage, yet not being accepted by the white population either. The response of many of these Native American youth was to turn to alcohol in an attempt to drown out the pain.

In 1978, the *Indian Child Welfare Act* (ICWA) (PL 95-608) was passed, which prevented the unjustified removal of Native American children from their homes. The act specifies that if removal is necessary, then the child must be placed in a home that reflects his or her culture and preserves tribal tradition. Tribal approval must be obtained prior to placement, even when the placement is a result of a voluntary adoption proceeding (Kreisher, 2002). This act has for the most part successfully stemmed the tide of mass removal of thousands of Native American children from their homes on the reservations, but unfortunately many caseworkers still do not understand the reason why such a bill was passed in the first place, or why it is necessary, and mistakenly believe that this act hampers placing needy children in loving homes (Martin, 2014). Further, a recent decision by the U.S. Supreme Court may reflect an attempt to dilute the ICWA. On June 25, 2013 in a 5-4 decision the Supreme Court reversed a lower court ruling, and decided in favor of the adoptive parents and against the Native American biological father contesting the adoption relying upon the ICWA. Justice Alito delivered the majority decision referencing the ICWA as a "trump card" that could be played by Native American biological fathers (Clinton, Goldberg, Tsosie, & Riley, 2013).

> ## Professional History
>
> *Understanding and Mastery: Historic and current legislation affecting service delivery*
>
> Critical Thinking Question: What are some of the precursors of the passage of the Indian Child Welfare Act (PL 95-608), and why is this legislation so important for advocates to be aware of?

Early Advocacy Efforts to Confront Child Welfare Abuses in America

Charles Loring Brace and the Orphan Train Movement

During the Industrial era, there were many child advocates working on behalf of poor and orphaned children, but they did not all agree on what types of activism was best, nor did they agree on the cause of the problem plaguing children. Rev. Charles Loring Brace, founder of the New York Children's' Aid Society, recognized the serious problem of children growing up on the streets of New York due to several tragic events from the middle of the nineteenth century. Brace estimated that as many as 5,000 children were homeless and forced to roam the streets in search of money, food, and shelter. Brace was shocked at the cruel indifference of most New Yorkers, who called these children street arabs with "bad blood." He was also appalled at reports of children as young as five years old being arrested for vagrancy (Bellingham, 1984; Brace, 1967). Brace described the problem, stating:

> … [t]he young ruffians of New York are the products of accident, ignorance, and vice. Among a million people, such as compose the population of this city and its suburbs, there will always be a great number of misfortunes; fathers die, and leave their children unprovided for; parents drink, and abuse their little ones, and they float away on the currents of the street; step-mothers or step-fathers drive out, by neglect and ill-treatment, their sons from home. *Thousands are the children of poor foreigners, who have permitted them to grow up without school, education, or religion.* All the neglect and bad education and evil example of a poor class tend to form others, who, as they mature, swell the ranks of ruffians and criminals. So, at length, a great multitude of ignorant, untrained, passionate, irreligious boys, and young men are formed, who becomes the "dangerous class" of society. [Emphasis Added] (Brace, 1967, p. 28)

Brace clearly blamed the parents for the orphan problem in New York, failing to truly recognize the social conditions at play during this era. Brace's primary concern was to keep orphans safe from the temptations of street life, which he believed would preclude any possibility that these children would grow up to be God-fearing, responsible adults. Since the focus of child welfare was developing a work ethic (versus becoming a "ruffian"). Brace reasoned that children who had no parents or whose parents could not or would not take care of them would be far better off living in the "clean open spaces" of the farming communities out West, where fresh air and the need for workers were plentiful. Because the rail lines were rapidly opening up the West, Brace developed an innovative program where children would be loaded onto trains and taken West to good Christian farming families. Notices were sent in advance of train arrivals, and communities along the train line would come out and meet the train, so that families who had expressed an interest in taking one or more children could examine the children and take them right then, if they desired. Brace convened committees of female volunteers (early caseworkers) who would interview families to ensure that they met the standards for qualified adoptive or foster families (Martin, 2014).

Survivors of these orphan trains have talked about how they felt like cattle, being paraded across a stage. Interested foster parents would often feel the children's muscles and check their teeth before deciding what child they would take. Few parents would take more than one child, thus siblings were most often split up, sometimes without even a passing comment made by the child-care agents or the new parents (Patrick, Sheets, & Trickel, 1990). It was as if the breaking of lifelong family bonds were considered trivial compared to the gift these children were receiving by being rescued from their hopeless existence on the streets (Martin, 2014).

Most children were not legally adopted but were placed with a family under an indentured contract, which served two purposes: First, this type of contract allowed the placement agency to take the children back if something went wrong with the placement; second, children placed under an indentured contract could not inherit property, thus farming families could take in boys to work on the farm or girls to assist with the housework but didn't have to worry about them inheriting the family assets (Martin, 2014; Trattner, 1998; Warren, 1995).

The orphan trains ran from 1854 to 1929, delivering approximately 150,000 children to new homes across the West, from the Midwestern states to Texas, and even as far West as California. Whether this social experiment was a glowing success or a miserable failure (or somewhere in between) depends on whom one asks. Some children were placed in wonderful, loving homes and grew up to be happy and responsible adults, but other survivors of the orphan trains shared stories of heartache and abuse. Some tell stories of lives no better than that of slaves, where they were taken in by families for no other reason than to provide hard labor for the cost of bed and board. Others tell stories of having siblings torn from their sides as families chose one child, leaving brothers and sisters on the train. And still others tell stories of failed placements, where farming families exercised their one-year return option, sending the children back to the orphanage or allowing the children to drift from farm to farm to earn their keep (Holt, 1992; Martin, 2014).

Eventually new child welfare practices caught up with new child development theories leading to a focus on childhood play rather than a focus on the virtue of work. By the early twentieth century, the practice of "farming out" children received increasing criticism, and the last trainload of children was delivered to its many destinations in 1929. Despite the controversy surrounding the orphan train movement and similar outplacement programs that followed, the orphan train movement is considered the forerunner to the current foster care system in the United States where children are placed in available private homes rather than in institutions (Trattner, 1998).

Assess your comprehension of Historic Treatment of Children and Efforts of Early Child Advocates by taking this quiz.

Contemporary Child Welfare: Advocating for Vulnerable Children

Children living in contemporary Western societies face very different challenges than 100 years ago. Child labor laws preclude child exploitation in the workforce; federal and state social welfare programs now exist in most developed nations, which have helped not only to alleviate poverty but also to protect families from the effect of various catastrophes, such as natural disasters and pandemics. Also, vulnerable groups of children are far better protected from disparity in treatment through the passage of such federal legislation as the Civil Rights Act of 1964 and the Americans with Disabilities Act, yet there remains disparity in treatment of children from certain ethnic groups, such as African American, Latinos, and Native Americans.

There remain serious issues with how some children are treated within society, particularly U.S. society. For instance, few truly effective systems are in place to assist runaway and homeless youth. Far too often, adolescents who experienced physical and sexual abuse in their homes are typically not served well by child protective services, and they often choose to live on the streets rather than remain in their homes or trust the "system" to provide for their care. Far too many children are charged as adults for crimes they committed as children, and most of these are children of color—primarily Africa-American boys. African-American girls also experience disparity in treatment by organizations charged with the responsibility for their protection. For instance, there is a growing recognition that African-American girls are far more likely to be victims of domestic sex trafficking, yet if they are apprehended, rather than being treated as victims, they are far more likely to be charged as prostitutes and sent back out onto the streets.

Gone are the days where the majority of children being placed into substitute care were orphaned due to industrial accidents, war, or illness. In the past 100 years, the protection of orphaned and neglected children in Western societies has slowly transitioned from a focus on institutionalized care to a system offering children in need of care and protection a substitute family in the form of foster care. Such changes were ushered in by federal legislation mandating the treatment and care of abused and neglected children, including the development of federal and state agencies that are responsible for the protection of children. And unlike earlier eras when orphanage placements were most often permanent, almost half of all children currently in the U.S. foster care have the goal of reunifying with their biological parents (U.S. Department of Health and Human Services, 2008). Yet there are significant problems with the U.S. foster care system, particularly with regard to disparity in treatment and the overrepresentation of certain ethnic minority groups.

The U.S. Foster Care System

The contemporary U.S. child welfare system exists to provide a safety net for children and families in crisis. A primary goal of the foster care system is to reunite foster care children with their biological parents whenever possible (Sanchirico & Jablonka, 2000). Federal and state laws have established three basic goals for children in its child welfare system:

- *Safety* from abuse and neglect
- *Permanency* in a stable, loving home (preferably with the biological parents)
- *Well-being* of the child with regard to their physical health, mental health, and developmental and educational needs

In 2011 (the most recent statistics available), there were approximately 400,540 children in the U.S. foster care system, which represents a decrease from prior years. Approximately 40% of all children in foster care are Caucasian, followed by 30% of African-American children, 20% Hispanic, and 10% multiracial groups. The majority of children in the child welfare system are in nonrelative foster care placement. The median length of stay in foster care is about 18 months, but it appears that if children aren't placed in the first 18 months of placement, the chance of remaining in placement for an extended number of years increases significantly (U.S. Department of Health and Human Services, 2012).

Children of color are overrepresented in the foster care system, comprising nearly 60% of all placements in the year 2004. This is nearly twice their representation in the general population. Of all children requiring child welfare intervention, the majority of African-American children requiring care are placed in foster care, whereas the majority of Caucasian children receive in-home services (Child Welfare League of America, 2002). In addition, African-American children remain in foster care far longer and are reunited with their families far less often. This overrepresentation of children of color in the foster care system, particularly African-American children, is fueled by other long-standing factors such as social oppression, negative social conditions, racial discrimination, and economic injustice. For instance, African-American children were initially excluded from the child welfare system but are now the most overrepresented of all racial groups (Smith & Devore, 2004).

Some reasons for this overrepresentation relate to complex social issues such as institutionalized racism, intergenerational poverty, and culturally based drug abuse. But other possible causes include racism within the child welfare system.

Types of racial discrimination include:

1. Racial bias in referring families for family preservation programs versus out-of-home placement. Certain special populations, including African-American families, are not consistently targeted for family preservation programs. Reasons for this include caseworker bias based on the belief that the needs of the African-American community may be too great to be appropriately handled by in-home family preservation programs (Denby & Curtis, 2003).

2. Racial partiality in assessing parent–child attachment leading to delays in returning children to their biological parents. A 2003 study of approximately 250 black and white children in foster care placement found that racial partiality existed in assessing the parent–child attachment when the caseworker was of a different race than the biological parent. Although this result was reciprocal (i.e., black caseworkers showed partiality to black families and white caseworkers showed partiality to white families), the effect of this trend has particular relevance to the African-American community because the majority of caseworkers are Caucasian, and African-American children are disproportionately represented among children in foster care. The results of this study revealed that Caucasian caseworkers might have erred when they concluded that African-American mothers were poorly attached to their children because of the caseworker's lack of understanding of cultural differences between Caucasian and African-American social customs (Surbeck, 2003).

3. Caseworkers who are poorly trained in cultural competencies. For a caseworker to accurately assess many of the factors necessary in determining whether out-of-home placement is warranted, such as the level of violence in the home, the ability of parents to protect their children, or the level of parental remorse, a caseworker must be aware of commonly held negative stereotypes of various racial groups. It is unacceptable for a member of the majority culture to claim not to hold any negative stereotypes, and it is only through the honest admission of overt and subtle negative biases toward other cultures that a caseworker can begin to work effectively with a variety of ethnic groups.

PLACING CHILDREN OF COLOR IN CAUCASIAN HOMES   Considerable controversy exists surrounding the placement of children of color in Caucasian homes. Many advocacy organizations do not support this practice, whereas others claim that it is not in the best interest of children to experience placement delays simply because there are no foster families available that are the same race as the child. From a "micro" perspective, the latter argument makes sense. If an African-American child is in desperate need of a long-term foster home, how much sense would it make to have a policy in place that prevents placement in a suitable home solely because the foster family is Caucasian? After all, all children deserve loving homes, and the color of their skin should not keep them from being placed in one, right?

Yet from a "macro" perspective, a different viewpoint is revealed. Consider the equity of a majority culture systematically destroying an entire race, as the United States has done to the African-American population during the slavery and post–Civil War eras or to the Native American population during colonial times and the era of early occupation of the United States. How do you think these racial groups would perceive this same majority culture then rushing in to rescue the children who were maltreated in great part because of this cultural genocide and the resultant social breakdown?

Advocates of placing children of color in homes of the parents of the same race often cite arguments based on a history of cultural genocide. Alternatives to transracial placement include the development of kinship care programs, where members of a child's extended family serve as foster parents, often made possible through some type of financial assistance. The National Association of Black Social Workers (NABSW) cites the long-standing tradition of informal kinship care within the African-American community, extending back to the Middle Ages and solidified during the slavery era, when many African Americans acted as surrogate parents for children whose biological parents were sold and sent away. Such cultural traditions can serve as a precursor for federally funded programs that promote kinship care foster programs, that respect cultural identity and tradition (NABSW, 2003).

> **Self-Development**

Understanding and Mastery: Clarification of personal and professional values

Critical Thinking Question: What are some ways that your personal background and values, particularly with regard to race may impact your perspectives on whether it is appropriate to place children of color in Caucasian homes?

Ultimately, the placement of children of color in the homes of members of the majority culture can be framed as a violation of human rights of the historically oppressed ethnic minority communities. The rationale for this stance is that Caucasian adoptive families are members of a majority culture that is collectively responsible for the historical oppression and social exclusion that in large part has resulted in the psychosocial issues involved in the breakdown of family and social structures in many ethnic minority homes and communities in the first place. This perception doesn't necessarily provide solid answers for children of color who are in need of loving homes, but it provides a paradigm for understanding this social problem in a way that both acknowledges and respects historical aggressions against ethnic minority populations, particularly African-American and Native American communities. Additionally, this framework provides a direction for advocates to head in developing policies and practice approaches that will focus on maintaining integrity within the communities of color. For instance, programs focusing on the recruitment of more ethnic minority adoptive homes, family preservation programs that address psychosocial issues within ethnic minority communities that have as their roots the historical oppression and racism that have been referenced in this section.

JUVENILE JUSTICE: CHARGING CHILDREN AS ADULTS Another area in which children need advocacy is in the juvenile justice system. There is a comprehensive alternate criminal court system for youth, based on the belief that youth are different from adults in a whole host of ways (psychologically, developmentally, biologically, etc.), Thus, youth need to be treated differently with regard to how culpability is perceived, as well as how consequences are meted out. For instance, within the juvenile justice system, the focus on rehabilitation is based on the belief that youth do not have the same intellectual reasoning ability as adults, or the same capacity for considering reasonable consequences for their behavior. Early in American history, criminal laws were based on English common law, which placed individuals in one of three categories: *infants* for children up to the age of seven (because they were deemed below the age of reason), *adults* for individuals over the age of 14 years (because they were deemed to be old enough to know the difference between right and wrong), and those in between, who fell into a gray area. Youth would fall into this middle category, being below the age of reason ("infants"), thus they would not be treated as an adult in the criminal court, or they could be treated as an adult, if the court determined that the youth understood the difference between right and wrong (Lawrence & Hemmens, 2008).

The first juvenile court was established in 1899 in Chicago, Illinois, as the result of the advocacy efforts of social reformers, Jane Addams and Julie Lanthrop. The concept of a separate court to deal with criminal infractions committed by juveniles caught on, and within a few decades, most states adopted a juvenile justice system. Juvenile courts allowed the state to act as the legal guardian of youth, if deemed necessary, with the goal of rehabilitation rather than solely punishment. Youth who engaged in repeated criminal activity were remanded to reform schools (now often referred to as residential treatment facilities), which allowed them to continue their education, while being rehabilitated (ABA Division for Public Education, n.d.). In the mid-1950s when the entire system of institutionalization of the mentally ill was for mental illness was being challenged in the United States, the institutionalization of "wayward youth" was challenged as well, and although the majority of Americans still believed that youth who broke the law should not be treated in the same manner as adults, overall faith in the juvenile justice system began to wane (Lawrence & Hemmens, 2008).

In the 1960s and 1970s, a shift occurred due to increased concerns about how youth were being treated, particularly the ongoing institutionalization of youth who were engaging in criminal activity on all levels, as well as how the informality of many juvenile courts were eroding juvenile legal rights. For instance, since youth were not treated as adults, they were not afforded similar rights in the court process. As a result of this growing concern within U.S. society, there were a number of U.S. Supreme Court decisions that increased the formality of the juvenile justice system in numerous respects. For instance, the courts determined that youth had the right to receive fair treatment under the law, including the right to receive official notice of all criminal charges, the right to obtain legal counsel, the right to confront their accusers, the right to cross-examination, the right to avoid self-incrimination, the right to a full transcript of any proceedings, and the right to an appellate review of their case. The motivation behind these decisions was to provide greater protection for youth. Other legislative actions included the passage of the *Juvenile Justice and Delinquency Prevention Act of 1974* (P.L. 93-415, 88 Stat. 1109), which set limits on the state's ability to institutionalize youth offenders and provided funding for community-based diversion programs. These reforms were based on the previously established principle that youth should not be held to the same standards as adults with regard to their level of understanding of right versus wrong, and their overall level of culpability for the crimes they committed since they were not yet adults, thus had not developed (cognitively and otherwise) to the level necessary to be able to reason as adults (ABA Division for Public Education, n.d.).

Yet, in the 1980s, this sentiment began to change, in large part due to the sharp rise in juvenile delinquency throughout the country, an increase that lasted through the mid-1990s. Juvenile arrests for rape, robbery, aggravated assault, and other serious felonies increased by 66% between 1980 and 1994, and juvenile arrests for murder increased by 167% during this same time period (Butts & Travis, 2002). This sudden and sustained increase in juvenile crime caught the attention of the entire country and ushered in a number of policy changes and legal reforms in attempts to address what Butts and Travis (2002) of the Urban Institute referenced as the public's fear of juvenile offenders, or what many referred to as "juvenile super predators" (p. 2). Starting in about 1992 (at just about the same time that juvenile crime started to decrease), most states in the United States made it easier to try juveniles as adults, especially for particularly egregious crimes, such as murder and other serious felonies. Some of these reforms included setting the upper age limit for juvenile court at 16 years of age (thus juveniles 16 through 18 years of age are charged as adults). In almost half of states, there are no minimum age thresholds where a juvenile cannot be charged as an adult, and by 2004, about a decade after juvenile crime peaked (it has now decreased considerably), 29 states had passed laws barring certain types of juvenile offenses from being handled by the juvenile court (in other words, certain crimes must be handled by adult criminal court, regardless of the age of the juvenile) (ABA Division of Public Education, n.d.).

At the heart of any argument about whether juveniles should be tried as adults is determining whether they have *diminished capacity* compared to adults. Advocates are concerned with at least two major issues regarding the evolution of the juvenile justice system. The first is whether youth who violate the law are being treated appropriately within the juvenile justice system. In other words, are the remedies being utilized reflective of the ways in which youth are different than adults? Are the remedies focused sufficiently on rehabilitation rather than punishment? Has the juvenile justice system finally found balance between providing juveniles all of the appropriate remedies mandated in the criminal court system (e.g., the right to due process, the right to know the charges against them, the right to legal counsel, the right to cross-examine), while maintaining the essence of a public service agency focused on rehabilitation? Second, are the remedies in juvenile court meted out equally? Are youth of all genders, races, religions, socioeconomic statuses, and sexual orientations treated equitably? Unfortunately, the answer to many of these questions appear to be no.

Research shows that race in particular is a delineating factor in whether a juvenile will be tried as an adult for a serious crime, with between 50% and 95% of all juvenile transfer cases involving African-American male youth, (97% of all transfer cases are male) who are lower socioeconomic (UCLA School of Law, 2010). A 2011 report on changing patterns for youth offenders in Missouri found that among all juveniles charged as adults in 2009, 64% were African American, double of that which was found in 2001 (Cooper, 2011). This appears to be reflective of an overall upward trend in juvenile cases, particularly in the last decade, toward charging youth of color as adults. For instance, three states automatically charge 16-and 17-year-olds as adults (Connecticut, New York, and North Carolina), and 10 states automatically charge 17-year-olds

A young African American boy is led into court where he is charged as an adult.

as adults (Georgia, Illinois, Louisiana, Massachusetts, Michigan, Missouri, New Hampshire, South Carolina, Texas, and Wisconsin) (Snyder & Sickmund, 2006).

A 2000 study that examined several jurisdictions across the United States found that 82% of all juvenile cases filed within a six-month period involved ethnic minority youth, including African American, Asian, Hispanic, and Native American, with African American by far constituting the largest percentage of all juvenile case transfers. The study also found that African-American youth were disproportionately charged with felonies, as well as being disproportionately charged as adults. In response to critics who may argue that African-American youth are simply committing more crimes, the study found that this was not the issue. Rather, the issue appears to be the charging decisions made by law enforcement. For example, the report cites a county in Alabama where African-American youth accounted for about 3 out of 10 felony arrests, but 8 out of 10 felony cases were filed in criminal court (Juszkiewicz, 2000).

More recent studies have found similar trends with Florida appearing to have one of the worst records of charging juveniles as adults, particularly black youth, with 54% of all juveniles with criminal cases transferred to adult court being black, compared to 29% who were white, and 12% who were Hispanic. In California and Arizona, among all serious juvenile crimes committed, the majority of cases transferred to adult court are those committed by Hispanic youth (Cooper, 2011). These statistics represent an overrepresentation of ethnic minority youth being charged with felonies (versus misdemeanors), and as an adult, despite the criminal offenses being committed by juveniles.

It is important to note that in many states, if a juvenile is charged with a felony, the case is automatically transferred to adult court; thus in addition to the issue of charging youth as adults, it is also important to consider the types of crimes youth are being charged with, and how such crimes are treated in the criminal court system, particularly with regard to racial disparity in charging decisions. For instance, it appears that African-American youth are about five times more likely to be charged with felony drug offenses, and prosecuted in adult court than white youth, despite similar behavioral patterns among both groups (Juszkiewicz, 2000). This is a very pertinent issue in consideration of very strict federal drug sentencing mandates, as well as state policies in how drug offences are handled. For instance, Illinois requires that all drug offenses committed by youth as young as 15 be transferred to adult court (UCLA School of Law, 2010).

It is also important to note that in many jurisdictions even relatively minor drug offenses are required to be charged as felonies due to federal sentencing mandates, thus it would be interesting to note whether white youth committing the same types of drug crimes as African-American youth are charged with lesser crimes. Another issue for advocates to consider is the type of legal counsel retained by juvenile offenders, and whether this impacts the ways in which criminal cases are handled. For instance, Juszkiewicz (2000) found that white youth were twice as likely to retain private legal counsel (versus being represented by a public defender), and cases handled by private legal counsel were less likely to be convicted, and far more likely to be transferred back to juvenile court. Similarly, black and Hispanic youth were far more likely to receive stricter sentences, which included incarceration, versus white youth, who were far more likely to receive probation. Similarly African-American youth are more likely to be charged with felonies and transferred to adult court (Arya & Augarten, 2008), and Native American youth are far more likely to be incarcerated in federal prison as adults (Arya & Rolnick, 2008).

There are very serious consequences of trying juvenile criminal offenders as adults, including being subject to adult penalties, including life without parole. They will receive little, if any, education, mental health treatment, or rehabilitation of any kind (since the adult prison system in the United States is based upon a punitive system, not a rehabilitative one). They will have an adult criminal record, which will severely affect their ability to receive an education due to limitations on federal financial aid, as well as limiting their future employment opportunities. They are at far greater risk of serious assault, and even death, when incarcerated alongside adults in an adult prison environment. Finally, being charged as an adult and serving time in an adult prison significantly increases the likelihood of recidivism (reoffending) (Arya & Augarten, 2008; Arya & Rolnick, 2008; Juszkiewicz, 2000; Snyder & Sickmund, 2006; UCLA School of Law, 2010).

> Assess your comprehension of Contemporary Child Welfare: Advocating for Vulnerable Children by taking this quiz.

Global Advocacy Practice: International Human Rights Violations against Children

Human Rights Violations against Children on an International Level

The human services professions evolved out of a firm commitment to meeting the needs of vulnerable and marginalized populations by using an ecological systems approach that considers the environmental context within which the individuals and communities function. Recognizing the reciprocal relationship between the individual and environmental forces lays a foundation for culturally competent intervention on both a micro and macro level. In addition to a commitment to culturally competent contextually sensitive intervention, the profession of social work is committed to advocating for social change in a manner that values and engages communities, a legacy begun by Jane Addams whose Settlement House Movement recognized the importance of meeting the needs of vulnerable populations within their own communities (Johnson, 2004). These foundational values and practice strategies place human services professionals in the unique position of being able to significantly contribute to finding solutions to many of the broad-based social problems currently plaguing the international community.

Unfortunately, the human services professions have gradually moved away from its social advocacy and community action, turning instead to a model of individualized care (Mizrahi, 2001). As those in the human services fields withdrew from macro-level work such as policy practice and other forms of advocacy, other disciplines have moved in to fill the gap, such as urban and public planning, the political sciences, and international studies disciplines. This professional shift has resulted in the human services professions often being out of the loop of community building and organizing efforts (Johnson, 2004), particularly on an international level. Concerns have also been expressed regarding macro and community practice being neglected in human services educational programs compounding the tendency for human services professionals to avoid macro practice since many recent graduates feel ill-equipped to enter into social advocacy or policy practice on an organizational or policy level (Polack, 2004; Weiss, 2005).

Human rights workers dealing with social problems affecting children in many countries in the Global South must be equipped to both understand and manage complex situations, some involving a long history of micro and macro interplay where governmental policy, cultural practices, and environmental forces frequently come together to create human rights crises effecting millions of vulnerable and marginalized populations requiring a cooperative international response. For social justice to be effectively achieved, human services professionals must once again find a place at the table working alongside other relevant disciplines, coordinating efforts with such human rights NGOs as Amnesty International and the International Red Cross, as well as UN agencies such as UNICEF and UNHCR.

The United Nations Convention on the Rights of the Child

The United Nations has responded to child protection issues in a variety of ways, using the UN human rights treaty the Convention on the Rights of the Child (UNCRC) as a template for how children *ought* to be treated. The UNCRC was adopted in 1989 and enacted in 1990, and is considered by many international child welfare experts to be a powerful international treaty establishing and enforcing human rights for all children. Every country in the world has signed and ratified the UNCRC except the United States and Somalia. Both countries have signed but not ratified the treaty, and while Somalia announced plans in 2009 to ratify the UNCRC, it is unable to do so because it does not currently have a functioning government.

The UNCRC consists of 41 articles setting forth basic rights of children (defined as any individual under the age of 18 years) based on the "best interest of the child" principle, which places the needs of children, particularly in decisions relating to their care, as a primary concern above all other interests. The ultimate goal of the UNCRC is to protect the survival, health, education, and development of children securing their well-being (UNCRC, 1989).

The UNCRC guarantees children basic rights, including the right to live, to develop in a healthy manner (including the right to play and enjoy a wide range of child-appropriate activities), to have a legal name and identity that is registered with the government (such as a birth certificate), to reside with parents (as long as this is in the child's best interest), to have access to appropriate health care, to have an education, and to have an adequate standard of living free from profound poverty. Several articles also guarantee a child's freedom of expression including having a voice in choices that affect them (as is deemed developmentally appropriate), appropriate freedom of expression, privacy, and access to information, with indigenous children even having the right to practice their own cultural traditions. Children are guaranteed the right to protection, including protection from violence, child labor, exposure to the drug trade, including drug abuse, sexual exploitation, abduction, trafficking, excessive detention, and punishment.

Relevant to the discussion on family preservation, several articles of the UNCRC set forth the rights of children who for whatever reason cannot reside with their families, including the right to be cared for in a manner that respects their religion, ethnic group, and cultural traditions, and the right to have all aspects of the UNCRC applied to them regardless of their residential or family status (UNCRC, 1989). Clearly, the international community recognizes the value of the biological family unit and supports all governmental efforts designed to support families maintain their bonds, particularly with their children. Such support can be in the form of "family-friendly" policies, financial and case management support for kinship care (increased since the passage of the Fostering Connections to Success and Increasing Adoptions Act of 2008), as well as other measures that focus on prevention and preservation rather than solely intervention.

The UNCRC requires governments to take all necessary and possible steps to guarantee that the rights of children are protected and fulfilled. Particular action steps ensuring the implementation, monitoring, and enforcement of the UNCRC were developed at the *World Summit for Children* (the Summit) held at the UN headquarters in New York in 1990. This global summit was widely attended by the majority of world leaders and delegates who had ratified the UNCRC. Tasks at the Summit involved the development of the *World Declaration on the Survival, Protection and Development of Children and a Plan of Action.* This action plan included the development of 27 goals relating to the survival, protection, physical health (including nutrition), and emotional health of all children in accordance with the UNCRC. This plan essentially put the UNCRC into action on both a national and international level, including specifying timelines for the development and implementation of UNCRC rights, as well as setting forth enforcement and monitoring strategies (UNICEF, 1990).

Human Services Delivery Systems

Understanding and Mastery: International and global influences on services delivery

Critical Thinking Question: What are the strengths and weaknesses of the UNCRC as a framework for providing protection mechanisms for children within the context of the range of global crises?

Despite the widespread support for the UNCRC as indicated by its comprehensive and expeditious ratification by most countries in the world, children remain one of the most vulnerable and marginalized groups on a global scale, consistently at risk of exploitation (such as trafficking and child labor), poverty, war, famine, and serious health crises such as infant mortality and HIV/AIDS (Inter-Agency, 2004). In fact, despite the general improvement of worldwide conditions for children since the ambitious development of *Plan of Action* goals, several catastrophic events, such as the 2004 tsunami, and the AIDS pandemic have rendered thousands of children at significantly increased risk of peril. These crises, as well as several others have contributed to the growing group of children who for whatever reason are without parental or familial care and protection. Such unaccompanied or displaced children present challenges to the international community, as well as the respective governments charged with their protection. The UNCRC and *Plan of Action* have and should continue to provide guidance in how individual nation-states and the international community provide for the needs of such children in a manner that fosters their developmental growth and protects their human rights.

Orphaned and Vulnerable Children in Developing Countries

The United Nations defines unaccompanied children as those children who are "separated from both parents and are not in the care of another adult who, by law or custom, has taken responsibility to do so" (Michel, 2001, p. 17). Unaccompanied children, also referred to as orphaned and other vulnerable children (OVC), are at a far higher risk of harm including being killed, sexually exploited, exploited in labor, tortured, and recruited as soldiers (Michel, 2001), as well as being at significantly higher risk for mental health problems, including depression, posttraumatic stress disorder (PTSD), social maladjustment, and delinquency (Betancourt & Khan, 2008; Goodman, 2004). There has been growing awareness in the international community of the need for a consistent and profound response to the growing problem of unaccompanied children, both within developed countries (i.e., unaccompanied child asylum-seekers and child refugees), as well as within developing countries, particularly those experiencing significant life-threatening crises (Inter-Agency, 2004).

Developed countries, such as the United States and the United Kingdom, have established child welfare strategies in response to unaccompanied children (such as unaccompanied child asylum-seekers) based on "best interest of the child" principles inherent in the UNCRC that places such children in family-based care whenever possible (Bhabha, 2004). Developing effective policy and practice responses to the growing crisis of unaccompanied and vulnerable children in developing countries has become of increasing concern to the international community of late, particularly since the majority of unaccompanied children in developing countries will not gain asylum or refugee status (Inter-Agency, 2004).

UNACCOMPANIED CHILDREN Children in developing countries may be separated from their families and communities for a variety of reasons. Although some may leave voluntarily, many are orphaned due to the death of one or both parents from health crises including pandemics, famine or war. Or, they may be temporarily separated or displaced due to forced migration in response to war or natural disaster. Any child in an unstable region may be at risk of being kidnapped for the purposes of trafficking or forced conscription into war as is the case with child soldiers, but orphaned children are at particular risk of being trafficked or conscripted into armed conflict due to their vulnerable and unprotected status, and because they may not see any other means for their own survival (Inter-Agency, 2004; Leatherman, 2011).

Global poverty is a multidimensional social problem with complex causes and manifestations, including a range of preventable illnesses resulting in death, such as malnutrition and diarrhea. AIDS, a life-threatening disease found disproportionately in sub-Saharan Africa, has had a devastating effect on families, particularly children. The life expectancy has dropped from 61 years of age to 35 in many African countries having a profound effect on children and their childhoods, with an estimated 12 million

Nature disasters often leave unaccompanied children to fend for themselves in dangerous and unsanitary conditions, such as this child in Bangladesh.

Xander Martin

children having been orphaned due to one or both parents dying of AIDS (Ansah-Koi, 2006; Dhlembeu & Mayanga, 2006; UNAIDS, 2009; UNICEF, 2006;). In fact, in Zimbabwe alone UNICEF estimates that 30% of all children have been orphaned due to AIDS (UNICEF, 2006). Unfortunately, many countries in the Global South that are the most affected by the HIV/AIDS pandemic have neither the funding nor the infrastructure capacity to place child welfare issues as a priority (Dhlembeu & Mayanga, 2006).

Natural disasters are another type of crisis that often leave children either permanently orphaned or temporarily separated from their parents. The 2004 tsunami in the Indian Ocean hit Sri Lanka, Indonesia, India, and Thailand, killing approximately 225,000 people and separating thousands of others from their families. Of the survivors, thousands of children were either orphaned or temporarily separated from their parents. Since so many children in these countries do not have birth certificates reuniting separated children with their parents is often an impossible task despite attempts by governments and NGOs (Dhlembeu & Mayanga, 2006; Peek, 2008).

In the last two decades, there have been between 17 to 25 armed civil conflicts at any one time leading to civil unrest and instability in several countries in the Global South. In the midst of a civil war, civilians are often forced to flee in search of safety, a phenomenon referred to as *forced migration*. If armed groups invade or raid villages without warning, residents who are able to escape flee quickly, with family members often becoming separated. In these situations children are often displaced, as well as temporarily separated from their parents (Roby & Shaw, 2006).

During the late 1980s and early 1990s, Ethiopia experienced several episodes of famine, an ongoing civil war, and a national government-sponsored mass resettlement program, all of which resulted in unaccompanied children, some temporarily displaced and

Michelle Martin

Many children were orphaned in the wars in the DRC and now live in refugee camps under the supervision of the UNHCR.

others permanently orphaned. One Ethiopian NGO estimated that civil war, famine, and forced migration in Ethiopia lead to approximately 250,000 children becoming orphaned and another 24,000 temporarily separated from their parents. Subsequent resultant trends included a dramatic increase in street children, an increase in exploitative household child labor, and a significant increase in juvenile delinquency (Seelig, 1994).

A similar situation arose in Sudan in the 1980s where an estimated 17,000 children, some as young as three years old, fled their villages after parents and relatives were killed when their villages were raided in Sudan's long-raging civil war. Thousands of these children eventually found their way to a refugee camp in Ethiopia (Goodman, 2004). Unaccompanied refugee youth are at increased risk of abuse and exploitation, as well as being at increased risk of mental health problems (Goodman, 2004).

CHILD SOLDIERS   A civil war involving armed nonstate rebel groups often involve a host of human rights violations against innocent civilians, including the recruitment and forced conscription of child soldiers (Wagner, 2009). A child soldier is defined as "… any person below the age of 18 who is a member of or attached to government armed forces or any other regular or irregular armed force or armed political group, whether or not an armed conflict exists" (Child Soldiers Global Report, 2012, p. 8). The Coalition to Stop the Use of Child Soldiers (2012) estimates that tens of thousands of children are currently being used by armies and rebel groups for a variety of purposes including combat, scouting and spying, messengers, laying land mines, and sexual slavery (the plight of most girls forced into armed conflict).

The majority of children in armed conflict are forcibly conscripted by nonstate armed groups, although between 2004 and 2007 there were approximately 19 countries or regions where state-sponsored armies recruited children, the majority of which are

Young boys recruited by Liberian rebel forces.

Christophe Calais/Corbis

in Africa, Asia, and the Middle East. Some of the most notorious nonstate-sponsored armed rebel groups that utilize child soldiers include the Revolutionary Armed Forces of Colombia (FARC) and the National Liberation Army (ELN) in Colombia, and the Lord's Resistance Army (LRA) in Uganda (Child Soldiers Global Report, 2012). Although some children are kidnapped from parents for use as child soldiers, children who have already been separated from their parents through death or other crises are particularly vulnerable to being forcibly conscripted into armed conflict since they are often targeted by rebel groups as being unprotected and vulnerable.

Many regions have established official Disarmament, Demobilization, and Reintegration (DDR) programs responsible for the demobilization of former rebels, including child soldiers. DDR programs manage the care and reintegration of child soldiers into society (which may or may not include reuniting with their families), yet research indicates that many of these programs are underutilized due to stigmatization, underfunding, or even government discouragement. In many instances, governments treat former child soldiers as adults, with reports of children as young as 9 years old being detained by military or government forces and subjected to ill treatment and even torture (Child Soldiers Global Report, 2012).

TRAFFICKING OF CHILDREN Other situations involving children becoming separated from their parents include the millions who are victims of sex trafficking, often across international borders (Hodge & Lietz, 2007; Robb, 2006). The International Labour Organization (ILO) estimates six million children are held in slavery and used for forced work and in armed conflict (ILO, 2002). In Europe, Roma children, who come from an ethnic group with a long history of societal marginalization persecution, predominate in institutions or special schools for the disabled (Ahern & Rosenthal, 2006). Finally, Rwanda, Bosnia, Sudan, Cambodia, and other parts of the world remain in the grip of post-genocidal crises, burdened with the task for caring for hundreds of thousands of children orphaned because their parents were slaughtered, or died of post-conflict disease or other conflict-related environmental conditions.

Advocacy Efforts on Behalf of Orphaned and Other Vulnerable Children

The general consensus among child welfare professionals is that children who are unable to live with their parents for any reason are best cared for in a family-based community care placements since such placements support a child's psychological, cultural, social, spiritual, and physical developmental needs (Arieli, Beker, & Kashti, 2001; Dhlembeu & Mayanga, 2006; Singletary, 2007; UNICEF, 2006), where decision making is democratic and parenting authoritative (Wolff & Fesseha, 2005). Alternately, years of research studies clearly indicate that institutionalized care of children is not an optimal choice, due to its artificial nature and minimal opportunity for the forming of significant and intimate attachment to parental figures. Several studies have found that healthy child development is often negatively affected by institutional care due to diminished opportunity for healthy socialization and increased risk of emotional, physical, and sexual abuse, as well as other human rights violations (Dunn, Jareg, & Webb, 2003; Williamson, 2004). In fact, several studies have found that children placed in institutional or residential group care, particularly at an early age, are far more likely to become emotionally disturbed, experience social isolation, experience higher rates of delinquency (Leve & Chamberlain, 2005; MacLean, 2003; Wolff & Fesseha, 2005), have difficulty forming lasting relationships, experience social stigmatization within their communities, and have significant difficulty attaining and maintaining self-sufficiency in adulthood (Dunn et al., 2003).

Despite the evidence supporting the value of family-based community care for children, many developing countries, particularly in Africa and Asia have faced

Xander Martin

Children in residential care in a rural community in India.

significant challenges in developing effective and comprehensive child protection networks with the capacity to provide support for family-based community care with effective monitoring and evaluation of placements (Miller, Gruskin, Subramanian, Rajaraman, & Heymann, 2006). In fact, a study focusing on governmental policy and program efforts in several African countries with the highest number of OVCs affected by the AIDS crisis found that although many developing countries had made some movement toward establishing policies and programs designed to protect OVCs, most had done little toward enforcing those policies. Virtually all countries experienced challenges with sufficiently supporting family-based community care in any real way often related to problems with funding, cultural, and political issues (Monasch, Stover, Loudon, Kabira, & Walker, 2007).

Assess your comprehension of Global Advocacy Practice: International Human Rights Violations against Children by taking this quiz.

Concluding Thoughts on Advocacy for Children

The world is changing quickly, and some of these changes are positive and have the potential to create increased opportunities for children and their families, but some of the changes are not positive and are creating significant challenges for children, particularly those with increased vulnerability. For instance, the sharp increase in conflicts around the globe have rendered millions of children orphaned or half-orphaned, particularly in conflict zones, such as countries in sub-Saharan Africa. The HIV/AIDS pandemic has had a marked impact on children, leaving millions orphaned, with many raising younger siblings with minimal adult assistance. Children are also being trafficked into the sex trade and labor markets in rates higher than previous decades. While globalization has helped advocacy efforts, particularly the globalization of communication technologies, by making global advocacy easier than ever before, it has also created challenges to social justice achievement in many regions of the world that have suffered in response to the exploitation that is commonly associated with the globalization of economic markets. Social justice advocates may be facing what seems like insurmountable odds in addressing these overwhelming challenges, but with increased tools available (i.e., the Internet), there is also reason to be hopeful. The UNCRC has provided a standard to which advocates everywhere can strive to reach with regard to advocacy, and while the UN treaty system is a top-down approach and often faces significant challenges with implementation, it still gives advocates a place to start. Much more work needs to be done though, and this reality illustrates the need for more human services professionals committed to child welfare on a global level to work in the area of international human services on some level.

Assess your analysis and evaluation of this chapter's content by completing the Chapter Review.

CHAPTER 7

Advocacy for Lesbian, Gay, Bisexual, and Transgender Populations

HUMAN RIGHTS ARE MY PRIDE

The Fight for Equal Treatment

Nikolas Georgiou/Alamy

On June 24, 1973, the last day of Pride Weekend, an unknown arsonist started a fire in the stairwell of a gay bar called the Upstairs Lounge, located in the French Quarter of New Orleans. The Metropolitan Community Church, the first lesbian, gay, bisexual, and transgender (LGBT) church in the United States, was holding a fundraiser at the bar that night, thus the club was crowded. The fire spread quickly, and since the fire was started in the stairwell, the bar's only exit was blocked. Thirty-two men died as a result of the fire, and 15 more were injured, some caught between the bars on the windows in an attempt to escape. The tragedy was compounded by local and national silence, including numerous churches that refused to hold a memorial service for the victims, and families that refused to claim the bodies of their loved ones because of embarrassment about their sexual orientation. This attack against LGBT people remains one of the deadliest in U.S. history.

On June 24, 1984, four friends, Timothy White, David Rogers, Donnie Clanton, and Doug Barr, all 21 years old, drove 40 miles to San Francisco for the sole purpose of "gay bashing." After attacking four men who the group identified as gay, they approached 40-year-old Dennis O'Connell and punched him in the face, causing him to hit his head on a curb. He died 10 days later. Witnesses heard one of the men yell, "Let's go beat up some Faggots!" before engaging in the attacks (Brewer, 1986).

On October 6, 1998, at around 8:00 p.m., 21-year-old gay Wyoming college student Matthew Shepard was kidnapped by two men, driven to a remote area, tied to a fence and beaten ruthlessly, and left for dead. The perpetrators, both 21-year-old locals, saw Shepard in a bar and pretended to be gay in order to gain Shepard's trust.

On December 13, 2008, a 28-year-old woman was attacked and gang raped by four men who sought her out solely because she was a lesbian. According to Richmond, California police, the victim was living openly as a lesbian, with a partner and had a rainbow sticker on her car. Her attackers, ranging in age from late teens to early 30s, admitted that they targeted her because of her sexual orientation. The attack lasted for 45 minutes, and during the beatings and rapes, the men used numerous insulting epitaphs referencing the victim's sexual orientation, ultimately leaving the victim naked and almost unconscious outside of an apartment complex.

The only commonality among these individuals is their sexual orientation. Another variable shared by most of the victims is the apathy expressed by witnesses, and sometimes, even social institutions that were charged with the responsibility of serve and protect. As a society, U.S. society has come a long way—from perceiving certain sexual orientations as illegal and members of the LGBT population as mentally ill, and from a society that sanctions crimes against the LGBT population as an understandable reaction to perceived "perversion," to a society that has at least on some levels allowed for a moderate level of mainstreaming of the LGBT population. We have Ellen DeGeneres, who while having experienced backlash for admitting she was a lesbian, is now a highly respected advocate and daytime talk show host and who has gained acceptance from populations historically resistant to sexual minorities. We have open debates on marriage equality and have made significant headway on providing protection to members of the LGBT population with the inclusion of sexual orientation in hate crimes' legislation. But advocates acknowledge that we still have a very long way to go in advocating for a population that has been marginalized and subject to discrimination and persecution for generations.

This area of advocacy is particularly complex because discrimination against the LGBT population extends far beyond the mistreatment of sexual minorities, as it includes the mistreatment and marginalization of many heterosexuals as well who are singled out because they do not conform to expected gender roles—men who think and act in ways considered more traditionally female, and women who think and act in ways that are considered more traditionally male. Thus, while throughout this chapter the term *LGBT* is used to refer to a diverse population of individuals who experience some level of same-sex attraction or who have a self-identity that does not conform to their biological gender (as is the case with transgender people), the dynamics addressed within this chapter also include issues related to conventional gender role expectation and gender role conformity. This is important to note since many hate crimes are committed against individuals who are *perceived* as gay or lesbian solely because they do not conform to traditional gender role expectations.

Terminology: The Importance of Words

Words and labels are important. They reflect attitudes, sentiments, and values. They also reflect societal acceptance and stigmatization. It is for this reason that I want to spend some time being explicit about the descriptive terms I am using in this chapter. Many labels have been used to describe a population of individuals who have a same-sex attraction and/or divergent sexual identity. Some terms that were once considered mainstream are now considered offensive to the gay and/or lesbian community. Using terminology that is not considered derogatory and offensive is the first step toward bridging differences and misunderstandings between diverse populations within society. As such I have taken great care to use terminology that is not offensive to the gay and/or lesbian population, and thus within this chapter I have adopted terminology endorsed by the Gay and Lesbian Alliance against Defamation (GLAAD), a highly respected advocacy organization.

According to GLAAD (2010), the term *homosexual* is an outdated clinical term that is considered offensive to many within the gay and/or lesbian population, yet is still consistently used in scholarly writings. Other offensive and derogatory language includes *homosexual relations, homosexual couple, homosexual lifestyle* or *gay lifestyle, homosexual agenda* or *gay agenda*, and *sexual preference*. GLAAD notes that these terms are often used by antigay advocates and extremists, and inaccurately reflect that sexual orientation and gender identity is a choice, and diverse sexual orientation is biologically or psychologically pathological. Rather than using the term *homosexual*, GLAAD suggests the terms *gay* and *lesbian*, terms used to describe individuals who have an enduring attraction to members of the same sex. Rather than using the term *sexual preference*, GLAAD (2010) suggests using the term *sexual orientation*, which reflects an individual's physical, psychological, and romantic attraction toward others, either the same sex or the opposite sex. Rather than using the term *gay* or *homosexual lifestyle*, GLAAD recommends using the term *gay lives* or *gay and lesbian lives*, which reflects diversity in the gay and lesbian community.

A very common acronym designed to be inclusive of the various orientations to sexuality and gender is LGBT (or GLBT), which stands for lesbian (women with an enduring attraction to women), gay (men with an enduring attraction to men), bisexual (people who have an enduring attraction to both genders), and transgender (people whose gender identity and/or expression is different from their assigned sex at birth). Sometimes this acronym is reflected with a "Q," (LGBTQ), where *Q* represents either queer (a pejorative that has been incorporated into the vernacular of some members of the LGBT community), or questioning (which refers to people who are questioning their sexual orientation or gender identity). In this chapter, I use the acronym *LGBT* as an umbrella term, reflecting inclusiveness and diversity within the community, except when I am referring to youth, where I use the acronym *LGBTQ* to reflect the increased hostility toward youth who are questioning their sexual orientation and gender identity. Also, while I avoid the terms *homosexual* and *homosexuality* as much as possible, in certain contexts I have found that I must use these terms for the purposes of clarity, particularly when exploring historic perspectives and attitudes toward the LGBT population. When I have used these terms, I have enclosed them in double quotations as an indication of unusual usage to denote my recognition that these words are not being used in a commonly accepted manner.

The Marginalization of the LGBT Population: Human Rights Violations on a Local and Global Level

Historically, individuals (primarily men) who were perceived as "homosexual" were considered sinful and immoral, committing what were perceived as unnatural acts, referred to as either sodomy or buggery. Men who were suspected of engaging in

Anita Bryant, a singer and television personality, and Evangelical Christian became a celebrated anti-gay activist in the 1970s when she headed up a political coalition called Save Our Children, Inc. The coalition worked to overturn a county ordinate in Florida, Bryant referred to as the "Metro Gay Blunder" that banned discrimination in housing and employment based on sexual orientation

"homosexual behavior" were often subjected to inhumane and unscientific examinations of their anuses in an attempt to determine if sexual intercourse with another man had occurred (this type of examination is still occurring in some parts of the world). In fact, not only was "homosexual activity" criminalized in the United States, it was considered a mental disorder by the American Psychiatric Association (APA) up until 1973.

In the first Diagnostic and Statistical Manual of Mental Disorders (DSM) published in 1952, "homosexuality" was considered a "sociopathic personality disturbance," and in the DSM-II published in 1968, it was considered a "sexual deviation." In 1973, after considerable debate, the APA made a compromised decision to remove "homosexuality" from the DSM and replace it with "sexual orientation disturbance" (SOD) to reflect the consensus of the APA that those who experienced clinical distress in response to their "homosexual orientation" were deemed to be suffering from a mental disorder, whereas those with a "homosexual orientation" who did not experience distress in response to their sexual orientation were not considered mentally ill (Spitzer, 1973). The controversy surrounding this decision centered on the argument that members of the LGBT community who may have experienced distress in response to their sexual orientation, likely did so because of societal stigmatization of "homosexuality," not because they were psychologically disordered.

The DSM-III published in 1987 replaced the SOD classification with "ego-dystonic homosexuality," defined as "a sustained pattern of overt homosexual arousal that is a source of distress" (3rd ed., rev.; DSM–III–R; American Psychiatric Association, 1987), but the revised version omitted all references to pathology in relation to one's sexual orientation because some initial distress in response to coming out (a term used to describe an individual openly admitting he or she is gay and/or lesbian) was deemed normative. These latter shifts in the attitudes of APA members were in large part due to the fact that more psychiatrists who were lesbian and gay were serving in decision-making roles and advocated strongly for the DSM to remove all references to sexual orientation, in particular references to "homosexuality" as a mental disorder (Krajeski, 1996). In addition, scientific evidence simply did not support the position that same-sex attraction and relationships were the result of pathology (Hooker, 1956, 1957).

Preceding this shift by the APA were the Alfred Kinsey studies on homosexuality in the 1940s and 1950s that found that homosexuality was not an either/or proposition but rather that sexual orientation occurred on a continuum. In fact, Kinsey created a scale where subjects rated their sexuality from 0 to 6, with 0 representing "exclusively heterosexual with no homosexual," and 6 representing "exclusively homosexual with no heterosexual," and each interim rank represented a graduated movement toward the "opposite orientation" (i.e., a rank of 2 represents "predominantly heterosexual, only incidentally homosexual," etc.). In describing this orientation continuum and what became known as the "Kinsey Scale," Kinsey stated:

> Males do not represent two discrete populations, heterosexual and homosexual. The world is not to be divided into sheep and goats. It is a fundamental of taxonomy that nature rarely deals with discrete categories ... The living world is a continuum in each and every one of its aspects. (Kinsey, Pomeroy, & Martin, 1948, p. 639)

> **Professional History**
>
> *Understanding and Mastery: How public and private attitudes influence legislation and the interpretation of policies related to human services*
>
> **Critical Thinking Question:** What are some of the reasons why it's important for advocates to be aware of historic incidences and trends of discrimination and marginalization of the LGBT population?

Although "homosexuality" has been declassified by the APA and many other mental health organizations, the social stigma remains, with many in the United States and certainly countries around the world continuing to believe that the "homosexual lifestyle" is disordered, demented, unnatural, and, generally, morally deficient. Just consider the arguments leveled against marriage equality (which will be discussed in more detail later in this chapter). The most common argument leveled by many within conservative religious organizations is that homosexuality is that a societal endorsement of same-sex marriage distorts biblical truth since homosexuality, according to the bible, is a sin. Focus on the Family, a conservative evangelical parachurch organization refers to attempts to change biblical interpretations of homosexuality and the definition of marriage as pro-gay revisionist theology, arguing that it "violates God's intentional design for gender and sexuality" (Focus on the Family, 2008, ¶ 4). It is important to note that while Focus on the Family has been a vocal opponent of normalizing homosexuality and marriage equality, it also cautions its readers to treat those in the LGBT community with love and compassion, stating on its website:

> There is no place for hatred, hurtful comments, or other forms of rejection toward those who experience same-sex attraction or identify themselves as gay, lesbian or bisexual. Because we humans are made in the image of God, Jesus teaches us to regard all humanity as having inherent value, worth and dignity. This includes those affirming or adopting labels or behaviors which we believe the Bible associates with sexual sin. The priority of love for the Christian is unquestionable, and the cause of love is advanced by telling the truth with grace and compassion. (Focus on the Family, 2013, ¶ 2)

This attitude of compassion is certainly not the case though for members of the Westboro Baptist Church (WBC), in Topeka, Kansas, founded in 1955, and led by Pastor Fred Phelps. This church, while professing to be an old school Baptist church, appears to exist solely to condemn the LGBT community, express hatred for them, and make known God's hatred for all "homosexuals." WBC argues that any theology that suggests that God loves everyone, or Jesus died for everyone's sin is based on lies. Many in the United States may be familiar with this church's tradition of picketing soldiers' funerals with signs stating "God Hates Fags!" and other profane messages. While the connection between "homosexuality" and the armed services is not clear, Phelps claims that God is killing American soldiers because of America's increasing tolerance of the "gay lifestyle." Featured prominently on its website is the following statement:

> WBC engages in daily peaceful sidewalk demonstrations opposing the homosexual lifestyle of soul-damning, nation-destroying filth. We display large, colorful signs containing Bible words and sentiments, including: GOD HATES FAGS, FAGS HATE GOD, AIDS CURES FAGS, THANK GOD FOR AIDS, FAGS BURN IN HELL, GOD IS NOT MOCKED, FAGS ARE NATURE FREAKS, GOD GAVE FAGS UP, NO SPECIAL LAWS FOR FAGS, FAGS DOOM NATIONS, THANK GOD FOR DEAD SOLDIERS, FAG TROOPS, GOD BLEW UP THE TROOPS, GOD HATES AMERICA, AMERICA IS DOOMED, THE WORLD IS DOOMED, etc. (WBC, 2013, ¶ 2).

WBC's hateful theology contributes to the stigmatization of the LGBT community by scapegoating them for all that is wrong with the world, including God's apparent wrath and condemnation. In fact, the WBC website makes this sentiment abundantly clear with its accusation that "the modern militant homosexual movement [...] pose[s] a clear and present danger to the survival of America, exposing our nation to the wrath of God" (¶ 3). Unfortunately, despite mainstream America's clear disdain for the WBC

Protesters led by Fred Phelps, of the Topeka, Kansas Westboro Baptist Church protesting at Lance Cpl. Snyder's funeral at his funeral service.

Jed Kirschbaum/Newscom

"family," the perspectives of its militant members, likely contributes to the scapegoating of the LGBT population for everything from the downfall of society to God's apparently abandonment of America.

Homophobia

Many of the hateful acts committed against the LGBT population can be better understood if viewed through the lens of homophobia. The term *homophobia* was first introduced in 1972 by George Weinberg, American psychotherapist, in his revolutionary book *Society and the Healthy Homosexual*, although he actually coined the phrase in the late-1960s. Weinberg's conceptualization of homophobia in essence turned the conceptualization of "homosexuality" as a mental disorder on its head in the sense that he proposed that it wasn't the "homosexual" who had the problem, but those who experienced an irrational prejudice against "homosexuals" and "homosexuality" that were suffering from some sort of psychological disorder. Weinberg discussed his experience with colleagues who were supposedly liberal and progressive but refused to socialize with members of the LGBT community due to a sense of dread that could not be explained rationally. He included this irrational dread, hostility toward, and prejudice against "homosexuality" in the same category as other phobias, due to the heightened sense of anxiety people exhibited at the thought of being in close quarters with "homosexuals" (Weinberg, 1972 as cited in Herek, 2004). In explaining his concept of homophobia, Weinberg states:

> I coined the word homophobia to mean it was a phobia about homosexuals.... It was a fear of homosexuals which seemed to be associated with a fear of contagion, a fear of reducing the things one fought for—home and family. It was a religious fear and it had led to great brutality as fear always does (Weinberg, 1972 as cited in Herek, 2004, p. 7).

According to Herek (2004), Weinberg's conceptualization of homophobia represents a true milestone in LGBT advocacy because

> [i]t crystallized the experiences of rejection, hostility, and invisibility that homosexual men and women in mid-20th century North America had experienced throughout their lives. The term stood a central assumption of heterosexual society on its head by locating the "problem" of homosexuality not in homosexual people, but in heterosexuals who were intolerant of gay men and lesbians. It did so while questioning society's rules about gender, especially as they applied to males (p. 8).

Weinberg's work in the area of homophobia was instrumental in effecting a change in attitudes within the APA, and his advocacy significantly contributed to the APA's 1973 decision to declassify "homosexuality" as a mental disorder. Weingberg's conceptualization of homophobia was an excellent first step in combating social injustices experienced by the LGBT population by "framing prejudice against homosexuals as a social problem" (Herek, 2004, p. 8). Yet, while Weinberg's conceptualization of homophobia significantly advanced LGBT advocacy, the term *homophobia* is now perceived as somewhat limited in the sense that it does not capture the totality of oppression the LGBT community has experienced that is rooted in stigma, sexual prejudice, and antigay hostility, thus contemporary conceptualizations of antigay attitudes and behaviors is far broader (Herek, 2004, 2009).

In the years since Weinberg's work, the stigmatization of LGBT people have declined considerably. For instance, in a recent Gallup poll 64% of people surveyed reported believing that gay or lesbian relations between consenting adults should be legal, compared to 43% in 1977. Eighty-nine percent of people polled reported believing that gay and lesbian people should have equal rights in terms of job opportunities, compared to 56% in 1978. This same Gallup poll also revealed a shift in how people viewed same-sex attraction, where in 1977 only 13% of people polled reporting a belief that people are born gay or lesbian, and 56% of people polled reporting that people become gay and lesbian through their upbringing. By 2012 these percentages had shifted to 45% and 36%, respectively.

Hate Crimes against the LGBT Population in a Western Context

Despite increased acceptance of LGBT people, hate crimes against the LGBT population are on the rise in the United States. In fact, according to the Federal Bureau of Investigations (FBI), hate crimes against those perceived to be gay or lesbian increased to over 20% of all documented hate crimes in the United States, representing an increase over 2010. This increase (see Figure 7.1) makes sexual orientation the second most common target of hate crimes in the United States, over religion, ethnicity/national origin, and disabilities (race remains the largest target of hate crimes in the United States).

In addition to an increase in the number of hate crimes in the United States is the fact that according to research, the level of violence in crimes against sexual orientation and gender identity–related crimes is considerably higher compared to hate crimes in response to other types of difference (Dunbar, 2006). For instance, the majority of hate crimes committed against LGBTs, or those perceived to be LGBT are against the person, not property and include physical assault, harassment, and intimidation. Also, the majority of hate crime murders committed in the United States were committed against members of the LGBT population (Marzullo & Libman, 2009). In fact, a recent national poll found that over 50% of LGBT people report being concerned about becoming victims of a hate crime, and of these, about one-quarter report being extremely concerned. This becomes even more meaningful when compared to that of the general population,

FIGURE 7.1
Number of Hate
Crimes by Bias Type

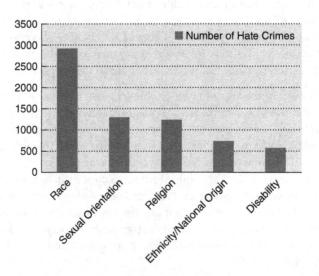

A gay rights demonstration in Northern Ireland.

where only about 6% people report being concerned about becoming a victim of a hate crime, and over half of the general population report no concerns at all about hate violence (Harris Interactive, 2006, as cited in Marzullo & Libman, 2009).

The recent passage of the Matthew Shepard & James Byrd Jr. Hate Crimes Prevention Act (P.L. 111-84) in the United States, signed into law in October 2009 by President Obama, makes it a federal crime to assault individuals because of their sexual orientation, gender, or gender identity. The passage of this somewhat contested legislation has been lauded by civil rights organizations as a significant step forward in the fight for equality and protection of the LGBT population, but far more must be done, particularly since hate crimes against LGBT people tend to be grossly underreported, particularly crimes that are highly violent (Human Rights Campaign, 2013).

Hate Crimes against the LGBT Population on a Global Level

The plight of LGBT people and people whose gender identity is questioned is quite bleak in many regions of the world. In many non-Western countries, same-sex relationships are illegal and may be punished with harsh prison sentences and even death. In addition, in many countries sexual minorities (LGBT people as well as those with nonnormative gender expression) are harassed and even tortured outside of the legal system, often by police, or others in positions of power. For instance, in Iran "homosexuality" is punishable by death (despite former president Mahmoud Ahmadinejad's 2007 assertion that there are no homosexuals living in Iran) (HRW, 2010a). In Senegal "homosexual conduct" is punishable by a minimum of five years in prison (HRW, 2010b).

Human Rights Watch (HRW) has reported on crimes against the LGBT population in Iraq, where death squads comb the country searching for men who appear gay. In what HRW describes as a "killing campaign," bands of armed men barged into private homes and abducted men who were perceived as gay, often for no reason other than

Two teenagers in Iran were executed due to perceptions that they were gay.

STR/AP images

they did not appear masculine enough. Evidence of torture was found on the discarded bodies, such as mutilated and severed genitals and glue injected into their anuses. HRW was informed that most of the death squads were from a militant militia group that openly denounces "homosexuality," professing effeminate men as a threat to society. The death squads have taken credit for the tortures and deaths, stating that they consider the killing as "social cleansing" (HRW, 2009, p. 4). Although these militia are from militant Islamic groups and may have been formed in response to a cleric's fatwa (order), neither the Iraqi government nor the Iraqi police have investigated the killings or made any arrests leading HRW and other advocates to believe that the government is not concerned about the actions of these death squads because they are targeting an undesirable and unsympathetic group.

South Africa is known for excessively high rates of violence, particularly against women, who are at risk of physical assault as well as rape (HRW, 2011). According to HRW, approximately 45% of all women in South Africa reported being a victim of rape, but in light of the fact that 8 out of 10 rape cases go unreported, it is quite likely that the actual number of female rape victims is significantly higher. In fact, in a recent study over 25% of men in South Africa admitted to having raped a woman, and many of them admitted to committing rape in gangs (Jewkes, Sikweyiya, Morrell, & Dunkle, 2009). Lesbians are particularly vulnerable to a type of rape called "corrective rape," which involves individual or gangs of men who rape women believed to be lesbians purportedly to teach them how to be more feminine. HRW's 2011 report on violence against black lesbians and transgender men reveals the high incidence of "corrective rape" against lesbian or women who do not conform to gender expectations. Often these rapes are brutal and may involve gangs of men beating their female victims, while calling them derogatory names. Several of the women interviewed by HRW reported being told by their rapists that they were being taught a lesson on how to act more like a woman.

South African men who rape lesbians often do so with complete impunity, confident that they will not be arrested, even if the victim does report the rape (although most often these rapes go unreported). These women are left not only traumatized and humiliated, but their rapes often leave them pregnant and HIV positive as well (HRW, 2011).

LGBT people in Saudi Arabia are often subject to public floggings and imprisonment for suspected homosexual behavior (Martin, 2014). In Egypt vice officers travel through towns in vans arresting as many as 100 men at a time for suspected "homosexual conduct." Many of these men were arrested because they knew what the word *gay* meant, a North American word assumed by Egyptian authorities to be known only by homosexual men. Men arrested on suspected "homosexuality" are then subject to severe beatings until they agree to sign arrest papers admitting to their "homosexuality." Signing these papers means a lifetime of certain harassment and refusing to sign them means certain death (Martin, 2014). In Jamaica LGBT people are often the targets of horrible human rights abuses, oftentimes fueled by the police who frequently invite bystanders to attack men suspected of "homosexual behavior." One incident reported to a human rights organization involved a man suspected of being gay who was attacked by police and ultimately beaten and stabbed to death in the middle of the street by bystanders who joined in the beating. Police in Jamaica also commonly stop individuals on the street who are suspected of being gay or lesbian. Once stopped, they are searched for any sign of "homosexual activity" such as condoms or lubricants. If these items are found, the men are often beaten and arrested (HRW, 2004).

Several countries in Africa, including Uganda and Nigeria, are currently considering antihomosexuality laws that would make "homosexual activity" illegal and

> ## Human Systems
>
> *Understanding and Mastery: Changing family structures and roles*
>
> **Critical Thinking Question:** The high rate of sexual violence in South Africa is alarming, particularly to social justice advocates. What are some of the underlying reasons why certain men in South Africa rape women they perceive do not conform to gendered female norms?

DESRUS BENEDICTE/SIPA/Newscom

A October 2010 edition of a popular Ugandan newspaper that published a list of names, addresses, and photographs of 100 "homosexuals" alongside a yellow banner reading "Hang Them" punishable by brutal penalties, including death. What is particularly disturbing about this recent antihomosexuality trend in Eastern Africa are reports that some U.S. evangelical leaders are behind the effort to criminalize same-sex relationships, based on a belief that the "homosexual agenda" threatens the traditional family (Gettleman, 2010). Human rights organizations have expressed outrage in response to the reported link between antigay legislation in some African countries and a segment of the U.S. evangelical church for a variety of reasons, chief among them is the potential for dictatorships with poor human rights records using such legislation to silence (either through long-term incarceration or death) anyone who opposes their autocratic rule (HRW, 2009).

Assess your comprehension of the Marginalization of the LGBT Population: Human Rights Violations on a Local and Global Level by taking this quiz.

Advocacy on Behalf of LGBT Populations: The Fight for Equality

The Right to Serve

Historically, gays and lesbians were systematically discharged from the military if their sexual orientation was discovered. In December 1993, in response to mounting pressure to change this policy, the Clinton administration compromised by implementing *Don't Ask Don't Tell* (DADT), an official policy of the U.S. government that prohibited the military from discriminating against gay and lesbian military personnel, as long as they kept their sexual orientation as secret. In other words, military personnel could no longer investigate one's sexual orientation, but if a member of the military admitted to being gay or lesbian, he or she could legally be discharged from the military. DADT was repealed by Congress in December 2010 pending review by military leadership who were to determine the effect on military readiness, but in July 2011 a federal court of appeals ruling barred further enforcement of the policy, and it was officially repealed by President Obama in September 2011.

Despite this accomplishment, gay and lesbian military personnel are still subject to intermittent harassment and discrimination due to their sexual orientation and gender identity, and thus are still in need of advocacy. The advocacy organization OutServe-SLDN cites numerous examples of harassment of active duty personnel, and in 2011 began a campaign requesting that the president sign an executive order barring harassment and discrimination based on sexual orientation and gender identity, since the antidiscrimination provision of DADT was dropped from the bill prior to being passed by Congress. Although OutServe-SLDN has not been successful in this advocacy campaign, they have been quite successful in several others, including their legal advocacy, which is offered on an individual basis to active duty personnel and their families, as well as veterans who believe they have been victims of harassment and/or discrimination based on their sexual orientation and/or gender identity (see OutServe-SLDN's website at http://www.sldn.org/).

Marriage Equality

The right of same-sex couples to get legally married is currently a battle fought on both a federal and state level. In 1996 the Defense of Marriage Act (DOMA) was passed, which defined marriage on a federal level as a union between one man and one woman (DOMA, 1996). Section 3 of DOMA provided that, for federal law purposes, the term "spouse" referred to someone of the opposite sex (a husband or a wife), rendering same-sex marriage unrecognized at the federal level. What this meant is that same-sex couples who were legally married in a state that permitted same-sex married, were denied all federal rights and benefits reserved for legally married couples. This did not stop gay rights advocates from continuing their fight for marriage equality on a state-by-state basis.

Arguments for same-sex marriage are typically based on rights of equality. The GLAAD website lists several protections that marriage offers that are currently unavailable to the LGBT population in same-sex partnerships. These include automatic inheritance, child custody/parenting/adoption rights, hospital visitation, medical decision-making power, standing to sue for wrongful death of s spouse, divorce protections, spousal/child support, access to family insurance policies, exemption from property tax upon death of a spouse, immunity from being forced to testify against one's spouse, domestic violence protections, and more (GLAAD, 2010, ¶ 7).

Arguments against same-sex marriages are often based on religious values that hold homosexuality as sinful and unnatural, and define traditional marriage as being between a man and a woman. There also appears to be a general fear that the normalization of homosexuality will lead to the lowering of moral standards in a variety of respects throughout society. Yet, advocates of same-sex marriage confront religious arguments by citing research that disputes allegation that same-sex marriage will somehow dilute "traditional" marriage or harm children. They also cite the increasing acceptance among U.S. citizens of same-sex marriage and of homosexuality in general (according to a series of Gallup polls, in 2009, 63% of the U.S. population surveyed stated that they believed that same-sex couples should be able to marry or have a legal civil union, compared to 55% in 2004).

In May 2012, President Obama officially declared his support for marriage equality, citing his daughters' friends with same-sex parents and his recognition that he could not defend a position that would prohibit them from having the same right to legally marry as heterosexual parents. In March 2013, the Supreme Court heard oral arguments on two cases related to same-sex marriage. The first case relates to the constitutionality of the DOMA (PL 104-199), a federal law enacted in 1996 that defined marriage as a union between a man and a woman, thus barring same-sex couples from receiving marital

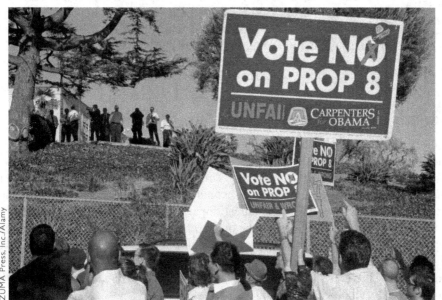

A group of voters demonstrating against the California Marriage Protection Act (Proposition 8), which amended the California constitution barring same-sex marriage. "Prop 8" has since been overturned by a U.S. District court.

benefits and federal protections, such as insurance benefits, Social Security survivors' benefits, immigration benefits, inheritance laws, and marital tax benefits (such as filing joint tax returns). DOMA also stipulates that no state is required to recognize same-sex marriages from another state. The second case relates to California's Proposition 8, the "California Marriage Protection Act," a ballot proposition voted into law in 2008 and California constitutional amendment that overturned the California Supreme Court's decision that made same-sex marriage legal in California. Proposition 8 (commonly known as "Prop 8") added a provision to the California Constitution that the only valid or recognized marriage in California was between a man and a woman (California Marriage Protection Act, 2008). A United States District court overturned Proposition 8 on the grounds that it was unconstitutional, and the U.S. Supreme Court agreed to hear oral arguments in December 2012. On June 28, 2013, the Ninth Circuit lifted its stay of the district court's ruling, enabling same-sex marriages in California, and on August 14, 2013 the court unanimously rejected challenges to Proposition 8, rendering it essentially dead. On June 26, 2013, the United States Supreme Court ruled DOMA Section 3 unconstitutional.

Human Systems

Understanding and Mastery: Processes to analyze, interpret, and effect policies and laws at local, state, and national levels

Critical Thinking Question: Why do many social advocates consider marriage equality a human right?

Many advocates of same-sex marriage argue that if laws such as California's Proposition 8 were voted on today, they would not pass because attitudes about same-sex marriage have changed within mainstream America. Recent Gallup polls show that American's perceptions of same-sex relationships have consistently reflected increasing acceptance in the last two decades in particular. In one Gallup poll asking whether gay/lesbian relationships were morally acceptable, 56% of respondents answered yes in 2011, compared to only 38% in 2002, and in a 2012 Gallup poll asking whether marriages between same-sex couples should be legally valid with the same rights as traditional marriage, 56% of those polled responded yes, that they should be considered legally valid with equal rights, compared to 27% in 1996 (the same year DOMA was signed into law). In 2008, the year that California Proposition 8 passed 40% of those polled about same-sex marriage responded in the affirmative, whereas 56% responded that same-sex marriage should not be legally valid (Gallup, 2011). Research conducted by the Pew Research Center shows a similar trend, with 57% of those polled in 2001 expressing opposition to same-sex marriage, and 35% expressing support, and in 2013 opposition to same-sex marriage dropped to 44% and support for same-sex marriage increased to 49% (Pew Research Center, 2013).

Assess your comprehension of Advocacy on Behalf of LGBT Population: The Fight for Equality by taking this quiz.

Advocacy for LGBT People from Special Populations

The vulnerability LGBT people experience to marginalization, injustice, and violence due to their sexual orientation and gender identity expression is magnified considerably with increasing levels of vulnerability. The theory of intersectionality (explored in Chapter 2), explores the interaction between multiple aspects of identity, such as gender, race, class, and sexual orientation, and their impact on social inequality (McCall, 2005). In the context of sexual orientation, the theory of intersectionality posits that societal oppression in the form of various types of social injustice, such as racism, sexism, ableism, ageism, and homophobia, do not act independent of one another, and in fact interact creating increasingly magnified forms of social oppression depending upon the number of vulnerabilities an individual possesses.

We already know from prior chapters that while all women experience some form of gender bias, an economically disadvantaged African-American woman will experience more social oppression than a middle-class Caucasian woman, because the into two identity categories of vulnerability (racial minority and poverty), but now add sexual orientation, a complex identity category, and the intersection of race, gender, sexual orientation, and perhaps gender identity expression will significantly increase this individual's vulnerability to social oppression, injustice, and likely bias-based violence (McCall, 2005; Meyer, 2012).

If the theory of intersectionality is applied to sexual orientation and gender-identity expression, then this means that social justice advocates must be even more vigilant when members of an LGBT community are also women, members of an historically marginalized ethnic minority group, experience economic disadvantage, are physically and/or mentally challenged in some manner, experience mental illness, are older adults, or are immigrants. On a global level, identity categories may also include caste level, geographic location, religious identity, ethnic group membership, and marital status. While exploring each area of identity vulnerability is beyond the scope of this chapter, I briefly explore a few key areas of increased vulnerability experienced by LGBT people who are members of other historically disenfranchised groups, including older adults, immigrants, and LGBT youth.

LGBT Older Adults

For years gerontology professionals working with the older adult population have ignored the needs of the LGBT older adult population (Shankle, Maxwell, Katzman, & Landers, 2003). Due to generational dynamics many older adults have never come out to family and friends, thus may be living secret lives, still fearing social ostracism and other forms of homophobia. LGBT older adults may experience greater levels of shame, than their younger "counterparts" and may have experienced considerably more discrimination and prejudice due to their sexual orientation, even if conclusions about their sexual orientation were based purely on speculation. Thus they are far likelier to be social cutoff, estranged from family and friends, be single, and childless (SAGE, 2010).

The specific needs of LGBT older adults are similar to heterosexual older adults, but are often magnified and include health-care needs, housing vulnerability, and economic instability. These needs are often magnified because LGBT older adults in same-sex partnerships have not been able to enjoy the same marital benefits of heterosexual married couples, such as inheritance laws, Social Security benefits, and domiciled partner health benefits (Altman, 1999). Social service and advocacy organizations that address the needs of the older adult population can better address the needs of LGBT older adults by bridging the gap between LGBT advocacy organizations and non-LGBT advocacy organizations, particularly because many older adults may not seek assistance from the former, due to fear of stigmatization (Shankle et al., 2003).

LGBT Immigrants

According to a recent report published by the Williams Institute, there are approximately 637,000 LGBT individuals among the adult documented immigrant population, the majority of which are Hispanic. This constitutes approximately 2.4% of the immigrant population in the United States. Additionally, there are an estimated 267,000 LGBT individuals living in the United States who are undocumented immigrants, which represents approximately 2.7% of the undocumented immigrant population. While these percentages may appear low, in reality these statistics reveal that almost one million immigrants living in the United States are self-identified as LGBT. Presumably the real number is much higher, in light of the high level of social stigmatization that occurs in the countries of origin of many of these immigrants.

In many respects LGBT immigrants face a substantially higher risk of homophobia, including societal oppression, social injustice, and bias-based violence due to xenophobia (the irrational fear of immigrants), and yet interestingly female immigrants who self-identified as lesbian typically have higher levels of education and higher levels of employment activity than do LGBT immigrants (Gates, 2013).

LGBT undocumented immigrants are at particular risk of economic insecurity and health-care inequities. Immigrant detention centers often fail to provide appropriate levels of protection for the LGBT undocumented immigrant population, particularly for those who are HIV-positive.

Areas of specific advocacy for LGBT immigrants include policies of keeping LGBT immigrants in isolation during detainment, marriage equality for binational same-sex couples, increased risk of sexual violence (particularly while being detained on alleged immigration violations), (Burns, Garcia, & Wolgin, 2013).

LGBTQ Youth

Students who are in the sexual minority, such as lesbian, gay, bisexual, transgender youth, and those students who are questioning their sexuality in some way (LGBTQ), are often the victims of bullying, including verbal harassment and physical violence. Many of these youth spend a considerable amount of time feeling different and isolated, often believing that no one will understand their feelings and accept them unconditionally (Martin, 2014). LGBTQ youth have an alarmingly high rate of suicide attempts, with over 30% admitting to having attempted suicide at some point in their lives. Also, approximately 75% of gay and lesbian students admit to having been verbally abused at school, and over 15% have been physically abused (Pope, 2003).

Most of the youth in Pope's study reported that the violence they experienced was a direct result of their sexual orientation, with boys being abused more often than girls. Pope discussed this type of abuse in terms of the pressure on most high school students to conform to the social norms of their peer group.

In 2009, the advocacy organization Gay, Lesbian, and Straight Educational Network (GLSEN) conducted a national survey of LGBTQ students on their experiences with the following issues:

- hearing biased and homophobic remarks in school;
- feeling unsafe in school because of personal characteristics, such as sexual orientation, gender expression, or race/ethnicity;
- missing classes or days of school because of safety reasons; and
- experiences of harassment and assault in school.

The results of the study found that a significant majority of LGBTQ youth experienced verbal and physical harassment on a daily basis in school, with little to no intervention or advocacy on the part of school personnel. For instance, between 75% and 90% of LGBTQ students surveyed heard homophobic terms used in a derogatory manner, such as *gay, dyke,* and *faggot* in school, which created immense psychological distress. Almost 85% reported that they had been verbally harassed at school due to their sexual orientation, and almost as many reported that they had been verbally harassed because of their gender-identity expression (not being feminine or masculine enough). About 40% of respondents reported that they had been victims of physical harassment at school because of their sexual orientation, and about 20% were physically assaulted. Over 50% of respondents were victims of cyberbullying and harassment through text messaging, emails, and social media. In most of these cases, there was little to no response on the part of school personnel, leaving the majority of these LGBTQ youth feeling very unsafe and unprotected. The consequences of this type of bias-based bullying is high and can include school avoidance and absenteeism, lower academic achievement, depression, anxiety, and lower levels of self-esteem.

GLSEN recommends that schools develop comprehensive programs to address homophobia in the schools, including the establishment of gay–straight alliance clubs (GSAs), inclusive curriculum (course curriculum that includes positive representations of LGBTQ people and events, currently and historically), supportive educators (training educators in LGBTQ awareness and advocacy), and the incorporation of strict bullying and harassment legislation and policies. Schools that had incorporated these remedies shows marked reductions in LGBTQ bias–based bullying (Kosciw, Greytak, Diaz, & Barkiewicz, 2010).

Assess your comprehension of **Advocacy for LGBT People from Special Populations** by taking this quiz.

Human Service Advocate's Response

Now that you have many facts associated with the plight of the LGBT population around the globe, what can you do? In addition to the suggestions included throughout this chapter, LGBT advocates stress a few actions that budding advocates can put into action immediately. First, social justice advocates must address their own feelings about the LGBT population, including any ambivalent feelings they might have about a need for advocacy on behalf of this population. Unfortunately, a 2009 study on social work attitudes toward the LGBT population found that 84% of social work students exhibited some level of homophobic attitudes toward the LGBT population, ranging from low homophobic to high homophobic. Those students with lower levels of homophobia were those who had friends, relatives, or acquaintances who were LGBT. The study also showed that female students and students who were more advanced in their studies tended to have lower levels of homophobic attitudes, reflecting the importance of socialization and the positive effect of education, if it includes material on sexual minorities (Kulkin, Williams, Boykin, & Ahn, 2009).

Those working in helper positions who may be in a position of advocating for the LGBT population can become more culturally competent by becoming more honest about their own attitudes, as well as gaining awareness about the issues and dynamics involved through professional and personal outreach efforts that will enable them to become more familiar with the experiences of LGBT people within different contexts. For instance, according to the Human Rights Campaign (HRC), an advocacy organization for the LGBT population, many within the LGBT population have had negative experiences with people of power in a variety of settings, including health care, thus they may be hesitant to disclose their sexual orientation, as well as same-sex behavior in a health-care setting out of fear of being stigmatized. HRC also suggests that a part of cultural competency includes increased sensitivity with regard to making appropriate referrals for the LGBT population. HRC also offers recommendations

The 5th Annual Miami Beach Gay Pride Parade on April 14, 2013 celebrated "Legacy couples"–members of the LGBT population who have been partnered for 20 years or longer. Ofelia Colunga & Betty Ortega have been together for 24 years. Legacy couples help dispel the myth that LGBT relationships are not enduring.

Jeff Greenberg/Alamy

on developing an open and nonjudgmental culture so that LGBT people will feel welcome and accepted.

There is also a greater need for social justice advocates to partner with international LGBT advocacy organizations to help combat harassment and violence against the LGBT population on a global scale. One way to do this is through assisting organizations in the preparation of global pride parade events, or even just attending a pride parade internationally, taking photos, and posting them to a social media website is an effective advocacy effort.

According to LGBT Movement Advancement Project (MAP), advocacy organizations currently addressing LGBT advocacy issues on a global scale include Amnesty International (International Secretariat), Anonymous, ARC International, Caribbean Vulnerable Communities Coalition/C-FLAG, Center for Women's Global Leadership, Equal Rights Trust, Front Line, Gender DynamiX, Global Rights, Heartland Alliance for Human Needs and Human Rights, Human Rights Watch, The Inner Circle, INTERIGHTS, International Commission of Jurists (ICJ), International Federation for Human Rights, International Gay and Lesbian Human Rights Commission, International Lesbian and Gay Association, ILGA-Europe, International Service for Human Rights, Press for Change, Sexual Rights Initiative, Sexuality Policy Watch, United and Strong, United Belize Advocacy Movement, and the World Organization Against Torture (for a complete list of international LGBT advocacy organizations, see the MAP report located at http://www.lgbtmap.org/file/international-lgbt-advocacy-organizations-and-programs.pdf).

Concluding Thoughts on Advocacy for the LGBT Population

Human services professionals and Human services professionals and social justice advocates around the globe are working tirelessly to reduce crimes against LGBT individuals through the passage of policies and legislation designed not only to protect individuals whose sexual orientation is not traditional but also to decriminalize homosexual behavior in all countries (Martin, 2014). It's difficult to imagine how or why any sane and decent person would condone abusive treatment of LGBT people, and yet advocacy efforts for this population do not tend to be broad-based. Could this be because mainstream America is unaware of the enormity of the problems facing the LGBT population, both in the United States and on an international level? If they became aware, would this awareness lead to a call of action on the part of the average heterosexual American? If not, why not?

Regardless of whether one considers same-sex attraction a lifestyle choice, a genetically predetermined orientation, a nontraditional sexual orientation no better or worse than heterosexuality, or an act of perversion and immorality, violence against someone based on their sexual orientation and gender-identity expression is never permissible under any conditions. Thus despite one's personal perspectives on issues relating to one's sexual orientation and same-sex relationships, all social justice advocates should be called to act to ensure that *all* individuals, despite their sexual orientation and/or gender-identity expression are treated with compassion, respect, and dignity.

Assess your analysis and evaluation of this chapter's content by completing the Chapter Review.

CHAPTER 8

Michelle Martin

Advocacy for Refugees and Migrants

· ·

Protection for Migrants on a Local and Global Level

Advocacy focusing on issues related to migration is complex and quite varied and is difficult to explore comprehensively in one chapter. In fact, there are entire books devoted to the subject of immigration that struggle to capture the comprehensive nature of this area of advocacy. Thus in this chapter, the goal is to provide a relatively cursory overview of the experiences of migrants within a local and global context, providing some examples of ways in which social justice advocates can make the migration process just a little bit easier, a little more straightforward, and a little less painful.

In this chapter I also explore the range of migration experiences and the need for advocacy by conceptualizing immigration in this way:

- Advocacy for political refugees within the context of *global forced migration* generated from conflict, and refugee resettlement primarily to the United States (including the political asylum experience); and
- Advocacy related to immigration focusing primarily on voluntary migrants, including authorized migrants through marriage, family ties and special skills, and unauthorized economic migrants to the United States, primarily from Latin America, (although it is important to note that immigrants entering the United States outside

of the refugee resettlement and political asylum process arrive from a wide range of countries outside of the Americas, including China and India), (Greenstone & Looney, 2010).

Refugees are often considered *involuntary immigrants* because they are limited in their decision-making processes, as they are forced into displacement most often due to conflict and are not given a choice of the country of resettlement, whereas all other migrants are often considered *voluntary immigrants* (including unauthorized immigration), because they have some decision-making power over leaving their country of origin and moving to a new country typically due to a lifestyle choice such as marriage or employment (Oliver-Smith & Hansen, 1982). Further, the adjustment process for involuntary migrants is considered a more challenging process due to their diminished power in decision making and at times a lack of desire to relocate (Gebre, 2002).

Categorizing immigrants as "voluntary" and "involuntary" while making sense on a variety of levels often fails to reflect the complex nature of immigration, including the often overlapping dynamics of each group (i.e., economic migrants who are escaping violence or life-threatening poverty in their countries of origin, political asylees who leave their country of origin voluntarily, but out of fear of persecution and/or death). Thus, it is important to note that while this chapter categorizes the migration experience into voluntary and involuntary, such classifications are somewhat artificial, and it should not be assumed that these categories are completely distinct.

Global Forced Migration and Mass Displacement

SUKREE SUKPLANG/Reuters /Landov

The Tham Hin refugee camp in in Thailand, along the Burmese/Thai border is one of nine UNHCR camps housing Karen refugees fleeing persecution in Burma (now called Myanmar)

Case Study 8.1
A New Life for Burmese Refugees

Candace and Stephan arrived at the airport just before the plane was landing. They were sent by the refugee resettlement agency to welcome Chicago's newest refugee family, the Phyo Pyaes from the Tham Hin refugee camp in Thailand. Phyo Pyae and his family—his wife and five children, ages 2 through 14, are members of the long-persecuted ethnic group, the Karen Burmese who fled from Myanmar (formerly Burma) decades ago to escape military rule. The Tham Hin refugee camp, where they have lived since 1997, was extremely overcrowded, and the conditions were quite poor. The camp has a very high crime rate and minimal services, despite being managed by the United Nations High Commissioner for Refugees (UNHCR). Phyo Pyae and his family lived in a one-room bamboo hut, and slept on grass mats. Their nutritional needs were not regularly met, thus Candace and Stephan have been told that the children may appear younger than they really are. Also, Stephan has been told to avoid direct contact with the women in the family since it is likely that they have all been victims of gender-based violence. The family moved into the camp when it first opened, thus they lived in the camp for over 15 years. Phyo Pyae's wife was pregnant with their first child when they entered the camp, which means that all five children were born in the camp and have known nothing else, but life in a refugee camp. Candace and Stephan were also told before heading to the airport that Phyo Pyae and his wife were civilians who were caught up in the major offensive against the Karen National Union (KNU), an ethnic group that has been fighting the Burmese dictatorship since 1949. Although Phyo Pyae was not a fighter, because he and his wife are members of the Karen ethnic group, they were forced to flee into Thailand along with about 1 million other Karen Burmese, seeking refuge. They received refugee status in 1999 when the UNHCR took control of the camps, which were initially developed by nongovernmental organizations (NGOs). Their path toward self-sufficiency will be a difficult one. Not only will they need to learn the English language, they will need to enter the workforce quickly because financial support for the U.S. refugee resettlement program has remained relatively stagnant, despite sharp increases in the influx of refugees. There will be little time for the family to adjust to U.S. society, let alone time to deal with their long-standing physical and psychological trauma. Their five children will likely face great challenges when entering the U.S. educational system, particularly since they never attended a formal school in the camp. But for today, all Candace and Stephan had to do was welcome the family to the country and drive them to their new apartment, filled with donations from a local church. The family looks intimidated and exhausted after their 26-hour flight. They have never been in a car before, and the youngest child cries when Candace attempts to put him in a car seat. The family knows they must trust these strangers, but trust is not something they have ever had the luxury of depending upon, in their 45 years on this earth. On the route to their new apartment, Candace and Stephan notice the looks on the family members' faces, but they aren't sure whether they are looks of awe or shock, or both. The primary responsibility of Candace and Stephan is to provide the family an orientation to their new apartment, which is challenging since the Phyo Pyae and his family do not speak English. They show the family how to turn the faucets on, how to flush the toilet (the camps do not have running water, or toilets), how to turn the shower on, and most important, how to turn on and off the stove. Candace touches the burner, making a pained expression on her face, and says "Ouch!" to signify that the stove gets hot. The family has never slept in beds and they all seemed to find the notion of the Western bed quite entertaining. But what was of most interest it seemed, especially to the kids, was the small tube television in the family room. Stephan showed Phyo Pyae how to turn the television and VCR on, and how to push the old VHS tape in. The kids screamed with delight when images of cartoon characters suddenly came to life. Before leaving, Candace confirmed that another Karen Burmese family, who had immigrated to the United States last year, would be bringing dinner for the family. When Candace and Stephan left, they both felt ill at ease about leaving the family with no working phone, and with no way to communicate that they would return the next day for their first case management meeting.

Refugees, IDPs, and Stateless Persons: Who Are They, Where Do They Come From, and Where Are They Going?

This case study, while fictionalized, illustrates several themes currently occurring within refugee situations and refugee resettlement, each of which involves various types of advocacy along the way. Factors such as *armed civil conflict, mass forced migration, protracted refugee situations* (PRS), and *refugee resettlement* into a host country were all a part of this vignette and will all be explored in more detail later in this chapter. Refugee resettlement has changed dramatically since the Cold War era, before the epidemic of armed civil conflict in Africa and southern Asia that has caused mass forced migration of millions across international borders, before the Internet that permits refugees to remain virtually connected with their home country and fellow countrymen and women, and before the September 11 terrorist attacks in 2001, which significantly altered U.S. immigration policy and general attitudes toward newcomers.

There are many reasons why people become refugees, but the primary cause of refugee displacement is conflict. The pattern of world conflict has changed considerably in the last few decades. As referenced in Chapter 1, there have been up to 33-armed conflicts in the Global South in the last two decades (SIPRI, 1993, 2008), which represents a shift from interstate conflict over territory, to armed civil conflict involving one or more rebel groups fighting against government forces. Often these newer conflicts involve ethnonationalism—loyalty to co-ethnics (versus nationalism, which involves loyalty to a nation-state) (Conversi, 2007). Conflicts that are ethnonationalist in nature tend to be far more violent (than traditional war), far more protracted, and involve numerous conflict cycles, meaning that the war doesn't have a beginning, a middle, and an end, but several cycles with no real end to the violence (Kahler & Walter, 2006). Related to this pattern of increased conflict is a new pattern in refugee flow, with an increase in refugees and political asylum-seekers migrating to host countries in the Global North.

Before exploring trends and dynamics related to refugees and their displacement experience, it is important to clarify what is meant by the terms most commonly used to signify an individual's migration status, since the various terms are legal in nature and not only specify elements of an individual's migration experience, but, in some circumstances, the rights a migrant may be entitled to on an international and national level.

Refugees are defined in international law as:

Any person who owing to a well founded fear of being persecuted for reasons of race, religion, nationality, membership of a particular social group or political opinion, is outside the country of his/her nationality and is unable, or owing to such fear, is unwilling to avail himself/herself of the protection of that country. (UN General Assembly, 1951)

In U.S. law a refugee is defined as:

(A) any person who is outside any country of such person's nationality or, in the case of a person having no nationality, is outside any country in which such person last habitually resided, and who is unable or unwilling to return to, and is unable or unwilling to avail himself or herself of the protection of, that country because of persecution or a well-founded fear of persecution on account of race, religion, nationality, membership in a particular social group, or political opinion, or (B) in such circumstances as the President after appropriate consultation [as defined in Section 207(e) of this Act] may specify, any person who is within the country of such person's nationality or, in the case of a person having no nationality, within the country in which such a person is habitually residing, and who is persecuted or who has a well-founded fear of persecution on account of race, religion, nationality, membership in a particular social group, or political opinion. The term "refugee" does not include any person who ordered, incited, assisted, or otherwise participated in the persecution of any person on account of race, religion, nationality, membership in a particular social group, or political opinion. (Immigration and Nationality Act, 2010).

> ## Professional History
>
> *Understanding and Mastery: Range of populations served and needs addressed by human services*
>
> **Critical Thinking Question:** What is the importance of making distinctions between different types of displacement?
>
> •

To be considered a "refugee" according to U.S. law, an individual must be referred by the UNHCR, a U.S. Embassy, or be a member of a particular group that has been granted priority status. Also, the individual must have fled across international borders, but not have been granted resident status or citizenship in that country. Further, the individual must not have an immediate relative who is a U.S. citizen (since this requires a different type of immigration process). The primary distinction between a refugee and a political asylum-seeker according to U.S. law is that the former receives refugee status prior to arriving in the United States, whereas a latter enters the United States (typically on another type of visa, such as a student or visitor visa), and then applies for legal resident status via the political asylum process, but must meet the same criteria as a refugee (Martin & Yankay, 2012). The UNHCR (2012a) definition of asylum-seeker is anyone who has sought international protection, but his or her refugee status has not yet been determined.

Internally Displaced Persons (IDPs) are defined as individuals, or groups of individuals who have been forced to flee their places of residence in response to armed conflict but have not fled across an international border. IDPs may also include situations involving general violence, natural disaster, or mass human rights violations. While the UNHCR recognizes a variety of reasons that individuals and groups may be internally displaced, they offer protection primarily to conflict-generated IDPs (versus disaster IDPs). In the past decade, the number global IDPs generated from conflict has remained relatively stable at between 24 and 27 million, but the number of IDPs that the UNHCR is responsible for protecting has increased significantly from around 4 million IDPs in 2001, to almost 16 million in 2011 (UNHCR, 2012a).

Stateless persons are defined by international law as people who are have no nationality. People become stateless for a variety of reasons, including situations where a nation-state ceases to exist, such as the case of the Palestinians living in Jordan (Human Rights Watch, 2010), and the Roma who have migrated throughout Europe for more than a century (Council of Europe: Commissioner for Human Rights, 2009). Another reason for statelessness relates to gender inequality, where women and their children are not granted nationality independently from men. According to the UNHCR, there are currently 40 nation-states that treat men and women differently with regard to granting nationality, with the rights associated with national nationality being severely limited where women are concerned (UNHCR, 2012b). Individuals who are stateless are often denied benefits that most of us take for granted, such as the ability to obtain a birth certificate, get a job, purchase a house, open a bank account, obtain an education, or access health care. They may also experience severe limitations in their ability to travel and may even be subject to detention for no reason other than the fact that they cannot provide documentation of their legal right to belong in any nation-state. It is for this reason, that statelessness is considered an international violation of human rights, and why the UN has made it a priority to reduce world statelessness, a priority articulated in the UN treaty, the 1961 Convention on the Reduction of Statelessness.

Assess your comprehension of Refugees, IDPs, and Stateless Persons by taking this quiz.

Global Trends in Forced Migration due to Natural Disasters

There are many reasons why people are forced to migrate, resulting in their official or unofficial status as a refugee, IDP, or stateless person. While the most significant dynamic involved in forced migration relates to conflict (explored in the next section), natural disasters also cause significant forced displacement around the globe (as well as the potential for considerable loss of life and property). Although many of these displacements are temporary in nature, not all are. In fact, many global situations involving extreme weather events, such as floods, tornados, hurricanes, and typhoons, and famines caused by drought, as well as non-weather-related disasters such as wild fires, and earthquake-related tsunamis, have resulted in millions of people being permanently displaced from their communities. (Williams, 2008).

A "natural disaster" is defined most commonly as an unexpected event that is contained in time and space (Fritz, 1961), that affects the majority of people in an affected community (Hossain, 2011), putting its members at extreme danger, causing significant loss (personal and environment), and the disruption in essential societal functioning (Fritz, 1961), at a level beyond the affected communities' capacity to respond (Hossain, 2011). Natural disasters also cause extreme collective stress due to the crisis nature of the event, often leading to significant psychological harm and life disruption among those affected by the disaster (Hossain, 2011).

In 2005 Hurricane Katrina hit the Gulf Coast of the United States resulting in 1,800 deaths, 1 million people being displaced, causing over $123 billion in damage. In 2012 Hurricane Sandy hit the Atlantic Basin, including New Jersey, resulting in 109 dead, 100,000 people being displaced, causing over $60 billion in damage to infrastructure and homes (Kaleem & Wallace, 2012). In December 2012 Typhoon Bopha hit the Philippines over a several day period resulting in over 2,000 deaths (some are still reported as missing), over 6 million people being displaced, causing over $584 million in damage to crops and infrastructure, including over 200,000 homes that were completely destroyed. As of March 2013, almost 850,000 people remained displaced. In December 2004, one of the world's largest recorded earthquakes, the Sumatra–Andaman earthquake, caused a series of tsunamis along the Indian ocean resulting in a death toll of almost 280,000 people across several countries, including Indonesia and Sri Lanka, almost 1.8 million people being displaced, and billions of dollars in damage and loss (resulting in over $14 billion pledged in humanitarian aid) (Jayasuriya & McCawley, 2010). According to the United Nations, more than 260,000 people died between 2010 and 2012 in the Somali famine, almost half of whom were children (UN, 2013). The famine has also resulted in over 1.5 million IDPs, as well as millions of dollars lost in cattle and lost productivity.

Disaster response and management has been defined in a variety of ways, but one of the most commonly accepted definitions is offered by the International Federation of Red Cross Red Crescent Societies (IFRC, n.d.), which defines disaster management as the facilitation and organization of all humanitarian-related activities involved in preparedness, response, and recovery to reduce the devastating impact of disasters. According to the Federal Emergency Management Agency (FEMA), there are four phases of emergency relief: mitigation (which involves prevention efforts), preparedness (which involves the development of disaster relief plans), response (which includes emergency actions taken during the disaster designed to save lives and protect individuals), and recovery (which includes actions taken to return life to normal) (FEMA, 2007). FEMA also notes the importance of all phases of emergency response efforts occurring within a framework that is comprehensive, progressive, integrated, collaborative, well-coordinated, flexible, and professional (FEMA, 2007).

Similarly, United Methodist Committee on Relief (UMCOR), an agency that responds to numerous natural disasters worldwide, categorizes the phases of disaster relief as:

(1) Readiness: being prepared for disasters, including developing a plan for response;
(2) Rescue: includes search and rescue efforts in the hours and days following the disaster;
(3) Relief: providing for the basic needs of those effected on an emergency basis, such as food, water, medicine, and shelter in the weeks and months following the disaster;
(4) Recovery: helping survivors find short, medium, and long-term solutions to the devastation they've endured in the months and years following a disaster. It includes community development efforts; and
(5) Review: evaluating the disaster response in order to make improvements for the next disaster, including disaster risk reduction. (Crutchfield, 2013)

Human services professionals play a key role in both natural disaster response and management, including emergency management, crisis response, and case management (coordination of services, and trauma services) (Williams, 2008). It is important to note that the world's most vulnerable—those struggling with chronic poverty and members of historically marginalized groups based on race and gender—are the most profoundly affected by natural disasters, whether in the United States or countries such as Haiti or Somalia. It is the members of these vulnerable populations that are most often the central focus of human services professionals engaging in advocacy work in the disaster relief area. Human service professionals can assist in all of these phases of disaster relief, coordinating with other professionals and paraprofessionals. Hossain (2011) describes the various case management tasks human services professionals engage in when they respond to a natural disaster, including such activities as building up a professional network, creating awareness about the disaster, transmitting important information about a disaster zone, participating in rescue operations in coordination with other agencies, and serving as a liaison between survivors and the government by conducting rapid surveys on losses and needs.

Williams (2008) recalls how the millions of individuals displaced after Hurricane Katrina created a modern-day diaspora with a significant portion of Gulf Coast residents being forced to relocate throughout the country, resulting in the largest forced migration episode in the history of the United States. Bell (2008) describes how in New Orleans, one of communities hit hardest by Hurricane Katrina is the economically vulnerable African American population. Many African Americans in New Orleans struggled with poverty prior to the hurricane at significantly higher rates than the rest of the population. Further, many of these communities existed in "pockets of poverty" and were more isolated from outside support networks. African Americans living in isolated pockets of poverty were disproportionately affected by Hurricane Katrina since were disproportionately affected by the hurricane since not only did many not have the means to evacuate but also their displacement resulted in the loss of a highly supportive community.

A children's aid worker with UNICEF who worked on an emergency response team shared that her team arrived on the scene of a natural disaster hours after it was determined that the environment was safe (relatively speaking). She discussed the importance of immediately mapping all agencies and NGOs working in the area so that services could be coordinated, as well as securing borders and engaging in a census of vulnerable members of the community, particularly women and children, to reduce the risk of trafficking and other forms of exploitation. She framed their initial work as emergency damage control to halt the potential of a runaway crisis. Once the community was mapped and all child protective measures were taken, her team would then act as an "emergency-response headquarters" with all NGO activities being coordinated through UNICEF, which would then take responsibility for communicating with government officials and the outside world, including other UN agencies, such as the World Health Organization (WHO) and UNHCR (C. Gale, personal communication, February 10, 2010).

Whether engaging in emergency response or working with survivors months after a crisis to connect them with valuable resources as they strive to get their lives back to normal, the case management services that human services professionals provide are valuable. One of the first tasks facing human service professionals engaging in disaster relief services is assessing the needs of survivors (Bell, 2008). This can be especially challenging since, as Williams (2008) noted, those with the greatest needs are often those who were in need prior to the natural disaster. Thus developing a case management plan that acknowledges the previous vulnerability, while remaining focused on the survivor's present needs related to the disaster is often a tangled process wrought with complicating factors and unforeseen challenges. Some examples of these challenges can be found in developing countries as well as countries, such as the United States. For instance, a study conducted by the Texas Health and Human Services Commission on Hurricane Katrina survivors living in Texas found that two years after the hurricane almost 60% of survivors were still unemployed, almost 50% relied on housing subsidies, and between 37% and 40% of those surveyed reported that they had significant physical and mental health needs (Texas Health and Human Services Commission, 2006, as cited in Bell, 2008). It's important for all human service professionals working in the area of disaster relief to recognize that case management services should be perceived as a long-term process.

The Role of Human Services in Disaster Relief and Management

Human service professionals possess skills that can meet many of the disaster survivors' needs (Pawar, 2008). The challenge though is determining what these needs are, as well as the best way to meet identified needs. An empirical review of 160 studies exploring the impact of natural disasters on 60,000 survivors (across all the studies in sample) found that survivors of natural disasters experienced a wide range of psychosocial and physical problems, including chronic problems with daily living; the loss psychosocial resources (coping mechanisms), such as optimism, resiliency, perceived control, and self-efficacy; and also experienced a range of somatic complaints. Psychological problems appeared to be the most frequently experienced and enduring consequence of enduring a natural disaster, the most significant of which was posttraumatic stress disorder (PTSD), followed by depression, anxiety, and loss of self-esteem (Norris, Friedman, & Watson, 2002). Additional responses to enduring a natural disaster include fear, anger, distress, sadness, and grief, all of which can increase the risk of psychiatric and psychological disorders, depending on an individual's past psychological history, current coping mechanisms, personal resiliency, and level of social support (Flynn & Norwood, 2004).

According to Flynn and Norwood (2004), human service professionals working in the area of disaster relief, disaster management, and postrelief services should focus on three factors when working with survivors of disasters: their psychosocial history, their personality characteristics and coping mechanisms (such as resiliency and attitude), and the nature and availability of social supports. They also note that the goal of all psychosocial intervention should be to reduce individual suffering and increase functioning and resiliency.

With regard to the effectiveness of current disaster relief and management efforts, Pawar's (2008) case study on the Krishna River flood in Maharashtra, India, highlighted several deficiencies including politicized and disorganized dissemination of humanitarian aid (food, kerosene, clothing, etc.); inadequacy of relief aid, including frequent distribution of aid to those who were not in need, and the failure to provide aid to many who were genuinely in need; and likely the most damaging of all deficiencies was a significant shortage of postdisaster relief programs, including case management and trauma counseling.

Pawar asserts that the problems in most disaster relief and management efforts that his case study discovered are areas where human service professionals can make significant contributions. In particular Pawar recommends that human service professionals engage in:

- coordination of better communication and coordination, including community education and awareness programs;
- development of more efficient method for accurately assessing affected community members' needs;
- coordination of equitable and timely aid distribution that reflects appropriate prioritizing based on need;
- serving as a liaison between community and political leaders and community members, encouraging a moral, rather than partisan response;
- fostering existing informal community support networks; and
- development and facilitation of postdisaster relief programs focusing on longer-term social welfare provision, including posttrauma counseling.

Global Trends in Conflict-Generated Mass Forced Migration

The UNHCR estimates that there are approximately 42.5 million individuals who were forcibly displaced from their homes due to conflict. Of these, 15.2 million have refugee status, 10.4 million are under the control of the UNHCR, and 4.8 million are Palestinian refugees who are under the control of the United Nations Relief and Works Agency for Palestine Refugees in the Near East (UNRWA). Counted among the broader figure of 42.5 million are also 895,000 asylum-seekers and 26.4 million IDPs, 15.5 million of whom were served in some capacity by the UNHCR (UNHCR, 2012a). According to the UNHCR, there were 4.3 million people who became newly forcibly displaced in 2011 (the most recent statistics available). Also among the world's refugees are approximately 12 million people who are considered stateless, without the protection of a nationality and with no place to call home.

The majority of the world's refugees are hosted in developing countries, with Pakistan hosting the most refugees. Other countries that accept a high number of refugees include Iran, Syria, Germany, Kenya, Jordan, Chad, China, Ethiopia, Tanzania and the United States. Countries that produce the most refugees include Afghanistan, which has produced over 2.6 million refugees as of 2011, Iraq, Somalia, Sudan, the Democratic Republic of the Congo (DRC), Myanmar (Burma), Colombia, Vietnam, Eritrea, and China (UNHCR, 2012a).

Currently countries in the Global North that accept the most refugees per year (in absolute numbers) includes Germany, Australia, the United States, Canada, and the United Kingdom, with the United States accepting the most refugees annually. The president of the United States, in consultation with Congress, determines the number of refugees admitted to the United States on an annual basis (often referred to as the "ceiling"), although the number of refugees actually admitted to the United States typically falls short of the ceiling. The highest the ceiling has ever been set was 142,000 in 1992, with 131,749 being admitted. The ceiling has fluctuated somewhat since then, with the lowest ceiling being 70,000 and the highest in recent years being 80,000. The number of refugees actually admitted to the United States has fluctuated far more dramatically, ranging from 80% to 98% of the ceiling in the 1990s. But after the September 11, 2001, terrorist attacks, the number of refugees admitted into the United States dropped

Michelle Martin

Newly arrived refugees from the most recent cycle of violence in the DRC, in a UNHCR camp in Rwanda, waiting in line for supplies.

significantly to only 27,070 refugees in 2002 (38.7% of the ceiling) and 28,117 in 2003 (40.2% of the ceiling). The numbers began to pick up in 2004 and have for the most part increased ever since, leveling off at a ceiling ranging from 70,000 to 80,000, with admittance averaging around 75,000 refugees per year.

The president also determines how the total number of refugee admission slots will be allocated among the world's refugees, based primarily on humanitarian concerns (although most would agree that political consideration is also a factor). For instance, for the fiscal year 2012, the president notified the secretary of state (who in turn notified Congress) that the allotted number of refugees was to be broken down in this way:

- Africa: 12,000
- East Asia: 18,000
- Europe and Central Asia: 2,000
- Latin America/Caribbean: 5,500
- Near East/South Asia (which includes the Middle East): 35,500
- Unallocated reserve: 3,000

In addition, Congress was instructed to consider persons in Cuba, Eurasia and the Baltics, and persons in Iraq for possible admission as well, if deemed appropriate.

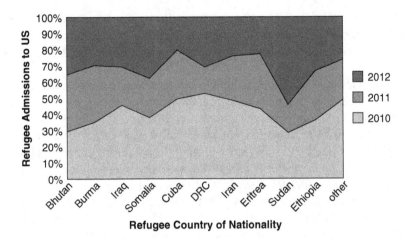

FIGURE 8.1

Trends in Refugee Admissions to the United States by Country of Nationality, 2010–2012

Source: DHS, Office of Immigration Statistics. (2013 April). Annual Flow Report, Refugees and Asylees 2012.

Historically, policies surrounding the admission of refugees were a component of overall U.S. foreign policy, thus during the U.S. fight against communism (which encompassed the Cold War with the former Soviet Union), refugees from communist countries, such as Russia and Cuba, received higher priority. Current refugee admittance priorities are often rooted in both need and foreign policy, and the list of countries where the majority of admitted refugees are from reflects both of these dynamics (see Figure 8.1).

Assess your comprehension of **Global Trends in Forced Migration** by taking this quiz.

A Contemporary Picture of Refugee Dynamics

Common Trends an Advocate Must Know

Before discussing common dynamics among refugee populations, it is very important to stress that refugees are not homogeneous populations but are in fact quite diverse, representing both genders, a wide range of nationalities, and a broad range of experiences and interests. Some harbor desires to return home, some do not. Some remain very attached to their ancestral territory, and some are not. Many refugees remain connected to their homelands, but do so in a wide range of ways, including providing financial remittance and supporting civil society, while some engage politically (Lyons, 2006). And finally, some make significant contributions to peace in their homelands while living abroad, while some contribute to conflict. The point is that while much is written about the common plight of the refugee, it is vitally important that advocates recognize that refugee populations, while certainly vulnerable, are also vibrant, fluid, and diverse, with personal agency, and despite their often dire circumstances, their individual stories reflect collective resiliency and hopefulness for a better future.

Most of the world's refugees are from Africa and Asia (which includes the Middle East) and remain in their region of origin, most often in neighboring countries (UNHCR, 2012a). For instance, of all refugees from the continent of Africa, 80% remain in the region and only 20% are relocated outside the region. Among refugees in Asia, 84% remain in the region and 16% are relocated outside the region (UNHCR, 2012a). UNHCR notes that Tunisia, Liberia, Pakistan, Chad, Afghanistan, and Iran have generated the most refugees globally, due to conflict, oppression, and civil unrest, yet despite the millions of refugees collectively generated in the last 10 years, over 9.1 million refugees returned home, 5.5 million refugees have returned to Afghanistan since 2002.

The goal of the UNHCR is to find durable solutions for refugee situations with the best option always being a resolution of the conflict so that refugees can return home. In 2011, tens of thousands of refugees returned home to Libya, Côte d'Ivoire, Afghanistan, Iraq, Sudan, and the DRC. Unfortunately, returning home does not always mean resuming (or initiating) a life of peace and safety since most of these countries remain at high risk of renewed violence. Thus, what refugees often experience is a revolving door of violence where repeating cycles of violence result in refugees experiencing ongoing disruptions in stability in every domain of their lives, affecting everything from individual and family psychosocial functioning to the ability to sustain a stable livelihood (Fagen, 2011).

Unfortunately, for many conflict-generated refugees and IDPs, life after displacement never returns to normal even if they do return home (presuming there ever was a normality that involved even relative peace in the first place). Also unfortunate is the fact that most refugees do not return home, but rather remain in a state of perpetual limbo as they wait for the international community to make determinations about their futures. In fact, of the 10.4 million refugees under the care of the UNHCR, approximately 75% (just over 7 million) are in what the *UNHCR calls protracted refugee situations* (PRS), defined as "refugee population of 25,000 persons or more that have been in exile for five or more years in developing countries" (Loescher, Milner, Newman, & Troeller, 2008, p. 21). Currently there are 30 PRS in the world, which represents a slight decrease from 1998 when there were 39 PRS (Department of State, 2011). Despite a decrease in PRS due to aggressive repatriation campaigns, global PRS remains a significant social problem, involving millions of people living in ongoing limbo often in situations that involve daily human rights violations, where they are unable to live their lives to their optimum levels. The 10 largest refugee populations that are considered to be protracted (mostly involving refugees living in UNHCR refugee camps for extended periods of time), include:

1. Over 1 million Afghan refugees in Pakistan
2. Nearly 1 million Afghan refugees in Iran
3. 350,000 Burundians in Tanzania
4. 215,000 Sudanese in Uganda
5. 174,000 Somalis in Kenya
6. 157,000 Eritreans in Sudan
7. 132,000 Angolans in the Democratic Republic of the Congo
8. 132,000 refugees from Myanmar in Thailand
9. 128,000 Congolese (DRC) refugees in Tanzania
10. 107,000 Bhutanese in Nepal. (UNHCR, 2008a)

In 2008, the UNHCR initiated a special initiative focusing on finding durable solutions to the world's longest PRS. This special initiative focuses specifically on five PRS, including the nearly 1 million registered Afghan refugees living in Iran since the 1980s, 1.6 million registered Afghan refugees living in Pakistan since the early 1990s; 30,000 registered Rohingya refugees in camps in Bangladesh since the early 1990s from Myanmar (Burma); 18,000 registered Bosnian refugees and 47,000 registered Croatian refugees living in Serbia since the Balkan wars in the early 1990s; over 25,000 registered

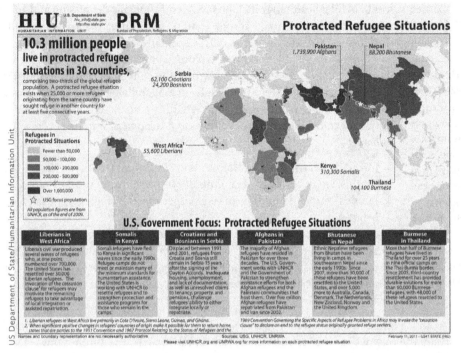

HIU U.S. Department of State
hiu_info@state.gov
http://hiu.state.gov
HUMANITARIAN INFORMATION UNIT

PRM Bureau of Population, Refugees & Migration

Protracted Refugee Situations

10.3 million people live in protracted refugee situations in 30 countries,

comprising two-thirds of the global refugee population. A protracted refugee situation exists when 25,000 or more refugees originating from the same country have sought refuge in another country for at least five consecutive years.

Pakistan
1,739,900 Afghans

Nepal
88,200 Bhutanese

Serbia
62,100 Croatians
24,200 Bosnians

West Africa¹
55,600 Liberians

Kenya
310,300 Somalis

Thailand
104,100 Burmese

Refugees in Protracted Situations

Fewer than 50,000
50,000 - 100,000
100,000 - 200,000
200,000 - 500,000
Over 1,000,000

☆ USG focus population

All population figures are from UNHCR, as of the end of 2009.

U.S. Government Focus: Protracted Refugee Situations

Liberians in West Africa¹	Somalis in Kenya	Croatians and Bosnians in Serbia	Afghans in Pakistan	Bhutanese in Nepal	Burmese in Thailand
Liberia's civil war produced several waves of refugees who, at one point numbered over 700,000. The United States has resettled over 30,000 Liberian refugees. The invocation of the cessation clause² for refugees may motivate the remaining refugees to take advantage of local integration or assisted repatriation.	Somali refugees have fled to Kenya in significant waves since the early 1990s. Refugee camps do not meet or maintain many of the minimum standards for humanitarian assistance. The United States is working with UNHCR to resettle refugees and to strengthen protection and assistance programs for those who remain in the camps.	Displaced between 1991 and 2001, refugees from Croatia and Bosnia still remain in Serbia 15 years after the signing of the Dayton Accords. Inadequate housing, unemployment, and lack of documentation as well as unresolved claims to tenancy, property, and pensions, challenge refugees' ability to either integrate locally or repatriate.	The majority of Afghan refugees have resided in Pakistan for over three decades. The U.S. Government works with UNHCR and the Government of Pakistan to strengthen assistance efforts for both Afghan refugees and the Pakistani communities that host them. Over five million Afghan refugees have repatriated from Pakistan and Iran since 2002.	Ethnic Nepalese refugees from Bhutan have been living in camps in southeastern Nepal since the early 1990s. Since 2007, more than 30,000 of these refugees have been resettled to the United States, and over 5,000 more to Australia, Canada, Denmark, The Netherlands, New Zealand, Norway and the United Kingdom.	More than half of Burmese refugees have lived in Thailand for over 25 years in nine official camps on the Thai-Burma border. Since 2005, third-country resettlement has provided durable solutions for more than 60,000 Burmese refugees, with 48,000 of these refugees resettled to the United States.

1. Liberian refugees in West Africa live primarily in Cote D'Ivoire, Sierra Leone, Guinea, and Ghana.
2. When significant positive changes in refugees' countries of origin make it possible for them to return home, states that are parties to the 1951 Convention and 1967 Protocol Relating to the Status of Refugees and the treaties and boundary representation are not necessarily authoritative.

1989 Convention Governing the Specific Aspects of Refugee Problems in Africa may invoke the "cessation clause" to declare an end to the refugee status originally granted refugee seekers.

Sources: USG, UNHCR, UNRWA
Please visit UNHCR.org and UNRWA.org for more information on each protracted refugee situation.

February 11, 2011 - U241 STATE (HIU)

Current protracted refugee situations worldwide

US Department of State/Humanitarian Information Unit

Burundi refugees in a camp in Tanzania since a conflict in Burundi in 1972 (UNHCR, 2010); and over 66,000 registered Eritrean refugees in eastern Sudan since the war of independence against Ethiopia between 1961 and 1991 (UNHCR, 2008b). Clearly these PRS represent only a small portion of the world's PRS, and while each situation is unique, they all involve conflict situations; people fleeing for their lives with few personal possessions, if any; loved ones and friends lost to violence, malnutrition and illness; trauma rooted in the conflict, displacement, and living in camps for decades.

Professional History

Understanding and Mastery: Range of populations served and needs addressed by human services

Critical Thinking Question: What are some of the reasons why protracted refugee situations exist, and what are some of the challenges related to finding durable solutions for the millions of refugees who remain in limbo for decades?

Psychosocial and Physical Consequences of Forced Migration due to Conflict

Human service professionals may work with refugee populations as a component of their work with a human rights organization, an international NGO, a UN agency, or as a social worker or counselor working in a refugee camp. The issues affecting refugee populations and the challenges they face are best understood within the broader socio-political context that resulted in their forced displacement. Developing a level of competency in the concrete details and cultural nuances surrounding a refugee's displacement is an integral part of an activist's ability to effectively advocate for the needs of a refugee, or an entire refugee community either in the camps or after resettlement.

There are numerous psychosocial and physical consequences of forced displacement due to conflict. Physical consequences can range of injuries due to conflict-related violence, illness, dehydration, and malnutrition due to food insecurity, as well as a host of other illnesses, such as chronic malaria, diarrhea, cholera, and tuberculosis.

Consequences to mental health may include severe and enduring depression and anxiety, intense shame, and amplified grief responses due to intense trauma and extended instability (Pedersen, 2002; Richards et al., 2011; Tempany, 2009).

Rape as a weapon of war was explored comprehensively in Chapter 5, but is explored again in this chapter within the context of refugee populations. Rape as a weapon of war often results in mass refugee flow because it is used to not only destroy the victim but the family system and the entire community. In fact, the consequences of rape as a weapon of war are severe and can include:

- forced dispersal of populations as they flee feared atrocity;
- submission of an invaded community through fear of reprisal rape;
- intensification of bonding among perpetrators through commission of brutal acts;
- demoralization of an entire people through violence against their women;
- genetic subversion through impregnation of women; and
- destruction of a social fabric by attacking women whose denigration or death often destroys the entire family unit. (Harvard Humanitarian Initiative, 2009, pp. 7–8)

In Chapter 5, I explored how rape was used as a weapon of war during the Rwandan genocide by government soldiers and their counterparts, the Interahamwe militia. When the genocide ended, unfortunately the rapes did not. Instead, the Interahamwe fled into the DRC (then Zaire) along with over 1.3 million other Rwandans, primarily ethnic Hutu. Once on the other side of the border between the DRC and Rwanda, the Interahamwe took over refugee camps set up along the border of Rwanda and used them as their military base (Orth, 2001; Prunier, 2009). While they continued to fight, in an attempt to retake Rwanda, they also continued to rape, and, in fact, they apparently introduced the concept of rape to the Congolese civilian population. In a recent report on civilian rape in the DRC, members of a community-based focus group in Eastern Congo reported that rape was very infrequent before the Rwandan genocide, but with the influx of the former Rwandan regime and Interahamwe, it became prolific in the civilian communities in Eastern DRC. In describing the increasing use of rape against mothers, wives, sisters, and daughters in Eastern Congo, one participant stated:

In my community, it is mostly militaries [who rape]. The Interahamwe are the ones who brought sexual violence here. There are also criminals wearing military uniforms, but finally it is becoming common for civilians to rape. Boys as young as ten are raping little girls who are five, to even younger. (Harvard Humanitarian Initiative, 2009, p. 23)

The respondents also discussed how rape was used to destroy a community, by tearing apart the family system, since most women who were raped were later rejected by their families due to the cultural stigmatization of rape. Also, women are often raped in public in the DRC (as they were in Rwanda), to traumatize the victim as well as the community members who are forced to watch. Advocates who are familiar with the context and specific dynamics of a conflict situation, as well as range of culturally based responses, will be much better equipped to effectively meet the advocacy needs of refugees on both a micro and macro level.

Michelle Martin

Many women and girls in refugee camps are at risk of gender-based violence, prompting many NGOs to develop advocacy programs similar to the one developed by the Danish Refugee Council.

Gender-based violence is an unfortunate aspect of life in refugee camps as well, despite the UNHCR and other NGOs working hard to prevent it. For instance, gender-based violence is a significant problem in the Yusuf Batil Camp in South Sudan's Upper Nile State and includes harassment of adolescent girls at water points and local roads, the sexual exploitation of young girls who are exchanging sexual favors for money and clothes, and the forced marriage of girls as young as 11 years old. The camp has undergone a recent mass influx of refugees from the continued fighting in the Sudan, swelling from 4,000 refugees to over 36,000 in a four-week period in June 2012. The Danish Refugee Council is an NGO that serves as the camp manager for the Yusuf Batil Camp and provides gender-based advocacy services in all four camps in the area that host a total of 110,000 refugees. In April 2013, the Danish Refugee Council announced an advocacy campaign called "16 Days of Activism" to raise awareness of gender-based violence in the camps. The campaign is a part of a broader global campaign focusing on violence against women. The campaign involves dramatic plays, singing, and a poster campaign all delivering the consistent message of "No to Gender-Based Violence!" (Danish Refugee Council, 2012). This campaign serves as an excellent example of an effective advocacy campaign facilitated on a mezzo and macro level, locally and globally.

Resettlement to the United States: Process and Practice

The decision about which refugees are selected for admittance to the United States is coordinated through the United States Resettlement Program (USRP), which is facilitated by the U.S. Department of State's Bureau for Population, Refugees, and Migration (PRM). For refugees to be considered for the resettlement program, they must be referred by the UNHCR or a U.S. embassy in the country of asylum that is most likely the country of their initial displacement. Refugee families are referred as a single group, and keeping immediate family members together is a priority, although this becomes challenging in camps and PRS where documentation of family relationships may not be available (or may not be accurate), and in cultures where surnames are not shared (Hollenbach, 2008). Applications for resettlement received by the State Department that are deemed eligible are then forwarded to the U.S. Citizenship and Immigration Services (USCIS) for processing and adjudication. Once a refugee has been cleared for resettlement, the International Organization for Migration (IOM) arranges for their travel in coordination with one of the 11 designated U.S. resettlement agency, approved by the U.S. State Department.

The U.S. Office of Refugee Resettlement (ORR) provides assistance to refugee populations in the resettlement process, including assistance with cultural acclimation and with gaining self-sufficiency in the host country. The ORR works with the U.S. State Department and other agencies in the placement process and also coordinates services for newly arrived refugees which includes case management, health and mental health services, and other outreach services. ORR benefits and services are available to refugees, political asylees, Cuban and Haitian entrants, Amerasians (typically Vietnamese children fathered by American soldiers during the Vietnam conflict), victims of human trafficking, unaccompanied minor children, and survivors of torture. Refugees receive benefits through existing U.S. social welfare programs, such as Temporary Assistance for Needy Families (TANF). They typically receive temporary work permits almost immediately, which allows them to legally work in the United States, and within two years they can become legal permanent residents, naturalized citizens after living in the United States for five years.

Advocacy on a Domestic and Global Level for Refugee Populations

An advocate can serve in several capacities, serving in many different roles, including providing advocacy services on a micro level, where they may advocate for refugee access to services and serve in a liaison role with members of the community, including advocating for better health services. They may provide advocacy on a macro level focusing on a range of issues impacting refugees in a particular region or on a global level.

Refugee Council USA (RCUSA), a coalition of 25 refugee resettlement and advocacy organizations, serves as an excellent example of a macro-level advocacy organization focusing on refugee populations. RCUSA provides macro-level advocacy efforts on a domestic and international level. Domestic areas of advocacy include making reforms to the U.S. Refugee Admissions and Resettlement Program, which RCUSA argues is outdated and based on refugee resettlement dynamics from several decades ago when the influx of refugees consisted of relatively large homogeneous groups from South Asia and the former Soviet Union. The current refugee resettlement program, according to RCUSA, does not take into account the role played by armed civil conflict in the current landscape of refugee displacement, the needs of torture survivors, and survivors of gender-based violence, the high number of "unaccompanied alien children" (UAC) (children who arrive in the United States without parents) and the vast number of incoming refugees from PRS. Additionally, welfare reform in the 1990s that involved a national shift away from entitlement programs such as Aid to Families with Dependent Children (AFDC) to a welfare-to-work program, such as TANF, which provides a relatively weak safety net, even for U.S. citizens. Refugees, unlike U.S. citizens, have not had enough time in the country

A recently arrived refugee is reunited with her family, previously resettled in the United States

ARMANDO ARORIZO/EPA/Newscom

to build up social support systems that can insulate them from difficult economic times, thus they often find that the current U.S. social welfare system is woefully inadequate to meet the complex needs of many incoming refugees (Adess et al., 2009; Martin, 2004).

Other domestic advocacy issues for refugees include increasing U.S. funding for refugee resettlement, as well as for their care globally, including funding for victims and surviving victims of torture; increasing funding, services, and awareness for UAC. For instance, a recent report by the United States Conference of Catholic Bishops (2012) cites an increase in UAC, particularly children from many Latin American countries, such as Guatemala, El Salvador, and Honduras, where crimes against children, including human trafficking (sex and labor) have increased significantly in recent years. While the average age of UAC entering the United States had remained relatively stable at between 7,000 and 8,000 annually, in 2012, that number spiked to over 14,000, and is expected to increase to 20,000 in the near future.

RCUSA advocates on an international level as well, advocating for greater awareness of the plight of refugees globally. In particular, RCUSA has current campaigns advocating for refugees with disabilities, unaccompanied refugee minors, and LGBT and intersex refugees–a particularly vulnerable group since many of the countries where refugees reside criminalize same-sex relationships, and sexual minorities. RCUSA also provides a policy framework that includes the need of special attention for groups of refugees that are perceived to be particularly vulnerable.

"Voluntary Migration": Immigration to the United States in Search of a Better Life

Trends in Authorized Immigration

There is considerable discussion and debate about U.S. immigration law and policy, with individuals from all partisan camps crying out for immigration reform. How that should be accomplished, and precisely what should be reformed is up for debate, and often involves sharply polarized perspectives on the nature of the immigration process and the inherent problems throughout the process, including perspectives on who is being exploited—U.S. citizens, the U.S. economy, or the migrants themselves, as well as what is doing the exploiting, U.S. companies or migrant populations. What is not up for debate is that the U.S. immigration LPR process is complex, made even more complex after the terrorist attacks on September 11, 2001. Providing a comprehensive overview of U.S. immigration policy is beyond the scope of this chapter, but a brief synopsis of the process is provided, to better understand areas where advocacy is most needed.

The United States has experienced many waves of immigration from its inception as a sovereign nation. Earlier waves of immigration were rooted in the need for human capital, particularly during the Industrial Revolution. Immigration during the eighteenth and nineteenth centuries were primarily from Europe. There was a significant shift in immigration demographics in the mid-twentieth century to immigrants coming from countries in the Global South (Latin America and Africa) and the East (Asia and South Asia) (West, 2011). Newly arrived immigrant groups have often been subject to varying levels of discrimination and social exclusion, but these newer immigrant groups were subjected to considerably high levels of discrimination and social exclusion than prior groups. One reason for this is that many of these newer immigrants did not speak English and came from cultures that were vastly different from Euro-centric Anglo American culture (West, 2011).

Historically, U.S. immigration policy was based on three underlying principles: (1) family reunification, (2) skill-based immigration that will enhance the U.S. economy, and (3) protection of refugees. Currently the three primary categories of entry, outside of the refugee and political asylum-seeking programs include *family sponsorship*, which includes marriage sponsorship, family reunification, and adoption; *employment-based programs*, which includes priority workers and professionals with advanced degrees; and *diversity programs*, which involves a lottery system that allows immigration from countries with typically low rates of immigration to the United States (Monger & Yankay, 2013; West, 2011).

The Immigration and Naturalization Act (INA), a body of laws that regulates immigration policy in the United States, currently sets an annual limit of permanent immigrants at 675,000 (not including family sponsorship or refugee admissions). 2012 limits for employment-based immigration was set at 140,000, and diversity-based programs was set at 50,000. Immigrants who have been granted legal residency in the United States are called *legal permanent residents* (LPR) and are legally allowed to live and work in the United States on a permanent basis. They are also granted certain rights and responsibilities, including the right to work, to own property, and to attend college and receive financial aid (Monger & Yankay, 2013). According to the DHS (2012) in 2012 1,031,631 immigrants were granted LPR status, 680,799 (66%) through family sponsorship, 143,998 (14%) through employer sponsorship, 40,320 (4%) through

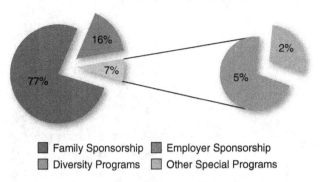

Breakdown by Immigration Program Type

- Family Sponsorship
- Employer Sponsorship
- Diversity Programs
- Other Special Programs

16% • 7% • 77% • 2% • 5%

FIGURE 8.2

Percentage Breakdowns of Immigrants Receiving LPR Status in 2012

Source: DHS, Office of Immigration Statistics (2013 April). Annual Flow Report, Refugees and Asylees 2012.

diversity programs, and 15,142 (1.5%) through other special programs, and the cancellation of approval proceedings (see Figure 8.2).

The majority of U.S. immigrants granted permanent residency in 2012 were from Asia (42%) and North America (32%), which includes the Caribbean and Central America. The top five countries of origin of 2012 LPRs include Mexico (14%), China (8%), India (6.4%), Philippines (5.6%), and the Dominican Republic (4%). The top five receiving states in 2012 often called *gateway communities* were California, New York, Florida, Texas, and New Jersey (DHS, 2012).

Trends in Unauthorized Immigration

The DHS defines unauthorized residents as "foreign-born non-citizens who are not legal residents" (Hoefer, Rytina, & Baker, 2012, p. 2). Unauthorized residents most commonly enter the United States without government approval or overstay a temporary visa. Current estimates put the unauthorized immigrant population at approximately 11 million, up from 8.4 million in 2000. Currently, authorized and unauthorized immigrants represent about 13% of the total U.S. population (Pew Research Center, 2013), although according to the Pew Research Center, migration from Mexico is currently at a standstill as of 2012 and may even be in a reverse trend (Passel, Cohn, & Gonzalez-Barrera, 2012). The majority of unauthorized residents (58%) migrated from Mexico and entered the United States through the Mexico-U.S. border (Passel & Cohn, 2011). Unauthorized immigration peaked in 2007 and as stated earlier has decreased since that time, likely due to the economic downturn in the United States, the unavailability of jobs, and an increase in U.S. border control, deportation measures, and workforce raids (Passel, 2008; Passel et al., 2012).

As of 2010, nearly two-thirds of unauthorized immigrants had lived in the United States for more than a decade, and almost half were parents of minor children, many of whom were born in the United States (Taylor, Lopez, Passel, & Motel, 2011). There are approximately 154 million people currently in the U.S. workforce, 8.3 million of which are unauthorized immigrants, which constitutes just over 5% of the workforce population (Pew Hispanic Center, 2013). The majority of unauthorized workers are employed in the farming industry. In fact, the Pew Hispanic Center estimates that approximately 25% of the farming workforce consists of unauthorized workers. Other industries where unauthorized workers tend to be employed include

A common sign warning of possible unauthorized immigrants crossings the freeways in Southern California.

grounds-keeping and maintenance (19% of the workforce), construction (17% of the workforce), food preparation and serving (12% of the workforce), production (12% of the workforce), transportation (7% of the workforce), and the civilian labor force (5.4% of the workforce). The Pew Hispanic Center also found that twice as many unauthorized immigrants as U.S.-born citizens live at or below the poverty level, half had a high school diploma, and approximately 59% had no health insurance (Passel & Cohn, 2009).

The Fight against Unauthorized Immigration

Attitudes toward unauthorized immigration and unauthorized immigrants in particular have never been overwhelmingly positive but have been increasingly the focus of a polarized debate centering on among other issues, whether unauthorized immigrants contribute positively or negatively to the U.S. economy (Varsanyi, 2011). Reflecting these polarized perspectives is a 2011 study conducted by Transatlantic Trends on global attitudes about immigration, which found that 51% of Americans perceived immigration in general as problematic, yet only 18% expressed concerns about legal immigration, which appears to indicate that the majority of those who express concerns about immigration are actually concerned about unauthorized immigration.

With regard to illegal immigration, despite strong anti-immigrant rhetoric on this topic in the United States, the Transatlantic Trends study found that respondents from the United States generally reflected lower levels of concern about illegal immigration compared to many European countries. For instance, 58% of U.S. respondents expressed being worried about illegal immigration, compared to 71% in the UK, 74% in Spain, and 80% in Italy. The study also found that 47% of U.S. respondents thought there were too many immigrants in the country (an attitude shared by a similar proportion of the population in the United Kingdom, Spain, and Italy but not by respondents in Germany and France) (Transatlantic Trends, 2011).

With regard to attitudes about illegal immigration, a March 2013 study conducted by the Pew Research Center found that while 70% of the U.S. population believed that there should be some way for unauthorized residents already living in the United States to remain (if they meet certain requirements), and almost half (49%) expressed a belief that unauthorized immigrants strengthened the country because they are hard workers, 41% stated that they were a burden to the U.S. economy because they took jobs and burdened the health-care system and housing market (Pew Research Center, 2013). These statistics reflect a slight increase in positive attitudes toward unauthorized immigrants compared to 2010 when 50% of Americans expressed a belief that immigrants in general were a burden on the U.S. economy. Additionally, approximately 52% of U.S. citizens reported a belief that new immigrants strengthened U.S. society, whereas 43% stated that they threatened traditional American values (Pew Research Center, 2013). Further, 86% of U.S. citizens reported a belief that immigrants are hard workers, but they seemed split on whether their work ethic was good for native-born U.S. citizens, with 51% expressing a belief that immigrants took jobs away from native-born U.S. citizens, while 61% believing that immigrants actually create jobs by establishing new businesses (Transatlantic Trends, 2008).

Attitudes toward unauthorized immigration tend to fall along educational and partisan lines, with those who have higher levels of education expressing more positive attitude about unauthorized immigration, and Democrats being generally far more positive about immigration in general and unauthorized immigration in particular than those with lower educational levels, and Republicans (Transatlantic Trends, 2008). Attitudes about granting citizenship to native-born children of unauthorized immigrant parents were far more polarized between the two political parties, with 65% of Democrats stating that they support children born in the United States to unauthorized parents being granted citizenship compared to 34% of Republicans. This polarization was not as apparent when members of each political party were asked whether they would support a law that would allow unauthorized immigrants a pathway to legal residency if they joined the military or attended college, where 55% of Republicans and 75% of Democrats expressed support for such legislation (Transatlantic Trends, 2011).

A controversial question that is often hotly debated is whether unauthorized immigration is good for the United States or causes harm, particularly on an economic level. The answer to this question depends in large part on how *good* and *harm* are defined. A recent report by the Migration Policy Institute (MPI) shows that unauthorized immigrants provide a very important contribution to the low-skilled workforce in the United States, including agriculture, construction, food processing, and other low-skill sectors. The report also found that "illegal inflow" is far more responsive to fluctuating U.S. workforce needs than is legal immigration, particularly since the official economic immigration process favors higher-skilled workers, thus it is virtually impossible under current U.S. immigration law to obtain a work visa for low-end positions. The report calculated that the economic cost of unauthorized immigration (such as providing health-care services) was ultimately balanced out with all of the benefits gained to

U.S. companies that hired unauthorized immigrants with lower than legal wages, and no benefits (Hanson, 2009). The study also found that the cost of border enforcement may not be money well spent, in light of the high cost associated with enforcement efforts and studies indicating that tighter border enforcement will not necessarily reduce unauthorized entry (Boucher & Taylor, 2007).

Despite a general increase in positive attitudes toward unauthorized immigrants, the U.S. response to illegal immigration has grown increasingly punitive. For instance, under the George W. Bush administration, efforts to control the U.S.-Mexico border were increased, as were workplace raids and efforts to deport unauthorized immigrants. The Obama administration has kept pace with previous deportation efforts, amidst increasing calls for reform from many sectors but particularly from immigrant, and Latino advocates (Lopez, Gonzalez-Barrera, & Motel, 2011). Justifications for increased border protection and harsher penalties for unauthorized entry into the United States are often based on the premise that individuals who immigrate to the United States without authorization are breaking the law, thus arguments about their contributions (or lack thereof) are moot since "the law is the law." This type of rhetoric makes a complex issue simple, when it is nothing of the sort and also does not account for U.S. companies that are suspected of having recruitment plans of illegal workers due to their lower cost (Barboza, 2001).

Effective Advocacy for Equitable Immigration Reform

Effective advocacy for immigration issues is aided by gaining an understanding of theoretical concepts that attempt to understand citizen reactions to foreign newcomers. *Xenophobia*, the irrational fear of immigrants, is one such concept that attempts to explain why members of a native-born population are inclined to feeling negatively toward migrant populations, particularly newcomers. Jones (2011) has described xenophobia as occurring on a continuum, starting with the lowest level, involving "exclusive xenophobia"—the belief that immigrants are fundamentally different and exist outside of one's community—a moderate level, involving "possessive xenophobia"—the belief that immigrants are fundamentally different, exist outside of one's community, and is attempting to take services from the community—and the highest level, involving "toxic xenophobia"—the belief that immigrants are fundamentally different, exist outside of the community, and are "trying to destroy that which we hold most dear, our freedom" (p. 35).

Xenophobia relies on "in-group/out group" dynamics, where the immigrant is considered "the other," as well as dehumanization, which makes it easier to experience diminished empathy for the plight of immigrants, particularly unauthorized immigrants, who most often experience high levels of poverty. An example of dehumanization is the use of the term *illegal alien*, which connotes the alternate term of the word *alien* (Weston, 2009). Weston notes how anti-immigrant political rhetoric often stokes the fire of xenophobia by linking "illegal aliens" with issues that will anger and create fear in some U.S. citizens, such as crime and economic exploitation. Understanding xenophobia, why it exists and how it develops, helps advocates to better understand the motives behind a lot of anti-immigrant rhetoric and can also inform strategies for combating political rhetoric that is based on xenophobic ideology.

Effective advocacy also depends in large part on a strategy that promotes truth over myth. In this respect, it is very important for immigration advocates to become familiar with factual information regarding immigration so that they can confront the many myths that far too often attempt to scapegoat immigrants, particularly unauthorized immigrants for problems in the host country that have little to no relationship with immigration, such as increases in crime, and job shortages. The following three common myths are explored briefly in this section: (1) "unauthorized immigrants pay no taxes," (2) "unauthorized immigrants move to the United States just for the social welfare benefits," and (3) "immigrants costs the United States millions of dollars, because the benefits they receive outweigh their contribution to society." The responses later in this section are not intended to provide a comprehensive response to these concerns but to provide fundamental information and a starting point for discussion.

Myth #1—*Unauthorized immigrants pay no taxes:* False. According to the U.S. Congressional Budget Office (2007) between 50% to 75% of unauthorized immigrants pay federal, state, and local taxes (see also Camarota, 2004 and Center for Comparative Immigration Studies, 2007). Additionally, since many unauthorized immigrants rely on false identification papers, they cannot receive tax refunds, which has resulted in billions of dollars of unclaimed tax refunds due to the inability to match worker identification with real Social Security numbers (Camarota, 2004).

Myth #2—*Unauthorized immigrants move to the United States just for the social welfare benefits:* False. There is no evidence that immigrants come to the United States to take advantage of the social welfare benefits. In fact under U.S. welfare reform (the Personal Responsibility and Work Opportunity Responsibility Act [PRWORA] of 1996), authorized immigrants who entered the United States after 1996 are barred from receiving benefits for the first five years they live in the United States. Additionally, most immigrants entering the United States after 1996 are barred from receiving other benefits for their first five years as well, including Medicaid, the State Children's Health Insurance Program, Supplemental Security Income, and food stamps (Tumlin & Zimmerman, 2003). Further, although authorized immigrants who entered the United States prior to 1996 remained eligible to receive public assistance, an Urban Institute report found that they experienced far greater reductions in approvals of their welfare applications and medical benefits than U.S. citizens after welfare reform legislation was passed. For example, the approval rate for immigrant applications for public assistance in Los Angeles County between 1996 and 1998 dropped by over 50%, while approvals for citizens' applications remained about the same (Tumlin & Zimmerman, 2003). Finally, unauthorized immigrants do not qualify to receive any benefits, except perhaps for their U.S.-born children.

Myth #3—*Immigrants costs the United States more than they contribute because the welfare benefits they receive outweigh their contribution to society:* True and false. Studies show conflicting findings on this issue because of the difficulty in tracking the income and benefits received by unauthorized immigrants. An early study estimated that unauthorized immigrants pay annual tax payments that are significantly more than their benefit use (Smith & Edmonston, 1997). Griswold (2012) contends that this is still the case, asserting that not only does immigration pose no long-term burden on U.S. taxpayers, but rather, immigrants and their descendants "pay more in taxes than they consume in government services in terms of net present value" (p. 159). Yet another study found that while there was no evidence to support the theory that unauthorized immigrants abuse social welfare benefits, they do create a net fiscal deficit on the federal level, and in some gateway states, because their average income level is lower due to lower educational levels. The study also found that while unauthorized immigrants only cost the federal government about half that of the average U.S. household due to lower benefit usage, this net savings is lost because their tax payments are lower as well, at only 28% of other U.S. households due to lower incomes and limited income mobility due to low education levels (Camarota, 2004). The issue of whether immigration, particularly from Mexico, helps or harms the U.S. economy is more complex than calculating the net cost (or benefit) of each immigrant though, and must include the net cost (or benefit) of an immigrant workforce, which often involves low-pay/low-benefit/high-productivity, as well as filling workforce shortages. For instance, the current severe labor shortage within the U.S. agricultural industry is believed to be caused in large part by U.S. government's increase in immigration enforcement, which as the 2012 Pew Research Center study, referenced earlier, notes has resulted in a standstill in Mexico-U.S. migration. Prior to the labor shortage, approximately 80% of the U.S. agricultural workforce was comprised of Mexican immigrants, 96% of which were unauthorized. This workforce shortage has not been filled by low-skilled U.S. workers who have consistently demonstrated an unwillingness to perform the "back-breaking labor-intensive operations" performed by the unauthorized workforce from Mexico (Devadoss & Luckstead, 2011, p. 859).

Immigration reform activists protest Arizona immigration laws at the White House on May 1, 2010, in Washington, DC.

Jim West/Alamy

Advocacy campaigns can take many forms, such as creating awareness among immigrant and nonimmigrant populations, engaging in outreach efforts focusing on legal issues, such as an immigrant's legal rights, and the immigration process, as well as advocating for and against particular immigration legislation. For instance, many immigration advocates have been actively engaged in the fight against Arizona's recent anti-immigration law "Support Our Law Enforcement and Safe Neighborhoods Act" (SB 1070, amended by HB 2162), which was signed into law on April 23, 2010. This controversial immigration enforcement legislation requires state and local law enforcement agencies, among other things, to verify the immigration status of individuals it encounters without probable cause that the individuals have committed a crime, other than being an unauthorized immigrant.

Critics of this legislation claim that it encourages racial profiling and circumvents federal law that requires probable cause (that a crime has been committed) (Immigration Policy Institute, 2012). The legislation has endured numerous legal challenges to its legality and its constitutionality, including a lawsuit filed by the U.S. Justice Department and the American Civil Liberties Union (ACLU). According to the ACLU website, despite numerous ongoing legal challenges, the Supreme Court has permitted many aspects of the law to take effect.

Another advocacy campaign focuses on the passage of the Development, Relief, and Education for Alien Minors Act, more commonly known as the DREAM Act. The DREAM Act is bipartisan legislation that seeks to address what is perceived by many advocates (as well as many U.S. citizens and politicians) to be the unjust situation of youth who have lived in the United States much of their lives, including having graduated from a U.S. high school, but who do not have legal status because their parents are unauthorized. Many of these children immigrated to the United States when they were very young, and in fact some were unaware of their unauthorized status until they attempted to apply for federal financial aid for college. The DREAM Act provides a pathway to legal residency and eventually citizenship for such youth who meet certain criteria, by allowing them to apply for temporary legal status (and eventually LPR and citizenship) if they attend college or serve in the U.S. military (National Immigration Law Center, 2011). To qualify applicants would need to be 15 years or younger when they migrated to the United States, and they must have lived in the U.S. at least five years prior to the enactment of the legislation. The legislation, in its current form, mandates that applicants attend an approved academic program or serve in the U.S. military for at least two years, and also mandates that these requirements be met within six years of application. Additionally, there is an exclusion clause for youth with poor moral character, which supporters assert will prohibit the legislation from serving as a "safe harbor" for criminals, while rewarding hardworking youth who have already contributed greatly to U.S. society (National Immigration Law Center, 2011). Although the bill was introduced in 2001 and was passed by the House of Representatives in 2010, it has not yet passed the Senate, despite its bipartisan support. Although the DREAM Act has not yet been passed on a federal level, several states have passed similar legislation at the state level, including California, Texas, New York, and Illinois.

Assess your comprehension of Effective Advocacy for Equitable Immigration Reform by taking this quiz.

Concluding Thoughts on Advocacy for Refugees and Immigrants

Advocacy for refugees and immigrants is a very broad area of advocacy and often deals with a wide range of issues pertaining to the rights of migrants within various contexts. While this chapter explores various types of migration experiences, it in no way attempts to address the global immigration process comprehensively. Gaining a general sense of the current trends in global migration, the role of conflict in forced migration, and the challenges in finding durable solutions for the millions of refugees and IDPs caught in the limbo of PRS is vital, as it enables human service professionals to better understand the role of social justice advocates in advocating for refugee populations in a variety of contexts. Similarly, gaining a general sense of the wide range of experiences among voluntary migrants within a U.S. immigration framework will provide human service professionals with the initial tools and fundamental framework for advocating for immigration reform, and immigrants in general, that respects the dignity and worth of all persons regardless of their immigration or nationality status.

Assess your analysis and evaluation of this chapter's content by completing the **Chapter Review**.

Epilogue

. . . .

The field of advocacy is growing, particularly on a global level, and is expected to continue to grow in the future. Prompting the need for social justice advocates are many factors, including globalization, driven in large part by dramatic technical advances. Other facilitating forces include dramatic increases on armed civil conflict, natural disasters and other social dynamics, causing mass forced migration and increases in human rights violations and crimes against humanity. Additional dynamics leading to an increased need for social justice advocates include enduring global poverty, food insecurity, and illnesses such as HIV/AIDS. All of these conditions create heavy burdens for the world's most vulnerable members, including marginalized groups based on ethnic group membership, gender, age, and religion.

Human services professions are ideally poised to be on the front lines of global advocacy due to the profession's roots in social justice movements, its theoretical base, and the profession's enduring commitment to vulnerable, disenfranchised, and marginalized populations. Human services professions must recognize the trends explored in this book to be prepared to not just take a seat at the table of advocacy for social justice on a global scale, but to take the lead. Areas to focus on include increasing global content in human services educational curriculum, increased funding for international internships, and minimum technology standards for human services professionals.

Advocacy for social justice in a global context is interdisciplinary in the sense that it depends on an interdisciplinary field of professions, including peace studies, human rights, public policy, political science, international relations, public health, community and clinical psychology, and the human services. Increasing interdisciplinary collaboration between these fields will ultimately strengthen the field of advocacy, by recognizing the strengths each of these disciplines has to offer in alleviating suffering of the world's most vulnerable members.

References for Chapter 1

Cohen, D., de la Vega, R. and Gabrielle Watson, G. (2001). *Advocacy for social justice: A global action and reflection guide.* Bloomfield, Connecticut: Kumarian Press.

Collier, P. (2000). Economic causes of civil conflict and their implications on policy. In C. Crocker, F. Hampson and P. Aall (eds.), *Leashing the dogs of civil war: Conflict management in a divided world.* Washington, D.C.: United States Institute of Peace (pp. 197–218).

Collier, P., & Hoeffler, A. (2002). On the incidence of civil war in Africa. *Journal of Conflict Resolution, 46*(1), 13–28.

Collier, P., & Hoeffler, A. (2004). Greed and grievance in civil war. *Oxford Economic Papers, 56*(4), 563–595.

Davidson, J. W. (2008). *"They say": Ida B. Wells and the reconstruction of race.* New York: Oxford University Press.

Donnelly, J. (1984). Cultural relativism and universal human rights. *Human Rights Quarterly, 6*(4), 400–419.

Falk, R. A. (2009). *Achieving human rights.* New York: Routledge Publishing.

Hamington, M. (2005). Public pragmatism: Jane Addams and Ida B. Wells on lynching. *Journal of Speculative Philosophy, 19*(2), 167–174.

Knight, L. (2010). *Jane Addams: Spirit in action.* New York: W. W. Norton & Co.

Kinzer, S. (2010). End human rights imperialism now. *The Guardian*, UK. Retrieved September 15, 2012, from http://www.guardian.co.uk/commentisfree/cifamerica/2010/dec/31/human-rights-imperialism-james-hoge.

Loewen, G., & Pollard, W. (2010). The social justice perspective. *Journal of Postsecondary Education and Disability, 23*, 1.

Longmore, P. (2003). *Why I burned my book and other essays on disability history.* Philadelphia, PA: Temple University Press.

Lundblad, K. S. (1995). Jane Addams and social reform: A role model for the 1990s. *Social Work, 40*(5), 661–669.

Lyons, T. (2004). Engaging diasporas to promote conflict resolution: Transforming hawks into doves. Working Paper presented at the Institute of Global Conflict and Cooperation Washington Policy Seminar, Washington, D.C., May 2004.

Martin, M. (2013). *Introduction to human services: Through the eyes of practice settings* (3rd ed.). Upper Saddle, NJ: Pearson Publishing.

Masner, c. M. (2008). *The Ethic of Advocacy.* Florida, USA: Universal Publishers.

Miller, D. (2001). *Principles of social justice.* Cambridge, MA: Harvard University Press.

Steen, J. (2006). The roots of human rights advocacy and a call to action. *Social Work, 51*(2), 101. Retrieved from MasterFILE Premier database.

Tilly, C. (2009). *Social movements, 1768–2008.* Boulder, CO: Paradigm Publishers.

Trattner, W. (1998). *From poor law to welfare state: A history of social welfare in America.* NY: Free Press.

Tusinski, K. (2007). *A Description of Lobbying as Advocacy Public Relations.* Originally published in the proceedings of 2007 International Public Relations Research Conference. pp. 563–570.

UN General Assembly. (1948). *Universal Declaration of Human Rights,* G.A. res. 217A (III), U.N. Doc A/810 at 71.

Zeitz, P. (2008). *What is advocacy? What is activism?* USA: George Washington University.

References for Chapter 2

"Welfare Queen" becomes issue in Reagan campaign. *New York Times* (1857–Current file), February 15, 1976. ProQuest Historical Newspapers the *New York Times* (1851–2005), p. 51.

Afisi, O. T. (2009). Tracing contemporary Africa's conflict situation to colonialism: A breakdown of communication between natives. *Philosophical Papers and Reviews, 1*(4), 59–66.

Alcock, P. (2006). *Understanding poverty.* Basingstoke: Palgrave Macmillan.

Barretto, M., & Parker, C. (2010). *May 2010 Washington Poll.* WISNER, University of Washington Institute for the Study of Ethnicity, Race & Sexuality. Retrieved from http://www.washingtonpoll.org/results/June1_teaparty.pdf

Betten, N. (1973). American attitudes toward the poor: A historical overview. *Current History, 65*(383), 1–5.

Blanton, R., Mason, T. D., & Athow, B. (2001). Colonial style and post-colonial ethnic conflict in Africa. *Journal of Peace Research 38*, 473–492.

Bloomberg News (2010, October). Poll: Tea party economic gloom fuels Republican Momentum. Retrieved from http://www .bloomberg.com/news/2010-10-14/tea-party-s-economic-gloom-fuels-republican-election-momentum-poll-says.html. [Actual poll available online].

Briar-Lawson K., Lawson, H., Hennon, C., & Jones, A. (2006). *Family-centered policies and practices: International implications.* New York: Columbia Press.

Brownridge, D. (2009). *Violence against women: Vulnerable Populations.* New York: Routledge.

Burghart, D., & Zeskind, L. (2010). Tea Party nationalism: A critical examination of the Tea Party movement and the size, scope and focus of its national factions. Institute for Research and Education for Human Rights. Special Report. Retrieved from naacp.3cdn.net/36b2014e1dddfe3c81_v7m6bls07.pdf

Callan, T., & Nolan, B. (1991). Concepts of poverty and the poverty line. *Journal of Economic Surveys, 5*(3), 243–261.

Carty, V., & Oynett, J. (2006). Protest, cyberactivism and new social movements: The reemergence of the peace movement post 9/11. *Social Movement Studies, 5*(3), 229–249.

Cohen, D., de la Vega, R., & Watson, G. (2001). *Advocacy for social justice.* Bloomfield, CT: Kumarian Press Inc.

Darwin, C. (2009). *The origin of species: By means of natural selection, or the preservation of favoured races in the struggle for life.* Boston: Cambridge University Press. (Original work published 1859.)

Feagin, J. R. (1975). *Subordinating the poor: Welfare and American beliefs.* Englewood Cliffs, NJ: Prentice Hall.

Feagin, J. R. (2004). Documenting the costs of slavery, segregation, and contemporary racism: Why reparations are in order for African Americans. *Harvard Black Letter Law Journal, 20*, 49–80.

Gollust, S. E., & Jacobson, P. D. (2006). Privatization of public services: Organizational reform efforts in public education and public health. *American Journal of Public Health, 96*(10), 1733–1739.

Gordon, D. (2006). The concept and measurement of poverty. In Pantazis, C., Gordon, D. & Levitas, R. (eds.), *Poverty and social exclusion in Britain.* Bristol, UK: The Policy Press, pp. 29–69.

Green, J. C., Rozell, M. J., & Wilcox, C. (2003). *The Christian Right in American politics: Marching to the millennium.* Washington, DC: Georgetown University Press.

Gustafson, K. (2009). The criminalization of poverty. *The Journal of Criminal Law and Criminology, 99*(3), 643–714.

Guth, J., & Green, J. C. (1986). Faith and politics: Religion and ideology among political contributors. *American Politics Quarterly, 14*(3), 186–199.

Hacker, J. S. (2002). *The divided welfare state: The battle over public and private social benefits in the United States.* Cambridge, MA: Cambridge University Press.

Hofstadter, R. (1992). *Social Darwinism in American thought.* Boston: Beacon Press.

Horvath, R. J. (1972). A definition of Colonialism. *Current Anthropology, 13*(1), 45–57.

Kluegal, J. R. (1987). Macro-economic problems, beliefs about the poor and attitudes toward welfare spending. *Social Problems, 34*(1), 82–99.

Knuckey, J. (2005). A new front in the culture war? Moral traditionalism and voting behavior in U.S. House elections. *American Politics Research, 33*, 645–671.

Knudsen, S. (2005). Intersectionality—A theoretical inspiration in the analysis of minority cultures and identities in textbooks. Presented at the Eighth International Conference On Learning and Educational Media. "Caught in the Web or Lost in the Textbook?" *IUFM DE CAEN* (France) October 26–29, 2005. Retrieved from http://www.caen.iufm.fr/colloque_iartem/pdf/knudsen.pdf on March 25, 2008.

Krugman, P. (2007). *Conscience of a liberal.* New York: W.W. Norton & Co.

Kunze, E.I. (2010). Sex trafficking via the Internet: How international agreements address the problem and fail to go far enough. *Journal of High Technology, 10*(24), 241–289.

Lee, P., & Murie, A. (1999). Spatial and social divisions within British cities: Beyond residualisation. *Housing Studies, 14*(5), 635–640.

Lessof, C. & Jowell, R. (2000). *Measuring social exclusion.* Working paper, No. 84, Centre for Research into Elections and Social Trends (CREST), University of Oxford.

Lister, R. (2004). *Poverty*. Cambridge, UK: Blackwell/Polity Press.

Martin, M. E. (2011). Philosophical and religious influences on social welfare policy in the United States. *Journal of Social Work, 11*(1), 1–14.

Martin, M. E. (2013). *Introduction to human services: Through the eyes of practice settings* (3rd ed.). Boston: Allyn & Bacon, Pearson Publishing.

Marx, I., & van den Bosch, K. (2007 September). *How poverty differs from inequality. On poverty measurement in an enlarged EU context: Conventional and alternative approaches*. Paper presented at the 34th CEIES Seminar, Helsinki.

Meyer, B. (2002). Extraordinary stories: Disability, queerness and feminism. *NORA, 3*, 168–173.

Morris, D., & Langman, L. (2002). Networks of dissent: A typology of social movements in a global age. In M. Gurstein & S. Finquelievich (eds.), *Proceedings of the 1st International Workshop on Community Informatics*. Montreal, Canada, October 8, 2002.

Nelson, J. I. (1992). Social welfare and the market economy. *Social Science Quarterly, 73*(4), 815–828.

New York Times/CBS News. (2010). *National survey of Tea Party supporters*. Retrieved from http://documents.nytimes.com/new-york-timescbs-news-poll-national-survey-of-tea-party-supporters?ref=politics.

Østergaard-Nielsen, E., (2006). *Diasporas and conflict: Part of the problem or part of the solution?* DIIS Brief no. Copenhagen: Danish Institute for International Studies (DIIS). Retrieved from http://subweb.diis.dk/sw20879.aspn.pdf

Pack, J. R. (1989). Privatization and cost reduction. *Policy Sciences, 22*(1), 1–25.

Polack, R.J. (2004). Social justice and the global economy: New challenges for social work in the 21st century. *Social Work, 49*(2), 281–290.

Ravallion, M. (1998). Poverty lines in theory and practice: Living standards measurement study. Working Paper 133, World Bank, Washington, DC.

Reese, E. (2006). Wedlock, worship, and welfare: The influence of social conservatives and the Christian Right on welfare reform. In *The promise of welfare reform: Results or rhetoric?*, Keith Kilty and Elizabeth Segal (eds.) (pp. 169–181). Binghamton, NY: The Hayworth Press, Inc.

Reno, W. (2011). *Warfare in independent Africa (new approaches to African history)*. New York: Cambridge University Press.

Rheingold, H. (2002) *Smart mobs: The next social revolution*. Jackson, TN: Perseus Books Group.

Roby J., & Shaw, S. (2006). The African orphan crisis and international adoption. *Social Work, 51*(3), 199–210.

Roy, O. (2007). *Le croissant et le chaos*. Paris: Hachette.

Samuels, G. M., & Ross-Sheriff, F. (2008). Identity, oppression and power: Feminisms and intersectionality theory. *Affilia, 23*, 5–9.

Scheim, B. (2011). What is an iReporter: CNN explains iReport and social media week. Social Media Week. Available online at: http://socialmediaweek.org/blog/2011/09/what-is-an-ireporter/#.UjP_r2TXiAM.

Schlesinger, M., Dorwart, R. A., & Pulice, R. T. (1986). Competitive bidding and states' purchase of services: The case of mental health care. *Journal of Policy Analysis & Management*, 5(2), 245–263.

Schonfeld, E. (2009). Images from the #iranelection. *TechCrunch*. Retrieved June 12, 2012 from http://www.washingtonpost.com/wp-dyn/content/article/2009/06/21/AR2009062100089.html.

Sclar, E. (2000). *You don't always get what you pay for: The economics of privatization*. A Century Foundation Book. Ithaca, NY: Cornell University Press.

Shonick, W., & Roemer, R. (1982). Private management of public hospitals: The California experience. *Journal of Public Health Policy, 3*(2), 182–204.

Simler. K. R., & Arndt, C. (2006). Poverty comparisons with absolute poverty lines estimated from survey data. FCND discussion papers, 211, International Food Policy Research Institute (IFPRI).

Stacks, J. (1995). 100 days of attitude. *Time*, April 10. Retrieved from http://www.time.com/time/magazine/article/0,9171,982782,00.html on December 23, 2011.

Stockholm International Peace Research Institute (SIPRI). (1993). *Yearbook of World Armaments and Disarmaments*. Oxford, UK: Oxford University Press.

Stockholm International Peace Research Institute (SIPRI). (2008). *Yearbook of World Armaments and Disarmaments*. Oxford, UK: Oxford University Press.

Structural Adjustment Participatory Review International Network (SAPRIN). (2002). *The policy roots of economic crisis and poverty: A multi-country participatory assessment of structural adjustment*. Washington, DC: SAPRIN Secretariat.

Townsend, P. (1979), *Poverty in the United Kingdom*. London: Penguin.

Uluorta, H. M. (2008). Welcome to the "All-American" fun house: Hailing the disciplinary neo-liberal non-subject. Millennium—Journal of International Studies, 36(2), 51–75.

UN General Assembly. (1997). Implementation of the declaration on the granting of independence to colonial countries and peoples—Report of the Secretary-General—Question of Western Sahara, September 26, 1997, A/52/364. Retrieved from http://www.unhcr.org/refworld/docid/3ae6af1d0.html on December 12, 2012.

Uzoigwe, G. N. (1985). European partition and conquest of Africa: An overview. In *General history of Africa, VII: Africa under colonial domination 1880–1935*, A. Adu Boahen (ed.). Berkeley, CA: University of California Press, 31.

Van Slyke, D. M. (2003). The mythology of privatisation in contracting for social services. *Public Administration Review, 63* (3), 296–315.

Yoon, M. Y. (2009). European colonialism and territorial disputes in Africa: The Gulf of Guinea and the Indian Ocean. *Mediterranean Quarterly, 20*(2), 77–94.

Zucchino, D. (1999). *The Myth of the Welfare Queen: a Pulitzer-Prize Winning Journalist's portrait of women on the Line*. New York: Touchstone.

References for Chapter 3

Allport, G. W. (1954). *The nature of prejudice*. Reading, MA: Addison-Wesley.

Bertalanffy, L. (1968). *General systems theory: Foundations, development, applications.* New York: George Braziller.

Chambers, D. E., & Wedel, K. R. (2013). *Social policy and social programs: A method for the practical public policy analyst* (6th ed.). Upper Saddle River, NJ: Pearson Education.

Cohen, D., de la Vega, R., & Gabrielle Watson, G. (2001). *Advocacy for social justice: A global action and reflection guide.* Bloomfield, CT: Kumarian Press.

Dale, O., & Smith, R. (2013). *Human behavior and the social environment: Social systems theory* (7th ed.). Upper Saddle River, NJ: Pearson Education.

Dobratz, B. A., Waldner, L. K., & Buzzell, T. (2012). *Power, politics, and society: An introduction to political sociology.* Boston: Pearson Education.

Gilbert, N., & Terrell, P. (2013). *Dimensions of social welfare policy* (8th ed.). Upper Saddle River, NJ: Pearson Education.

Haynes, K. S., & Mickelson, J. S. (2010). *Affecting change: Social workers in the political arena* (7th ed.). Upper Saddle River, NJ: Pearson Publishing.

Higley, J., & Burton, M. (2006). *Elite foundations of liberal democracy.* Lanham, MD: Rowman & Littlefield.

Hindman, H. D. (2009). *The world of child labor: An historical and regional survey.* Armonk, NY: M.E. Sharpe.

Kozol, J. (2012). *Amazing grace: The lives of children and the conscience of a nation.* New York: Broadway Books.

Kuhn, T. S. ([1962] 1996). *The structure of scientific revolutions* (3rd ed.). Chicago: University of Chicago Press.

Levin, J., & Nolan, J. (2011). *The violence of hate: The confronting racism, anti-Semitism, and other forms of bigotry* (3rd ed.). Boston: Pearson Education.

Marger, M. (1987). *Elites and masses.* Belmont, CA: Wadsworth Publishing.

Martin, M. E. (2013). *Introduction to human services: Through the eyes of practice settings.* Upper Saddle River, NJ: Pearson Publishing.

Marx, K. ([1962] 1996). *The economic and philosophical manuscripts of 1844.* In D. J. Struik (Ed.), Reprint. New York: International.

Miller, D. (1970). *International community power structures: Comparative studies of four world cities.* Bloomington, IN: Indiana University Press.

Miller, M., Azrael D., Hepburn L., Hemenway, D., & Lippmann, S. J. (2006). The association between changes in household firearm ownership and rates of suicide in the United States, 1981–2002. *Injury Prevention, 12,* 178–182. doi:10.1136/ip.2005.010850.

Moscicki, E. K. (2001). Epidemiology of completed and attempted suicide: Toward a framework for prevention. *Clinical Neuroscience Research, 1*(5), 310–323.

Netting, F. E., Kettner, P. M., McMurtry, S. L., & Thomas, M. L. (2012). *Social work macro practice* (5th ed.). Upper Saddle River, NJ: Pearson Education.

Neville, H. A., Worthington, R. L., & Spanierman, L. B. (2001). Race, power, and multicultural counseling psychology: Understanding White privilege and color-blind racial attitudes. In J. Ponterotto, J. M. Casas, L. A. Suzuki, & C. M. Alexander (Eds.), *Handbook of multicultural counseling* (pp. 257–288). Thousand Oaks, CA: Sage.

Pinterits, E., Poteat, V., & Spanierman, L. B. (2009). The White Privilege Attitudes Scale: Development and initial validation. *Journal of Counseling Psychology, 56*(3), 417–429. doi:10.1037/a0016274.

Rothman, J. C. (2008). *Cultural competence on process and practice: Building bridges.* Upper Saddle River, NJ: Pearson Publishing.

Schatz, M., Jenkins, L., & Sheafor, B. (1990, Fall). Milford redefined: A model of initial and advanced generalist social work. *Journal of Social Work Education, 26*(3), 217–231.

Skocpol, T., & Fiorina, M. P. (1999). *Civic engagement in American democracy.* Washington, DC: Brookings.

Warren, R. L. (1978). *The community in America* (3rd ed.). New York: University Press of America.

Yoder, K. A., Whitbeck, L. B., & Hoyt, D. R. (2001). Event history analysis of antecedents to running away from home and being on the street. *American Behavioral Scientist, 45*(1), 51–65.

Zetzer, H. (2005). White out: Privilege and its problems: Identity and the politics of location. In S. K. Anderson & V. A. Middleton (Eds), *Explorations in privilege, oppression, and diversity* (pp. 9–10). Belmont, CA: Brooks/Cole.

References for Chapter 4

Archer, J. (2004). Sex differences in aggression in real-world settings: A meta-analytic review. *Review of General Psychology, 8*(4): 291–322.

Arredondo, P., Toporek, M. S., Brown, S., Jones, J., Locke, D. C., Sanchez, J. & Stadler, H. (1996) *Operationalization of the multicultural counseling competencies.* Alexandria, VA: AMCD.

Bouchard, T. 1, Jr., Lykken, D. X, McGue, M., Segal, N. L., & Tellegen, A. (1990). Sources of human psychological differences: The Minnesota study of twins reared apart. *Science, 250*, 223–228.

Buss, D. M., & Schmitt, D. P. (1993). Sexual strategies theory: An evolutionary perspective on human mating. *Psychological Review, 100*, 204–232.

Bussey, K., & Bandura, A. (1999). Social cognitive theory of gender development and differentiation. *Psychological Review, 106*, 676–713.

Dahlström, E., & Liljeström, R. (1983). The patriarchal heritage and the working-class women. *Acta Sociologica (Taylor & Francis Ltd), 26*(1), 3–20.

De Cordier, B. (2010). On the thin line between good intentions and creating tensions: A view on gender programmes in Muslim contexts and the (potential) position of Islamic aid organisations. *European Journal of Development Research, 22*(2), 234–251. doi:10.1057/ejdr.2010.2.

Fausto-Sterling, A. (1992). *Myths of gender: Biological theories about women and men.* NY: Basic Books Publishing.

Freud, S. (1905/1930). *Three contributions to the theory of sex.* New York: Nervous and Mental Disease Publishing Co. (Original work published in 1905).

Gilder, G. (1981). *Wealth and poverty.* New York: Basic Books.

hooks, b. (2000). *Feminist theory from margin to center.* Brooklyn, NY: South End Press.

Hunnicutt, G. (2009). Varieties of patriarchy and violence against women: Resurrecting "patriarchy" as a theoretical tool. *Violence Against Women, 15*(5), 553–573.

Kandiyoti, D. (1988). Bargaining with Patriarchy. *Gender & Society, 2*(3), 274–290.

Karlsen, C. (1989). *The devil in the shape of a woman: Witchcraft in colonial New England.* New York: Vintage Books.

Kohlberg, L. (1966). A cognitive-developmental analysis of children's sex-role concepts and attitudes. In E. E. Maccoby (Ed.), *The development of sex differences* (pp. 82–173). Stanford, CA: Stanford University Press.

Lippert-Rasmussen, K. (2010). Gender constructions: The politics of biological constraints. *Distinktion—Scandinavian Journal of Social Theory*, Symposium on Essentialism vs. Constructivism, no. 20, pp. 73–91.

Meier Tetlow, M. (2004). *Women, crime and punishment in ancient law and society: The ancient Near East.* New York: The Continuum International Publishing Group.

Plomin, R., Chipuer, H. M., & Neiderhiser, J. M. (1994). Behavioral genetic evidence for the importance of nonshared environment. In E. M. Hetherington, D. Reiss, & R. Plomin (eds.), *Separate social worlds of siblings: Impact of nonshared environment on development* (pp. 1–31). Hillsdale, NJ: Erlbaum.

Plomin, R., & Daniels, D. (2011). Why are children in the same family so different from each other? *International Journal Epidemiology, 40*, 563–582.

OECD (2011). Aid in support of gender equality and women's empowerment: Statistics based on DAC Members' reporting on the Gender Equality Policy Marker, 2008–2009 Creditor Reporting System database. OECD-DAC Secretariat. Retrieved from http://www.oecd.org/dataoecd/9/34/47335126.pdf.

Rowe, D. C. (1994). *The limits of family influence: Genes, experience, and behavior.* New York: Guilford Press.

Rowland, D. (2004). *The boundaries of her body: The troubling history of women's rights in America.* Naperville, IL: Sphinx Publishing.

Roy, O. (2008). *The politics of chaos in the Middle East.* New York: Columbia University Press.

Sanday, P. R. (2002). *Women at the center: Life in a modern matriarchy.* Ithaca, NY: Cornell University Press.

Schaus M. (Ed.). (2006). Women and gender in medieval Europe: An encyclopedia (Vol. 14, p. 421). New York: Routledge.

Smith, A. (2005). *Rape and the war against Native women.* In I. Hernández-Avila (Ed.), *Reading Native American women: Critical/creative representations.* Lanham, MD: AltaMira Press.

United Nations Development Program [UNDP]. (2000). Millennium development goals. Retrieved from http://www.un.org/millenniumgoals/ on June 22, 2011.

United Nations. (1995). Beijing Declaration and Platform of Action, adopted at the Fourth World Conference on Women, 27 October 1995. Retrieved from http://www.unhcr.org/refworld/docid/3dde04324.html on June 19, 2011.

UN General Assembly. (1979). Convention on the elimination of all forms of discrimination against women, December 18. United Nations, Treaty Series (vol. 1249, p. 13). Retrieved from http://www.unhcr.org/refworld/docid/3ae6b3970.html on December 14, 2012.

Ussher, J. M. (1992). *Women's madness: Misogyny or mental illness?* Boston: University of Massachusetts Press.

Westerkamp, M. J. (1999). *Women and religion in early America, 1600–1850: The Puritan and Evangelical traditions.* New York: Routledge.

Whitaker, D. J., Baker, C. K., Pratt, C., Reed, E., Suri, S., Pavlos, C., & Silverman, J. (2007). A network model for providing culturally competent services for intimate partner violence and sexual violence. *Violence Against Women, 13*(2), 190–209.

References for Chapter 5

Aronowitz, A. A. (2009). *Human trafficking, human misery: The global trade in human beings.* Westport, CT: Praeger Publishing.

Basile, K. C., & Saltzman, L. E. (2002). *Sexual violence surveillance: Uniform definitions and recommended data elements* (Version 1.0). Atlanta, GA: Centers for Disease Control and Prevention, National Center for Injury Prevention and Control. Retrieved from http://www.cdc.gov/ncipc/pub-res/sv_surveillance/sv.htm on September 14, 2005.

Bennett, L., Riger, S., Schewe, P., Howard, A., & Wasco, S. (2004). Effectiveness of hotline, advocacy, counseling and shelter services for victims of domestic violence: A statewide evaluation. *Journal of Interpersonal Violence, 19*(7), 815–829.

Black, M. C., Basile, K. C., Breiding, M. J., Smith, S. G., Walters, M. L., Merrick, M. T., Chen J., & Stevens, M. R. (2011). *The National Intimate Partner and Sexual Violence Survey (NISVS): 2010 Summary Report.* Atlanta, GA: National Center for Injury Prevention and Control, Centers for Disease Control and Prevention.

Blumer, H. (1971). Social problems as collective behavior. *Social problems, 18*(3), 298–306.

Bogecho, D., & Upreti, M. (2006). The Global Gag Rule—An antithesis to the rights-based approach to health. *Health and Human Rights, 9,* 17–32.

Bohner, G., Reinhard, M., Rutz, S., Sturm, S., Kerschbaum, B., & Effler, B. (1998). Rape myths as neutralizing cognitions: Evidence for a causal impact of anti-victim attitudes on men's self-reported likelihood of raping. *European Journal Social Psychology, 28,* 257–268.

Burt, M. R. (1991). *Rape myths and acquaintance rape.* In A. Parrot, & L. Bechhofer (Eds.), *Acquaintance rape: The hidden crime* (pp. 26–40). New York: Wiley.

Catalano, S., Rand, M., Smith, E., & Snyder, H. (2009). Female victims of violence. Bureau of Justice Statistics. Retrieved from http://bjs.ojp.usdoj.gov/index.cfm?ty=pbdetail&iid=2020.

Center for Reproductive Rights. (2003). *Breaking the silence: The Global Gag Rule's impact on unsafe abortion.* Retrieved from http://reproductiverights.org/en/document/breaking-the-silence-the-global-gag-rules-impact-on-unsafe-abortion.

Centers for Disease Control and Prevention (CDC). (2005). *Sexual violence: Fact sheet.* Atlanta, GA: National Center for Injury Prevention and Control. Retrieved from http://www.cdc.gov/ncipc/factsheets/svfacts.htm on September 15, 2006.

Centers for Disease Control and Prevention (CDC). (2008, February). Adverse health conditions and health risk behaviors associated with intimate partner violence—United States, 2005. *MMWR Weekly, 57*(5), 113–117. Retrieved from http://www.cdc.gov/mmwr/preview/mmwrhtml/mm5705a1.htm on September 15, 2009.

Cohen, D., de la Vega, R. & Watson, G. (2001). *Advocacy for social justice: A global action and reflection guide.* Bloomfield, Connecticut: Kumarian Press.

Dallaire, R. (2003). *Shake hands with the devil: The failure of humanity in Rwanda.* Cambridge, MA: Da Capo Press.

DiLillo, D., Giuffre, D., Tremblay, G. C., & Peterson, L. (2001). A closer look at the nature of intimate partner violence reported by women with a history of child sexual abuse. *Journal of Interpersonal Violence, 16,* 2, 116–132.

Domestic Violence Awareness Project (DVAP). (2011). The costs of domestic violence. Retrieved from http://penigma.blogspot.com/2011/10/costs-of-domestic-violence-october-is.html.

El-Bassel, N., Caldeira, N. A., Ruglass, L. M., & Gilbert, L. (2009). Addressing the unique needs of African American women in HIV prevention. *American Journal of Public Health, 99*(6), 996–1001.

Feagin, J. R. (1975). *Subordinating the poor: Welfare and American beliefs.* Englewood Cliffs, NJ: Prentice Hall.

Federal Bureau of Investigation. (2011). Crimes in the United States 2011: Forcible rape. Retrieved from http://www.fbi.gov/about-us/cjis/ucr/crime-in-the-u.s/2011/crime-in-the-u.s.-2011/violent-crime/forcible-rape.

Global Justice Center. (2010). A call for all member states of the human rights council: End the gross violations of the rights of girls and women raped and impregnated in armed conflict, to non-discriminatory medical care, including abortions, under the Geneva Conventions. Retrieved from http://www.globaljusticecenter.net/news-events/news/2010/GJC%20Call%20to%20Action%20at%20US%20Review%20by%20UNHRC.pdf.

Gordon, K. C., Burton, S., & Porter, L. (2004). Predicting the intentions of women in domestic violence shelters to return to partners: Does forgiveness play a role? *Journal of Family Psychology, 18*(2), 331–338.

Hildebrandt, E., & Stevens, P. (2009). Impoverished women with children and no welfare benefits: The urgency of researching failures of the Temporary Assistance for Needy Families Program. *American Journal Public Health, 99*(5), 793–801, doi: 10.2105/AJPH.2006.106211.

Hogan, M. C., Foreman, K. J., Naghavi, M., Ahn, S. Y., Wang, M., Makela, S. M., Lopez, A., Lozano, R., & Murray, C. (2010). Maternal mortality for 181 countries, 1980–2008: A systematic analysis of progress towards Millennium Development Goal 5. *The Lancet, 375*(9726), 1609–1923. doi:10.1016/S0140- 6736(10)60518-1. (Epub before print.)

Hooks, B. (2000). *Feminist theory from margin to center.* Brooklyn, NY: South End Press.

Hudson, K., & Coukos, A. (2005). The dark side of the Protestant ethic: A comparative analysis of welfare reform. *Sociological Theory*, 23(1), 1–24.

Human Rights Watch (HRW). (1995a). Rape for profit: Trafficking of Nepali girls and women to India's brothels. Retrieved from http://www.hrw.org/legacy/reports/1995/India.htm.

Human Rights Watch (HRW). (1995b). Rape as a weapon of war and a tool of political repression. In *Global report on women's human rights*. Retrieved from www.hrw.org/reports/pdfs/g/general/general958.pdf.

Human Rights Watch (HRW). (2002). The war within the war: Sexual violence against women and girls in Eastern Congo. Retrieved from http://www.hrw.org/en/node/81076/section/1.

Human Rights Watch (HRW). (2009). Stopping rape as a weapon of war in Congo. [Press Release]. Retrieved from http://www.hrw.org/en/news/2009/09/18/stopping-rape-weapon-war-congo.

Human Rights Watch (HRW). (2010). Iraqi Kurdistan: Girls and women suffer the consequences of Female Genital Mutilation: Kurdistan Regional Government should outlaw the practice. Retrieved from http://www.hrw.org/news/2010/06/16/iraqi-kurdistan-girls-and-women-suffer-consequences-female-genital-mutilation.

International Committee of the Red Cross. (ICRC). (1949). Geneva Convention Relative to the Protection of Civilian Persons in Time of War (Fourth Geneva Convention). Geneva August 12, 1949, 6 U.S.T. 3516, 75 U.N.T.S. 287, Article 27.

International Committee of the Red Cross. (ICRC). (1987). *Commentary on the additional protocols of 8 June 1977 to the Geneva Conventions of 12 August 1949* (p. 1375, paragraph 4539). Geneva: Martinus Nijhoff Publishers.

International Planned Parenthood Federation. (2007). Witnesses tell U.S. Congressional Committee that President Bush's Global Gag Rule fails women [News Release]. Retrieved from http://www.ippf.org/en/News/Press-releases/Witnesses+tell+US+Congressional+Committee+that+President+Bushs+Global+Gag+Rule+fails+women.htm.

International Women's Health Coalition. (2009). Putting politics before public health: The Global Gag Rule. Retrieved from http://www.iwhc.org/index.php?option=com_content&task=view&id=3529&Itemid=1217.

Institute for Global Labour and Human Rights. (1996). Children exploited by Kathie Lee/Wal-Mart. Available at http://www.globallabourrights.org/alerts?id=0246.

International Committee of the Red Cross (ICRC), Geneva Convention Relative to the Protection of Civilian Persons in Time of War (Fourth Geneva Convention), 12 August 1949, 75 UNTS 287, available at: http://www.refworld.org/docid/3ae6b36d2.html [accessed 12 November 2013]

Lexow, J., Berggrav, M., & Taraldsen, S. (2009). Prevention and eradication of female genital mutilation (FGM) and other harmful traditional practices (HTPs). Norad Collected Reviews. Retrieved from http://www.norad.no/en/Tools+and+publications/Publications/Publication+Page?key=125122

Lightfoot-Klein, H. (1991). Prisoners of ritual: Some contemporary developments in the history of female genital mutilation. Presented at the Second International Symposium on Circumcision in San Francisco, April 30–May 3, 1991.

Lipson, J. G., Lenburg, C. B., & Demi A. S. (Eds.). (1995). *Promoting Cultural Competence in and through nursing education: A critical review and comprehensive plan for action*. Washington, DC: American Academy of Nursing.

Martin, M. (2012). Philosophical and religious influences on social welfare policy in the United States: The ongoing effect of reformed theology and social Darwinism on attitudes toward the poor and social welfare policy and practice. *Journal of Social Work*, 12(1), 51–64. doi:10.1177/1468017310380088.

Martin, M. E. (2014). *Introduction to human services: Through the eyes of practice settings* (3rd ed.). Upper Saddle River, NJ: Pearson Education.

Max, W., Rice, D. P., Finkelstein, E., Bardwell, R. A., & Leadbetter, S. (2004). The economic toll of intimate partner violence against women in the United States. *Violence and Victims, 19*(3), 259–272.

McDermott, M. J., & Garofalo, J. (2004). When advocacy for domestic violence victims backfires. *Violence Against Women, 10*(11), 1245–1266.

National Coalition Against Domestic Violence (NCADV). (2007). Domestic violence fact sheet. Retrieved from http://www.ncadv.org/files/DomesticViolenceFactSheet(National).pdf.

Nunez, R., & Fox, C. (1999). A snapshot of family homelessness across America. *Political Science Quarterly, 114*(2), 289–307.

Phanor-Faury, A. (2012). The high price of Haute Couture. *Black Book Magazine*. Retrieved from http://www.blackbookmag.com/fashion/the-high-price-of-haute-couture-1.48170.

Polack, R. J. (2004). Social justice and the global economy: New challenges for social workers in the 21st century. *Social Work, 49*(2), 281–290.

Saunders, W., & Fragoso, M. (2009). Obama, the U.N. and women's rights: The Obama administration veers to the left on abortion at the United Nations [Issue Brief]. Family Research Council. Retrieved from http://downloads.frc.org/EF/EF09D44.pdf.

Schow, D. (2006). The culture of domestic violence advocacy. Values of equality/behaviours of control. *Women and Health 43*(4), 49–68.

Schuyler, M. (1976). Battered wives: An emerging social problem. *Social Work, 21*, 488–491.

Shepard, M. F. (1999). Advocacy for battered women: Implications for a coordinated community response. In M. F. Shepard, & E. L. Pence (Eds.), *Coordinating community responses to domestic violence: Lessons from Duluth and beyond* (pp. 115–125). Thousand Oaks, CA: Sage.

Siegel, J., & Williams, L. (2003). The relationship between child sexual abuse and female delinquency and crime: A prospective study. *Journal of Research in Crime and Delinquency, 40*(1), 71–94.

Truman, J. L., & Planty, M. (2012, October). Criminal victimization, 2011. Bureau of Justice Statistics Bulletin. Washington D.C.: Bureau of Justice Statistics. Retrieved from http://www.bjs.gov/content/pub/pdf/cv11.pdf.

Tjaden, P., & Thoennes, N. (2000). *Extent, nature, and consequences of intimate partner violence.* Washington, DC: US Department of Justice, Office of Justice Programs.

United Nations, *Beijing Declaration and Platform of Action, adopted at the Fourth World Conference on Women,* 27 October 1995, available at http://www.refworld.org/docid/3dde04324.html (accessed 13 October 2013).

United Nations Committee on the Elimination of Discrimination Against Women (CEDAW), *UN Committee on the Elimination of Discrimination against Women: State Party Report, Brazil,* 7 November 2002, CEDAW/C/BRA/1-5. Retrieved from http://www.unhcr.org/refworld/docid/3f8d51da4.html on June 7, 2011.

United Nations Development Fund for Women (UNIFEM). (2007). Liberia supporting women's engagement in peace building and preventing sexual violence: Community-led approaches. Retrieved from http://www.unifem.org/afghanistan/docs/pubs/07/DFID/liberia.pdf.

United Nations Development Program (UNDP). (2000). Millennium development goals. Retrieved from http://www.undp.org/mdg/basics.shtml.

United Nations Department of Public Education (2007). Lessons from Rwanda: Supporting survivors—victims of sexual violence. Retrieved from http://www.un.org/preventgenocide/rwanda/support.shtml.

United Nations Population Fund (UNFPA). (2011). Population dynamics in the least developed countries: Challenges and opportunities for development and poverty reduction. Retrieved online from http://unfpa.org/webdav/site/global/shared/documents/publications/2011/CP51265.pdf.

United Nations Population Fund (UNFPA). (2009). The end is in sight: Moving toward the abandonment of female genital mutilation/cutting. Annual Report 2009. UNFPA/UNICEF Joint Programme.

United Nations Population Fund (UNFPA). (1997). Women: The right to reproductive and sexual health. United Nations Department of Public Information (DPI/1877). 1997.

United Nations Women. (2011). Fourth United Nations Conference on the Least Developed Countries. Retrieved from http://www.un.org/wcm/content/site/ldc/home.

United Nations Women. (n.d.). Women, poverty, & economics. Retrieved from http://www.unifem.org/gender_issues/women_poverty_economics/.

United Nations. (1995). Beijing Declaration and Platform of Action, adopted at the Fourth World Conference on Women, October 27, 1995. Retrieved from http://www.unhcr.org/refworld/docid/3dde04324.html on June 19, 2011.

United Nations. (1968). Final Act of the International Conference on Human Rights, Tehran, May 13, 1968. Retrieved from http://www.unhcr.org/refworld/docid/3ae6b36f1b.html on June 19, 2011.

United Nations. (2005). Beijing Declaration and Platform of Action, adopted at the Fourth World Conference on Women, 27 October 1995. Retrieved from http://www.unhcr.org/refworld/docid/3dde04324.html on May 27, 2011.

United States Department of Justice. (2012). Attorney General Eric Holder announces revisions to the Uniform Crime Report's definition of rape: Data reported on rape will better reflect state criminal codes, victim experiences (Press Release). Retrieved from http://www.justice.gov/opa/pr/2012/January/12-ag-018.html.

United States Department of State. (2013). *Trafficking in persons report.* (USDS Publication No. 11252). Washington, DC: U.S. Government Printing Office. Retrieved from http://www.state.gov/documents/organization/210737.pdf.

U.S. Department of Justice. (1997). An analysis of data on rape and sexual assault: Sex offenses and offenders. *Bureau of Justice Statistics.* Available online http://www.bjs.gov/content/pub/pdf/SOO.PDF.

Walker, L. (1979). *The battered woman.* New York: Harper and Row.

Weaver, K., Shapiro, R., & Jacobs, L. (1995). The polls–trends: Welfare. *Public Opinion Quarterly, 59*(4), 606–627.

Wolfe, D. A., & Jaffe, P. G. (1999). Emerging strategies in the prevention of domestic violence. *The Future of Children, 9*(3), 133–144.

World Health Organization (WHO). (2008). Eliminating female genital mutilation: An interagency statement UNAIDS, UNDP, UNECA, UNESCO, UNFPA, UNHCHR, UNHCR, UNICEF, UNIFEM, WHO. Geneva: World Health Organization.

World Health Organization (WHO). (2013). Female genital mutilation: Fact sheet. Retrieved from http://www.who.int/mediacentre/factsheets/fs241/en/index.html.

World Health Organization (WHO), UNICEF, & UNFPA. (1997). Female genital mutilation. A Joint WHO/UNICEF/UNFPA Statement. Geneva: World Health Organization.

Wright, T. (2000). Resisting homelessness: Global, national and local solutions. *Contemporary Sociology, 29*(10), 27–43.

References for Chapter 6

ABA Division for Public Education. (n.d.). Part I: The history of juvenile justice: Dialogue on youth and justice. Retrieved from http://www.americanbar.org/content/dam/ aba/migrated/publiced/features/DYJpart1.authcheckdam.pdf/

Adams, D. (1995). *Education for extinction: American Indians and the boarding school experience, 1875–1928*. Lawrence, KS: University Press of Kansas.

Addams, J. (2011). *Twenty years at Hull House*; with autobiographical notes (Kindle Locations 3331–3332). Kindle Edition (original work published 1910).

Ahern, L., & Rosenthal, E. (2006). Hidden suffering: Romania's segregation and abuse of infants and children with disabilities. A report by Mental Disability Rights International. Mental Disability Rights International: Washington, DC: Retrieved from www.mdri.org on March 25, 2009.

Ansah-Koi, A. (2006). Care of orphans: Fostering interventions for children whose parents die of AIDS in Ghana. *Families in Society, 87*, 4, 555–559.

Arieli, M., Beker, J. & Kashti Y. (2001). Residential group care as a socializing environment: Toward a broader perspective. *Child and Youth Care Forum, 30*, 403–414).

Arya, N., & Augarten, R. (2008). Critical condition: African-American youth in the justice system. Campaign for Youth Justice. Retrieved from http://www.campaignforyouthjustice.org/documents/AfricanAmericanBrief.pdf.

Arya, N., & Rolnick, A. (2008). A tangled web of justice: American Indian and Alaska Native youth and federal, state, and tribal justice systems. Campaign for Youth Justice. Retrieved from http://www.campaignforyouthjustice.org/documents/CFYJPB _TangledJustice.pdf.

Bellingham, B. (1984). *Little wanderers: A socio-historical study of the nineteenth century origins of child fostering and adoption reform, based on early records of the New York Children's Aid Society*. Unpublished doctoral dissertation, University of Pennsylvania (available from University Microfilm Incorporated (UMI), Ann Arbor, MI).

Bender, T. (1975). *Toward an urban vision: Ideas and institutions in nineteenth century America*. Baltimore, MD: The John Hopkins University Press.

Betancourt, T. S., & Khan, K. T. (2008). The mental health of children affected by armed conflict: Protective processes and pathways to resilience. *International Review of Psychiatry, 20*(3), 317–328.

Bhabha, J. (2004). Seeking asylum alone: Treatment of separated and trafficked children in need of refugee protection. *International migration, 42*(1), 141–148.

Brace, C. L. (1967). *The dangerous classes of New York and twenty years of work among*. New York: Wynkoop & Holland Publishers (original published in 1872).

Brown, D. (2001). *Bury my heart at wounded knee: An Indian history of the American west*. New York: Henry Holt and Company.

Butts, J., & Travis, J. (2002). *The rise and fall of American youth violence: 1980–2000*. Urban Institute Justice Policy Center. Washington, DC Retrieved from http://www.danielcarter.us/juvenile_info/410437.pdf. Centers for Disease Control and Prevention (CDC). (2002). Infant mortality and low birth weight among black and white infants—United States, 1980–2000. *MMWR, 51*(27), 589–612.

Child Soldiers Global Report. (2012). Louder than words: An agenda for action to end state use of child soldiers. Child Soldiers International. Retrieved from http://www.child-soldiers.org/global_report_reader.php?id=562 on October 14, 2013.

Child Welfare League of America. (2002). Minorities as majority: Disproportionality in child welfare and juvenile justice. *Children's Voice*. Retrieved from http://www.cwla.org/articles/cv0211minorities.htm on March 4, 2005.

Child Soldiers International, Louder than words: An agenda for action to end state use of child soldiers. (2013), Available at: http://www.refworld.org/docid/5208bcdb4.html [accessed 17 November 2013]

Clinton, R.N., Goldberg, C.E., Tsosie, R. & Riley, A. (2013). *American Indian Law: Native Nations and the Federal System* (6th edition). LexisNexis. Available online at http://www.lexisnexis.com/store/images/Supplements/3009_2013%20Fall %20Supplement.pdf.

Cooper, K. J. (2011). Despite law on racial disparities, black teens are overly tried as adults. St. Louis Post-Dispatch. Retrieved from https://www.stlbeacon.org/#!/content/16224/black_teens_disproportionately_tried_as_adults.

Denby, R. W., & Curtis, C. M. (2003). Why special populations are not the target of family preservation services: A case for program reform. *Journal of Sociology & Social Welfare, 30*(2), 149–173.

Dhlembeu, N. & Mayanga, N. (2006). Responding to orphans and other vulnerable children's crisis: Development of Zimbabwe's national plan of action. *Journal of Social Development in Africa, 21*(1), 5–49.

Dunn, A., Jareg, A., & Webb, D. (2003). A last resort: The growing concern about children in residential care. Washington, DC: International Save the Children Alliance.

First Nations Orphan Association. (n.d.). Retrieved from http://www.angelfire.com/falcon/fnoa on March 28, 2006.

Fryer, D. (2007). "Improved" and "very promising children" growing up rich in eighteenth century South Carolina. In J. Marten (Ed.), *Children in Colonial America*. New York: New York University Press.

Galenson, D. W. (1984). The rise and fall of indentured servitude in the Americas: An economic analysis. *The Journal of Economic History, 44*(1), 1–26.

Goodman, J. H. (2004). Coping with trauma and hardship among unaccompanied refugee youths from Sudan, *Qualitative Health Research, 14*(9), 1177–1196.

Hindman, H. D. (2002). *Child labor: An American history*. New York: M.E. Sharp.

Hodge, D., & Lietz, C. (2007). The international sexual trafficking of women and children: A review of the literature. *AFFILIA Journal of Women & Social Work, 22*(2), 163–174.

Holt, M. (1992). *The orphan trains: Placing out in America*. Lincoln: University of Nebraska Press.

Honeyman, K. (2007). *Child workers in England, 1780–1820 (studies in labour history)*. Hampshire, England: Ashgate Publishing Unlimited.

Inter-Agency, *Inter-agency guiding principles on unaccompanied and separated children*, January 2004. Retrieved from http://www .refworld.org/docid/4113abc14.html on October 15, 2013.

International Labour Organization (ILO). (2002). A future without child labour: Global report under the follow up to the ILO Declaration on Fundamental Principles and Rights at Work. Geneva: International Labour Office.

Johnson, A. K. (2004). Social work is standing on the legacy of Jane Addams: But are we sitting on the sidelines? *Social Work, 49*(2), 319–322.

Juszkiewicz, J. 2000. *Youth crime/adult time: Is justice served?* Washington, DC: Pretrial Services Resource Center for the Building Blocks for Youth Initiative.

Katz, M. B. (1996). *In the shadow of the poorhouse: A social history of welfare in America*. New York: Basic Books.

Kreisher, K. (2002, March). Coming home: The lingering effects of the Indian adoption project. *Children's Voice*. Child Welfare League of America. Retrieved from http://www.cwla.org/articles/cv0203indianadopt.htm on July 10, 2004.

Lawrence, R., & Hemmens, C. (2008). *Juvenile justice*. Thousand Oaks, CA: Sage Publications.

Leatherman, J. (2011). *Sexual violence and armed conflict*. Cambridge: Polity Press.

Leve, L. D., & Chamberlain, P. (2005). Association with delinquent peers: Intervention effects for youth in the juvenile justice system. *Journal of Abnormal Child Psychology, 33*(3), 339–347.

Marten, J., & Greven, P. J. (2007). *Children in colonial America*. New York: New York University Press.

MacLean, K. (2003). The impact of institutionalization on child development. *Development and Psychopathology, 15*(04), 853–884.

Martin, M. (2014). *Introduction to human services: Through the eyes of practice settings* (3rd ed.). Upper Saddle, NJ: Pearson Publishing.

Michel, G. (2001). *The impact of war on children: A review of progress since the 1996 United Nations report on the impact of armed conflict on children*. Vancouver, BC: University of British Columbia Press.

Miller, C. M., Gruskin, S., Subramanian, S. V., Rajaraman, D., & Heymann, S. J. (2006). Orphan care in Botswana's working households: Growing responsibilities in the absence of adequate support. *American Journal of Public Health, 96*(8), 1429–1435.

Mizrahi, T. (2001). The status of community organization in 2001: Community practice context, complexities, contradictions, and contributions. *Research on Social Work Practice, 11*, 176–189.

Monasch, R., Stover, J., Loudon, M., Kabira, D, & Walker, N. (2007). National response to orphans and other vulnerable children in sub-Saharan Africa: The OVC Policy and Planning Effort Index, 2004. *Vulnerable Children and Youth Studies, 2*(1), 40–59,

Morgan, K. (2001). *Slavery and servitude in colonial North America: A short history*. New York: New York University Press.

National Association of Black Social Workers (NABSW). (2003). *Kinship care*. Retrieved from http://www.nabsw.org/mserver/ KimshipCare.aspx?menuContext=760 on October 23, 2005.

O'Conner, S. (2004). *Orphan trains: The story of Charles Loring Brace and the children he saved and failed*. Chicago: The University of Chicago Press.

Patrick, M., Sheets, E., & Trickel, E. (1990). *We are a part of history: The orphan trains*. Virginia Beach, VA: The Donning Co.

Peek, L. (2008). Children and disasters: Understanding vulnerability, developing capacities, and promoting resilience—An introduction. *Children Youth and Environments, 18*(1), 1–29.

Piaget, J. (1926). *The language and thought of a child*. New York: Trench, Trubner & Co., Ltd.

Polack, R. (2004). Social justice and the global economy: New challenges for social work in the 21st century. *Social Work, 49*(2), 281–290.

Ressler, E. M., Boothbay, N., & Steinbock, D. J. (1988). *Unaccompanied children: Care and protection in wars, natural disasters, and refugee movements*. New York: Oxford University Press.

Robb, M. (2006). International child sex trafficking: Ravaged innocence. *.Social Work Today, 6*(5), 22–25.

Roby, J. L., & Shaw, S. A. (2006). The African orphan crisis and international adoption. *Social Work, 51*(3), 199–210.

Romero, T. (2007). Colonizing childhood: Religion, gender, and Indian children in southern New England, 1620–1720. In James Marten, & Philip J. Greven (Eds.), *Children in colonial America (children and youth in america)* (p. 33). NYU Press reference. Kindle Edition.

Rossen, L. M., & Schoendorf, K. C. (2013). Trends in Racial and Ethnic Disparities in Infant Mortality Rates in the United States, 1989–2006. *American journal of public health*, (0), e1–e8.

Sanchirico, A., & Jablonka, K. (2000). Keeping foster children connected to their biological parents: The impact of foster parent training and support. *Child and Adolescent Social Work Journal, 17*(3), 185–203.

Schultz, C. B. (1985). Children and childhood in eighteenth century. In Joseph M. Hawes & N. Ray Hiner (Eds.), *American childhood: A research guide and historical handbook* (pp. 70, 79–80). Westport, CT: Greenwood Press.

Seelig, J. M. (1994). Child welfare issues in Ethiopia. John Michael Seelig and Andargatchew Tesfaye. *International Social Work* (SAGE, London; Thousand Oaks, CA; and New Delhi), *37*, 221–237.

Silverman, D. J. (2001). The Impact of Indentured Servitude on the Society and Culture of Southern New England Indians, 1680–1810. *The New England Quarterly, 74*(4), 622–666.

Singletary, J. (2007). Community and family models of care for orphans and vulnerable children in Africa. *Social Work and Christianity, 34*(3), 298–316.

Smith, C. J., & Devore, W. (2004). African American children in the child welfare and kinship system: From exclusion to over inclusion. *Children & Youth Services Review, 26*(5), 427–446.

Snyder, H. N., & Sickmund, M. (2006). Juvenile offenders and victims: 2006 national report. Washington, DC: U.S. Department of Justice, Office of Justice Programs, Office of Juvenile Justice and Delinquency Prevention.

Surbeck, B. C. (2003). An investigation of racial partiality in child welfare assessments of attachment. *American Journal of Orthopsychiatry, 73*(1), 13–23.

Trattner, W. (1998). *From poor law to welfare state: A history of social welfare in America*. New York: Free Press.

U.S. Agency for International Development [UNAIDS]. (2009). *AIDS epidemic update: December 2009*. Geneva: WHO Regional Office Europe.

UCLA School of Law. (2010). The impact of prosecuting youth in the adult criminal justice system: A review of the literature. UCLA School of Law, Juvenile Justice Project.

United Nations Children's Fund (UNICEF). (2006). Africa's orphaned and vulnerable generations: Children affected by AIDS. Retrieved from http://www.unicef.org/publications/files/Africas_Orphaned_and_Vulnerable_Generations_Children_Affected_by_AIDS.pdf.

United Nations Children's Fund (UNICEF), & U.S. Agency for International Development (USAID). (2004). *Children on the brink 2004: A joint report of new orphan estimates and a Framework for Action*. The Joint United Nations Programme on HIV/AIDS. New York: United Nations Children's Fund.

United Nations Children's Fund (UNICEF). (2008). The state of the world's children: Child survival. Retrieved from http://www.unicef.org/sowc08/docs/sowc08.pdf on April 4, 2009.

United Nations Children's Fund (UNICEF). (1990). First call for children: World declaration and plan of action from the World Summit for Children. Convention on the Rights of the Child. Retrieved from http://www.unicef.org/about/history/files/WSC_declaration_first_call_for_children.pdf.

United Nations Convention on the Rights of the Child (UNCRC). (1989). Resolution adopted by the U.N. General Assembly, 44th Session, 20 November, A/RESZ.

U.S. Department of Health and Human Services, Administration for Children & Families, Administration on Children, Youth and Families, Children's Bureau. (2012). *The AFCARS report*. Retrieved from http://www.acf.hhs.gov/programs/cb/stats_research/afcars/tar/report14.htm on June 22, 2009.

U.S. Senate. (1974). *Hearings before the Subcommittee on Indian Affairs of the Committee on Interior and Insular Affairs,* 99th Cong., 2nd Session (testimony of William Byler). Washington, DC: U.S. Government Printing Office.

Wagner, C. (2009, March). Stopping the use of child soldiers. *Futurist, 43*(2) 9–9. Retrieved April 5, 2009, from Business Source Elite database.

Warren, A. (1995). *Orphan train rider: One boy's true story*. Boston: Houghton Mifflin Co.

Weiss, I. (2005). Is there a global common core to social work? A cross-national comparative study of BSW graduate students. *Social Work, 50*(2), 102–110.

Williamson, J. (2004). A family is for a lifetime. USAID Office of HIV/AIDS. Washington, DC: The Synergy Project.

Wolff, P. H., & Fesseha, G. (2005). The orphans of Eritrea: What are the choices? *American Orthopsychiatry, 75*(4), 475–484.

References for Chapter 7

Altman, C. (1999). Gay and lesbian seniors: Unique challenges of coming out in later life. *Siecus Report, 27*(3), 14–17.

American Psychiatric Association. (1987). *Diagnostic and statistical manual of mental disorders* (3rd ed., revised). Washington, DC: Author.

Brewer, S. (1986, January 26). 'Gay bashing': A growing threat to homosexuals. *Los Angeles Times*. Retrieved from http://articles.latimes.com/1986-01-26/news/mn-160_1_gay-community/.

Burns, C., Garcia, A., & Wolgin, P. (2013). *Living in dual shadows: LGBT undocumented immigrants*. Washington, DC: Center for American Progress,. Retrieved from http://www.americanprogress.org/wp-content/uploads/2013/03/LGBTUndocumentedReport-5.pdf.

California Marriage Protection Act of 2008 [Proposition 8]. CA. Const. art. II, § 7.5.

Defense of Marriage Act (DOMA), 1 U.S.C. § 7 and 28 U.S.C. § 1738C.

Dunbar, E. (2006). Race, gender, and sexual orientation in hate crime victimization: Identity politics or identity risk? *Violence & Victims, 21*(3), 323–337.

Federal Bureau of Investigations. (2012). Hate crimes accounting: Annual report released. Retrieved from http://www.fbi.gov/news/stories/2012/december/annual-hate-crimes-report-released/annual-hate-crimes-report-released.

Focus on the Family. (2008). Our position (pro-gay theology). Retrieved from http://www.focusonthefamily.com/socialissues/social-issues/same-sex-revisionist-theology/our-position.aspx.

Focus on the Family. (2013). Can you explain and defend your ministry's perspective on homosexuality and same-sex marriage? Retrieved from http://family.custhelp.com/app/answers/detail/a_id/26078.

Gallup Organization. (2011, May 5–8). Gay and lesbian rights [Graph]. Retrieved from http://www.gallup.com/poll/1651/Gay-Lesbian-Rights.aspx.

Gates, G. (2013, March). LGBT adult immigrants in the United States. The Williams Institute, UCLA School of Law. Retrieved from http://williamsinstitute.law.ucla.edu/wp-content/uploads/LGBTImmigrants-Gates-Mar-2013.pdf.

Gettleman, J. (2010). America's role seen in Uganda's anti-gay push. *The New York Times.*

GLAAD. (2010). *Media reference guide* (8th ed.). Retrieved from http://www.glaad.org/files/MediaReferenceGuide2010.pdf.

Herek, G. M. (2004). Beyond "homophobia": Thinking about sexual prejudice and stigma in the twenty first century. *Sexuality Research & Social Policy, 1*(2), 1–24.

Herek, G. M. (2009). Sexual stigma and sexual prejudice in the United States: A conceptual framework. In D. A. Hope (Ed.), *Contemporary perspectives on lesbian, gay & bisexual identities: The 54th Nebraska Symposium on Motivation* (pp. 65–111). New York: Springer.

Hooker, E. 1956. A preliminary analysis of group behavior of homosexuals. *Journal of Psychology, 42*, 217–225.

Hooker, E. 1957. The adjustment of the male overt homosexual. *Journal of Projective Techniques, 21*, 18–31.

Human Rights Campaign. (2013). LGBT cultural competence. Retrieved from http://www.hrc.org/resources/entry/lgbt-cultural-competence.

Human Rights Watch (HRW). (2004). Hated to death: Homophobia, violence, and Jamaica's HIV/AIDS epidemic. Retrieved from http://www.hrw.org/reports/2004/11/15/hated-death-0.

Human Rights Watch (HRW). (2009, August 17). "They want us exterminated": Murder, torture, sexual orientation and gender in Iraq. Retrieved from http://www.hrw.org/sites/default/files/reports/iraq0809web.pdf.

Human Rights Watch (HRW). (2010a, December 15). We are a buried generation: Discrimination and violence against sexual minorities in Iran. Retrieved from http://www.hrw.org/node/94978.

Human Rights Watch (HRW). (2010b, November 30). Fear for life: Violence against gay men and men perceived as gay in Senegal. Retrieved from http://www.hrw.org/reports/2010/11/30/fear-life.

Human Rights Watch (HRW). (2011). "We'll show you you're a woman": Violence and discrimination against black lesbians and transgender men in South Africa. Retrieved from http://www.hrw.org/sites/default/files/reports/southafrica1211.pdf.

Jewkes, R., Sikweyiya, Y., Morrell, R., & Dunkle, K. (2009). Understanding men's health and use of violence: Interface of rape and HIV in South Africa. Retrieved from http://www.mrc.ac.za/gender/violence_hiv.pdf.

Kinsey, A. C., Pomeroy, W. B., & Martin, C. E. (1948). *Sexual behavior in the human male*. Philadelphia, PA: W. B. Saunders.

Kosciw, J. G., Greytak, E. A., Diaz, E. M., & Bartkiewicz, M. J. (2010). The 2009 National School Climate Survey: The experiences of lesbian, gay, bisexual, and transgender youth in our nation's schools. New York: GLSEN.

Krajeski, J. 1996. Homosexuality and the mental health professions. In R. Cabaj & T. Stein (Eds.), *Textbook of Homosexuality and Mental Health* (pp. 17–31). Washington, DC: American Psychiatric Press.

Kulkin, H. S., Williams, J., Boykin, L, & Ahn, B. (2009). Social work students and homophobia: What are their attitudes? *Journal of Baccalaureate Social Work, 14*(2), 79–88.

Martin, M. E. (2014). *Introduction to human services: Through the eyes of practice settings* (3rd ed.). Upper Saddle River, NJ: Pearson Education.

Marzullo, M. A., & Libman, A. J. (2009). Hate crimes and violence against lesbian, gay, bisexual, and transgender people. Human Rights Campaign. Retrieved from http://www.hrc.org/files/assets/resources /Hatecrimesandviolenceagainstlgbtpeople_2009.pdf.

McCall, L. (2005). The complexity of intersectionality. *Journal of Women in Culture and Society, 30*(3), 1771–1800.

Meyer, D. (2012). An intersectional analysis of lesbian, gay, bisexual, and transgender (LGBT) people's evaluations of anti-queer violence. *Gender & Society, 26*(6), 849–873. doi:10.1177/0891243212461299.

Pew Research Center. (2013, March). Changing attitudes on gay marriage. Retrieved from http://features .pewforum.org/same-sex-marriage-attitudes/.

Pope, M. (2003). Sexual minority youth in the schools: Issues and desirable counselor responses. Washington, DC: Education Resources Information Center (ERIC Document Reproduction Service No. ED480481).

Services and Advocacy for Gay, Lesbian, Bisexual and Transgender Elders and Movement Advancement Project (SAGE). (2010). Improving the lives of LGBT older adults. New York: SAGE. Retrieved from http://www .lgbtagingcenter.org/resources/pdfs/ImprovingtheLivesofLGBTOlderAdultsFull.pdf.

Shankle, M. D., Maxwell, C. A., Katzman, E. S., & Landers, S. (2003). An invisible population: Older lesbian, gay, bisexual, and transgender individuals. *Clinical Research & Regulatory Affairs, 20,* 159–182.

Spitzer, R. L. (1973). A proposal about homosexuality and the APA nomenclature: Homosexuality as an irregular form of sexual behavior and sexual orientation disturbance as a psychiatric disorder. *American Journal of Psychiatry, 130,* 1214–1216.

Westboro Baptist Church (WBC). (2013). WBC website, "GodHatesFags". Retrieved from http://www.godhatesfags.com/wbcinfo/aboutwbc.html.

References for Chapter 8

Adess, S., Goodman, J., Kysel, I., Pacyniak, G., Polcyn, L., Schau, J., & Waddell, A. (2009). Refugee crisis in America: Iraqis and their resettlement experience. Georgetown University Law Center, Human Rights Institute. Retrieved from http://scholarship.law. georgetown.edu/hri_papers/4.

Barboza, D. (2001, December 20). Tyson foods indicted on plans to smuggle illegal workers. *New York Times.* Retrieved from http://www.nytimes.com/2001/12/20/us/tyson-foods-indicted-in-plan-to-smuggle-illegal-workers.html.

Bell, H. (2008). Case management with displaced survivors of Hurricane Katrina: A case study of one host community. *Journal of Social Service Research, 34*(3), 15–27. doi: 10.1080/01488370802085932.

Boucher, S. R., &J. E. Taylor. (2007). Policy shocks and the supply for Mexican labor to U.S. farms. *Choices, 21,* 1st quarter, 37–42.

Camarota, S. A. (2004). *The high cost of cheap labor: Illegal immigration and the federal budget* (Vol. 23). Washington, DC: Center for Immigration Studies.

Center for Comparative Immigration Studies. (2007). In W. A. Cornelius & J. M. Lewis (Eds.), *Impacts of border enforcement on Mexican migration: The view from sending communities. La Jolla.* San Diego, CA: University of California at San Diego.

Congressional Budget Office. (2007). The impact of unauthorized immigrants on the budgets of state and local governments. Retrieved from http://www.cbo.gov/sites/default/files/cbofiles/ftpdocs/87xx/doc8711/12-6-immigration.pdf.

Conversi, D. (2007-03-16). *Ethnonationalism in the contemporary world* (Routledge advances in international relations and global politics) (p. 288). Taylor & Francis, Kindle Edition.

Council of Europe: Commissioner for Human Rights. (2009, July 6).Many Roma in Europe are stateless and live outside social protection. Retrieved from http://www.unhcr.org/refworld/docid/4a7023c72.html on April 12, 2013.

Crutchfield, M. (2013). Phases of disaster recovery: Emergency response to the long term. United Methodist Church on Relief (UMCOR). Retrieved from http://www.umcmission.org/Find-Resources/New-World-Outlook-Magazine/2013/March-April-2013/0430-Phases-of-Disaster-Recovery-Emergency-Response-for-the-Long-Term.

Danish Refugee Council (DRC). (2012). A sexual and gender-based violence rapid assessment: Doro Refugee Camp, Upper Nile State, South Sudan [Press Release]. Retrieved from http://reliefweb.int/report/south-sudan-republic/sexual-and-gender-based-violence-rapid-assessment-doro-refugee-camp.

Department of State. (2011). Protracted refugee situations. Bureau of Populations, Refugees and Migration. Retrieved from http://www.state.gov/j/prm/policyissues/issues/protracted/.

Devadoss, S., & Luckstead, J. (2011). Implications of immigration policies for the U.S. farm sector and workforce. *Economic Inquiry, 49*(3), 857–875.

Fagen, P. W., (2011, April). Refugees and IDPs after conflict: Why they do not go home. United States Institute of Peace, Special Report 268. Retrieved from http://www.usip.org/files/resources/SR268Fagen.pdf.

Federal Emergency Management Agency (FEMA). (2007). The four phases of emergency management. FEMA Training Module. Retrieved from http://usasearch.fema.gov/search?utf8=%E2%9C%93&sc=0&query=four+phases&m=&affiliate=fema&commit=Search.

Flynn, B. W., & Norwood, A. E. (2004). Defining normal psychological reactions to disaster. *Psychiatric Annals, 34*(8), 597–603.

Fritz, E. C. (1961). Disaster. In R. K. Merton & R. A. Nisbet (Eds.), *Contemporary social problems: An introduction to the sociology of deviant behavior and social disorganization.* New York: Harcourt, Brace & World.

Gebre, Y. (2002). Contextual determination of migration behaviors: The Ethiopian resettlement in light of conceptual constructs. *Journal of Refugee Studies, 15*(3), 265–282.

Greenstone, M., & Looney, A. (2010). Ten economic facts about immigration. The Hamilton Project. Retrieved from http://www.brookings.edu/~/media/research/files/reports/2010/9/immigration%20greenstone%20looney/09_immigration.

Griswold, D. T. (2012).Immigration and the welfare state. *Cato Journal, 32*(1), 159–174.

Hanson, G. H. (2009). *The economics and policy of illegal immigration in the United States.* Washington, DC: Migration Policy Institute. Retrieved from http://www.migrationpolicy.org/pubs/Hanson%20-Dec09.pdf.

Harvard Humanitarian Initiative. (2009). Characterizing sexual violence in the Democratic Republic of the Congo: Profiles of violence, community responses and implications for the protection of women. Retrieved from http://hhi.harvard.edu/sites/default/files/publications/final%20report%20for%20the%20open%20society%20institute%20-%201.pdf on May 23, 2011.

Hoefer, M., Rytina, N., & Baker, B. (2012). Estimates of the unauthorized immigrant population residing in the United States: January 2011. Office of Immigration Statistics, Policy Directorate, U.S. Department of Homeland Security. Retrieved from http://www.dhs.gov/xlibrary/assets/statistics/publications/ois_ill_pe_2011.pdf.

Hollenbach, D. (2008). *Refugee rights*. Washington, DC: Georgetown University Press.

Hossain, F. (2011). Disaster management in Bangladesh: Regulatory and social work perspectives. *Journal of Comparative Social Work, 27*(1), 91–101.

Human Rights Watch. (2010, February 2). Stateless again: Palestinian-origin Jordanians deprived of their nationality. Retrieved from http://www.unhcr.org/refworld/docid/4b6ae5702.html on April 12, 2013.

Immigration and Nationality Act (last amended March 2010) [United States of America] (2010, March 4). Retrieved from http://www.refworld.org/docid/4e663ba42.html on October 17, 2013.

Immigration Policy Institute. (2012). Arizona SB 1070: Legal challenges and economic realities. Retrieved from http://www.immigrationpolicy.org/clearinghouse/litigation-issue-pages/arizona-sb-1070%E2%80%8E-legal-challenges-and-economic-realities.

International Federation of Red Cross and Red Crescent Societies (IFRC). (n.d.). About disaster management. Retrieved from https://www.ifrc.org/en/what-we-do/disaster-management/about-disaster-management/.

Jayasuriya, S., & McCawley, P. (2010). The Asian tsunami: Aid and reconstruction after a disaster. Northampton, MA: Edward Elgare Publishers.

Jones, R. (2011). Intolerable intolerance: Toxic xenophobia and pedagogy of resistance. *High School Journal, 95*(1), 34–45.

Kahler, M., & Walter, B. (Eds.). (2006). *Territoriality and conflict in an era of globalization*. Cambridge, MA: Cambridge University Press.

Kaleem, J., & Wallace, T. (2012). Hurricane Sandy vs. Katrina infographic examines destruction from both storms. *Huffington Post*. Retrieved from http://www.huffingtonpost.com/2012/11/04/hurricane-sandy-vs-katrina-infographic_n_2072432.html.

Loescher, G., Milner, J., Newman, E., & Troeller, G. G. (Eds.). (2008). *Protracted refugee situations: Political, human rights and security implications*. Tokyo: United Nations University Press.

Lopez, M. H., Gonzalez-Barrera, A., & Motel, S. (2011). As deportations rise to record levels, most Latinos oppose Obama's policy. Washington, DC: Pew Hispanic Center, December. http://www.pewhispanic.org/2011/12/28/as-deportations-rise-torecord-levels-most-latinos-oppose-obamas-policy.

Lyons, T. (2006). Diasporas and homeland conflict. In M. Kahler and B. Walter (Eds), *Globalization, territoriality, and conflict*. Cambridge: Cambridge University Press.

Martin, D. A. (2004). The United States Refugee Admissions Program: Reforms for a new era of refugee resettlement. *Columbia Human Rights Law Review, 36*, 299–321.

Martin, D. C., & Yankay, J. E. (2012).Refugees and asylees: 2011. Annual Flow Report. DHS Office of Immigration Statistics. Retrieved from http://www.dhs.gov/xlibrary/assets/statistics/publications/ois_rfa_fr_2011.pdf.

Monger, R., & Yankay, J. (2013). U.S. legal permanent residents: 2012. Office of Immigration Statistics, Policy Directorate, U.S. Department of Homeland Security. Retrieved from http://www.dhs.gov/sites/default/files/publications/ois_lpr_fr_2012_2.pdf.

National Immigration Law Center. (2011). The Dream Act: Summary. Retrieved from http://nilc.org/dreamsummary.html.

Norris, F., Friedman, M., & Watson, P. (2002). 60,000 disaster victims speak: Part II. Summary and implications of the disaster mental health research. *Psychiatry, 65*(3), 240–260.

Oliver-Smith, A., & Hansen, A. (1982). Involuntary migration and resettlement: Causes and contexts. In A. Hanson & A. Oliver-Smith (Eds.), *Involuntary migration and resettlement*. Boulder, CO: Westview Press.

Orth, R. (2001). *Rwanda's Hutu extremist insurgency: An eyewitness perspective*. New Haven, CT: MacMillan Center for International and Area Studies.

Passel, J. (2008). *Trends in unauthorized immigration: Undocumented inflow now trails legal inflow*. Washington, DC: Pew Hispanic Center. Retrieved from http://pewhispanic.org/reports/report.php?ReportID=94.

Passel, J. S., & Cohn, D. (2009, April). *A portrait of unauthorized immigrants in the United States*. Washington, DC: Pew Hispanic Center. Retrieved from http://www.pewhispanic.org/2009/04/14/a-portrait-of-unauthorized-immigrants-in-the-united-states/.

Passel, J. S., & Cohn, D. (2011). *Unauthorized immigrant population: National and state trends, 2010*. Washington, DC: Pew Hispanic Center. Retrieved from http://www.pewhispanic.org/2011/02/01/unauthorized-immigrant-populationbrnational-and-state-trends-2010/.

Passel, J. S., Cohn, D., & Gonzalez-Barrera, A. (2012). *Net migration from Mexico falls to zero—and perhaps less*. Washington, DC: Pew Research Center. Retrieved from http://www.pewhispanic.org/files/2012/04/Mexican-migrants-report_final.pdf.

Pawar, M. (2008). The flood of Krishna River and the flood of politics: Dynamics of rescue and relief operations in a village in India. *Asia Pacific Journal of Social Work Development, 18*(2), 19–35.

Pedersen, D. (2002). Political violence, ethnic conflict, and contemporary wars: Broad implications for health and social well-being. *Social Science & Medicine, 55*(2), 175–190.

Pew Hispanic Center. (2013). *A nation of immigrants: A portrait of the 40 million, including 11 million unauthorized.* Washington, DC: Pew Research Center. Retrieved from http://www.pewhispanic.org/files/2013/01 /statistical_portrait_final_jan_29.pdf.

Pew Research Center. (2013). Most say illegal immigrants should be allowed to stay, but citizenship is more divisive. Retrieved from http://www.people-press.org/files/legacy-pdf/3-28-13%20Immigration%20Release.pdf.

Prunier, G. (2009). *Africa's world war: Congo, the Rwandan genocide, and the making of a continental catastrophe.* New York: Oxford University Press.

Richards, A., Ospina-Duque, J., Barrera-Valencia, M., Escobar-Rincón, J., Ardila-Gutiérrez, M., Metzler, T., & Marmar, C. (2011). Posttraumatic stress disorder, anxiety and depression symptoms, and psychosocial treatment needs in Colombians internally displaced by armed conflict: A mixed-method evaluation. *Psychological Trauma: Theory, Research, Practice, and Policy, 3*(4), 384.

Smith, J. P., & Edmonston, B. (Eds.). (1997). *The New Americans: Economic, demographic, and fiscal effects of immigration.* Washington, DC: National Academy Press.

Stockholm International Peace Research Institute (SIPRI). (1993). Yearbook of World Armaments and Disarmaments. Oxford, UK: Oxford University Press.

Stockholm International Peace Research Institute (SIPRI). (2008). Yearbook of World Armaments and Disarmaments. Oxford, UK: Oxford University Press.

Taylor, P., Lopez, M. H., Passel, J. S., & Motel, S. (2011, December). *Unauthorized immigrants: Length of residency, patterns of parenthood.* Washington, DC: Pew Hispanic Center. Retrieved from http://www.pewhispanic .org/2011/12/01/unauthorized-immigrants-length-of-residency-patterns-of-parenthood/.

Tempany, M. (2009). What research tells us about the mental health and psychosocial wellbeing of Sudanese refugees: A literature review. *Transcultural Psychiatry, 46*(2), 300–315.

Transatlantic Trends. (2008). Immigration: Key findings 2008. Retrieved from http://www.gmfus.org/wp-content /blogs.dir/4/files/archived/doc/TTI_2008_Final.pdf.

Transatlantic Trends. (2011). Immigration: Key findings 2011. Available at: http://www.gmfus.org/publications _/TT/TT2011_final_web.pdf.

Tumlin, K. C., & Zimmerman, W. (2003). *Immigrants and TANF: A look at immigrant welfare recipients in three cities.* Washington, DC: The Urban Institute. Occasional Paper No. 69.

UN General Assembly. (1951). Convention Relating to the Status of Refugees, 28 July 1951, United Nations, Treaty Series, vol. 189, p. 137. Retrieved from http://www.refworld.org/docid/3be01b964.html on October 17, 2013.

UN High Commission for Refugees (UNHCR). (2012b). Statelessness and women. Retrieved from http://www .unhcr.org/pages/4ab1eb446/gallery-5045ef2f6.html on April 12, 2013.

UN High Commissioner for Refugees (UNHCR). (2008a). Outline for the oral update on protracted situations which would benefit from international support. Report presented at the 41st Meeting of the Standing Committee, March 6–8, 2008. Retrieved from http://www.unhcr.org/refworld/pdfid/47d6a6762.pdf.

UN High Commissioner for Refugees (UNHCR). (2008b). *Protracted refugee situations,* November 20, 2008. Retrieved from http:// www.unhcr.org/refworld/docid/492fb92d2.html on April 12, 2013.

UN High Commissioner for Refugees (UNHCR). (2010). Evaluation of the protracted refugee situation (PRS) for Burundians in Tanzania. Retrieved from www.oecd.org/countries/sudan/47164501.pdf on April 13, 2013.

UN High Commissioner for Refugees (UNHCR). (2012a). UNHCR global trends 2011: A year of crises, June 18, 2012. Retrieved from http://www.unhcr.org/refworld/docid/4fdeccbe2.html on April 12, 2013.

United Nations (UN). (2013). Somalia famine killed nearly 260,000, half of them children—reports UN. UN News Centre [Press Release]. Retrieved from http://www.un.org/apps/news/story.asp?NewsID=44811#.UddbtD7714E.

United States Conference of Catholic Bishops. (2012). The changing face of the unaccompanied alien child: A portrait of foreign-born children in federal foster care and how to best meet their needs. Retrieved from http://www.rcusa.org/uploads/pdfs/ A-Portrait-of-Foreign-Born-Children-in-Federal-Foster-Care-and-How-to-Best-Meet-Their-Needs_USCCB-December-2012 .pdf on October 21, 2013.

Varsanyi, M. W. (2011). Neoliberalism and nativism: Local anti-immigrant policy activism and an emerging politics of scale. *International Journal of Urban and Regional Research, 35*(2), 295–311.

West, D. M. (2011). The costs and benefits of immigration. *Political Science Quarterly, 126*(3), 427–443.

Weston, D. (2009). *Immigrating from facts to values: Political rhetoric in the U.S. immigration debate.* Washington, DC: Migration Policy Institute. Retrieved from http://www.migrationpolicy.org/pubs/tcm-politicalrhetoric-westen.pdf.

Williams, S. A. (2008). Impact of natural disasters: Implications for human and social services. *Journal of Social Service Research, 34*(3), 1–3.

Index